Shahzada Firoz Shah

A Forgotten Hero of 1857

Shahzada Firoz Shah

A Forgotten Hero Of 1857

Prof. Suresh Mishra

Radha Publications
New Delhi - 110002

First Edition : 2018

ISBN : 978-93-86439-52-9

ISBN 93-86439-52-2

9 789386 439529

The publication of this book has been financially supported by the Indian Council of Historical Research. The responsibility for the facts stated or opinions expressed is entirely of the author and not of the council.

Radha Publications

4231/1, Ansari Road, Daryaganj
New Delhi-110002
Phone : 23247003, 23254306
Email : radhapub@gmail.com

Published by Nitin Garg for Radha Publications and printed by Asian Offset Press, Shahadra, Delhi-32

Preface

The present work is the culmination of my study about the role of Shahzada Firoz Shah in the great uprising of 1857. At the young age of 20-22, this Mughal prince – sans resources and only by dint of his sheer courage and his ancestors' prestige – mustered a massive following in Mandsaur and soon we find him traversing Bundelkhand, Awadh, Ruhelkhand and Rajputana working shoulder to shoulder with towering personages such as Laxmibai – the Rani of Jhansi – Bakhatbali of Shahgarh, Mardansingh of Mardanpur, Begam Hazrat Mahal of Lucknow, Maulvi Ahmadulla Shah, Rana Beni Madhav, Nana Saheb Peshwa, Khan Bahadur Khan of Bareilly, Rao Saheb and Tatya Tope himself. From July 1857 to the end of 1859 he was actively engaged in his struggle against the British with utmost courage, confidence, determination, tenacity and willpower.

Once the flame of insurgency simmered down in India, he journeyed to Afghanistan, Turkey, Iran and Mecca to gather support against the British but in vain. As fate would have it, his efforts failed to bear fruit and he died at the age of 40 – disabled and penniless – in holy Mecca.

His military daring, hair-breadth escapes and skilful horsemanship are the stuff of legend and spoken of with admiration. Although confronting dire circumstances, he declined to barter self-respect, personal liberty or the claims of his House. The Shahzada had been an intrepid fighter and his faith in his beloved country's destiny remained unshaken till the bitter end.

I have tried to be objective in my narrative, which is based mainly on archival sources. Whatever sources are available about Firoz Shah, They are in English showing the British point of view, but looked with keen eyes, a clear picture of the exploits and role of Firoz Shah in the great struggle comes out.

My thanks are due to the Indian Council of Historical Research, New Delhi for giving me an opportunity to delve in the life and works of this valiant warrior by granting me the Senior Academic Fellowship for two years and the publication grant too. I also thank the authorities of Shri Natnagar Shodh Sansthan, Sitamau, District Mandsaur, MP, who allowed me to take up this research work under their prestigious institution and to use the library of the Sansthan. Its Director Dr. Manohar Singh Ranawat was nice enough to discuss with me some important points regarding Firoz Shah's movement in Malwa. I also thank my friend Mr. K.C. Pande of Mandsaur for providing me the Urdu Ms. of *Baghawat-e-Malwa* and a *Malwi* folk song on Firoz Shah.

Next to be thanked is my late wife Sheela, who, as always, relieving me of the household chorus, allowed me to busy myself with my books and laptop for the entire period of fellowship.

Bhopal

1st February 2017 **Suresh Mishra**

Contents

Abbreviations

Ball	History of the Indian Mutiny, London, Vol. I and II by Charles Ball
F. S. U. P.	*The Freedom Struggle in Uttar Pradesh- The Source Material*, edited by S.A.A. Rizvi and M.I. Bhargava, 6 Volumes 1957-61.
Tarikh-e-Malwa	*Tarikh-e-Malwa* (Urdu) 1874. (In by the library of Shri Natnagar Shodh Sansthan, Sitamau) by Munshi Karim Ali.
Luniya	Freedom Movement in Madhya Bharat, 1956 by B.N. Luniya.
Raghubirsinh	*Malwa ke Mahan Vidroh Kaleen Abhilekh* (Hindi), 1986 by Raghubirsinh (ed).
Showers	A Missing Chapter of the Indian Mutniy, 1888, by C.L. Showers.
Tarikh-e-Jaora	*Tarikh-e-Jaora* (Urdu), 1947 by Ashfaq Ahmad Jahidi (Ms in the Library of Shri Natnagar Shodh Sansthan, Sitamau, M.P.)
Sen	Eighteen Fifty Seven, 1958, by S.N. Sen
Shrivastava	The Revolt of 1857 in Central India- Malwa 1966, by K.L.Shrivastava.

Chapter - 1
Political Condition of Malwa prior to 1857

Amongst the principle leaders of the great uprising of 1857, mostly Rani Laxmibai of Jhansi, Tatya Tope, Nana Saheb, Begum Hazrat Mahal are talked about, but a person, who took no lesser part in the uprising, is usually forgotten. This person plunged himself in to the great struggle at the tender age of twenty and starting his exploits from Malwa, he fought along with the great leaders of insurgency and roamed in Bundelkhand, Awadh, Ruhelkhand and Rajputana. When the fire of insurgency died down in India, he went to Afghanistan, Turkey, Iran and Mecca to gather support against the British, though in vain. He was none other than Firoz Shah, more popularly known as Shahzada Firoz Shah. Unfortunately his efforts did not bear fruit and he died at the age of 40 as a disabled poor man at Mecca.

"If Robert Bruce[1] was a patriot" says Surendra Nath Sen, "Firoz Shah was certainly one. Alone he traveled from Mecca to Bombay and from Bombay to Central India to organise the revolt there. A young man without any following or financial resource, he built up an army and fought against heavy odds for two long years. His hands were not stained with innocent blood. He believed in the ultimate success of his cause but feared that it had been deferred by the murder of helpless. No other rebel leader condemned the massacres so openly and in such unreserved terms. His youth, his piety, and his imperial descent made a saintly hero of him and it was in the fitness of things that he should die at Mecca, an end coveted by every pious Muslim. It is a pity that he left no account of his peregrinations for he traversed the greater part of the Middle East and Central Asia during the years of his exile. It is a greater pity that few of his countrymen remember him to-day.[2]

This work is an effort to bring to light the part played by this valiant warrior in the great uprising. Since he started his career from Malwa, we have to first have an overview of the political condition of Malwa prior to 1857.

The British in Malwa

The British had defeated the *Pindaries* and the Marathas in 1818 and Malwa was brought under the control of the East India Company. The Company's government now had to solve a number of problems. It had to fix the boundaries of the various States, had to codify the laws according to British notions, regulate the trade to suit British commercial interest, control the manufacture of arms and close down local mints to introduce uniform British coinage throughout India. The solution of such grave problems left many bitter memories in the minds of several persons in Malwa whose interests were adversely affected by the Company's decision. The seeds of disaffection lay undetected for a while, but they sprouted into an organized revolt when circumstances were favourable. The spirit of military adventure dominated the people of Malwa, for there was abundant scope for freebooting and pillage. The cost and difficulties of putting large British armies into operation against such people were enormous. The territories of most of the important rulers in Central India were intermixed and this afforded a chance to these people to plunder some village in one State and immediately take to flight and seek shelter in another. Coupled with this, there was natural unwillingness on the part of many rulers to co-operate whole-heartedly with the Company in maintaining law and order. The police force was inadequate to cope with the situation which was worsened on account of the existence of trackless jungles.

Besides, a few influential people were in league with these freebooters and secretly encouraged them.[3]

During this time several proposals for the suppression of military adventurers were discussed. After much deliberation it was decided to raise a Corps of the Bhils of Malwa. Law courts in Malwa were proposed to be established to try the culprits, but due to First Afghan War of 1839-42 nothing could be taken up in this direction. Further, Wars with the Amirs of Sind, the Sindhia, the Sikhs and the Burmese occupied the British and nothing concrete could be done to improve the affairs of Malwa.

It was a coincidence that between 1845 and 1857, several Malwa states were under minority administration and were more or less under the British supervision. There was a minority administration at Gwalior after the Gwalior army was defeated at the battle of Maharajpur in 1843 and it continued till 1873 when at Gwalior, Jayaji Rao Sindhia became major. In 1843 the Resident was replaced by an Assistant and the affairs of the Gwalior State were to be communicated to the Central Government through the Resident at Indore. From 1844 to 1852 the Indore state was under minority administration till Tukoji Rao II became major. So was the case with Bhopal State where the administration was under the Regency Council under the British Resident at Indore, due to the minority of Shah Jahan Begum. During minority administration of the above states the British had immense control over these states giving rise to the dissatisfaction amongst the people of Malwa.

The main purpose of the Company was to exploit the resources of Malwa for waging wars in India and abroad. The native states hardly devoted time for developing roads and communication in their respective states and enough attention was not paid for the education and uplift of the masses of the region. Hardly there was a road in Malwa which could be called metal road and this impeded commerce and transportation of that region to a great extent. Some schools were opened by the Christian missionaries, but these were not liked by the people who were suspicious of the intentions of the British. The soil of Malwa was very productive and produced enough food for the habitants of that region, but the disturbed conditions and ravages of the freebooters rendered the condition of the people precarious. The other natural resources of Malwa were still untapped and the revenues of the States did not increase for a considerable period. The British were only interested in the cultivation of opium, which they found very profitable. They encouraged its cultivation and tried to collect opium as much as possible and earned great profit by exporting it to China.

Events from 1818 to 1857 led the people of Malwa to believe that by different treaties their rulers were made subordinate to the British, they had to disband their large armies and were compelled to keep small armies. Though the British did not interfere in their internal administration, the rulers of Malwa had to keep Residents or other representatives of the Company in their territories. They have lost territories to the British and had to keep British contingents in their territories on the expense of the state concerned. Thousands of soldiers became out of job and their life of military adventure was brought to an end. By introduction of new regulations people felt that their economic resources were exploited, and the British aimed at the destruction of their caste and religion.

There were four major states viz. Indore, Gwalior and Bhopal and Dhar, and eight minor states, viz. Dewas, Ratlam, Amjhera, Jhabua, Jaora, Sitamau, Rajgarh and Sailana.

Indore State

By the treaty of Mandsaur, signed in January 1818, Malhar Rao Holkar of Indore lost his considerable territories. He had to relinquish his claims upon the Rajputana states and had to cede all the territory south of the Narmada to the British. The capital of the Holkar state was transferred from Maheshwar to Indore. He had to limit his armies and pay for the British contingent troops maintained at Indore under the British Commander. A British Resident was to be kept at Indore.

Malhar Rao Holkar faced an insurrection headed by Krishna Kumar but was suppressed. Soon erupted the second insurrection headed by Hari Rao, a cousin of Malhar Rao Holkar II but he was defeated and imprisoned in Maheshwar fort. This was followed by two unsuccessful local insurrections. The Minister Tatia Jog was not a good administrator and the State suffered financial losses due to bribery and private trade. Tatia Jog died in 1826 and now there was no control over the expenditure of Malhar Rao Holkar II who now squandered lot of money in luxury. Pay was not disbursed to the troops and their mutiny could only be avoided by the money provided by the mother of Malhar Rao II.

Malhar Rao II died in 1833 and his widow adopted Martand Rao, who ascended the throne in January 1834. Just after a month, Hari Rao, the cousin of Malhar Rao II escaped from the prison of Maheshwar and occupied the throne on 17th April 1834. His minister Ravaji Phanse proved incapable and the state was plunged into anarchy and the state treasury became empty with the result that the discontented troops attacked the palace. Though they were repulsed, the condition was not changed. The gross management of state affairs was such that in 1838 the Company government threatened to assume the administration of the State in its own hand. In 1843 Hari Rao died and was succeeded by Khande Rao, his adopted son. Within a year he too died issueless and the Company nominated a minor Tukoji Rao II as ruler of Holkar state and appointed a minority Council to look after the administration. In 1852 Tukoji Rao Holkar attained majority and became a full fledged ruler of the State. Although Tukoji Rao was young, he was wise enough to manage the administration.

Gwalior State

Gwalior state was a huge state with its territories scattered in most parts of Malwa. Its earlier capital was Ujjain but then it was shifted to Gwalior, further north of Malwa. When in 1794 Daulat Rao Sindhia began his political life as a ruler of the Sindhia state, the Marathas had the de facto control over the throne of Delhi and were masters of a might and extensive dominion. He fought bravely in the Second Maratha War, but unfortunately lost a large portion of his territory in the end. The Marathas did not find Daulat Rao Sindhia of any help to them in their last struggle against the British power. His neutrality possibly brought about the ruin of the Maratha Confederacy.[4] He helped the British in crushing the Pindaris and during third Anglo Maratha war, he remained neutral when the British forces defeated the Holkar of Indore, the Bhonsla ruler of Nagpur and Peshwa Baji Rao II. With the fall of three major Maratha states, the decline of Sindhia was not far away. Very soon Daulat Rao Sindhia had to sign a treaty with the British on 5th November 1817 and Sindhia's army was cut to size and had to agree to provide five thousand troops against the campaign against the Pindaris. He had to hand over the forts of Asirgarh and Handia because these were situated in strategic places. While Asirgarh was a strong force in Nimar territory, controlling the route to the Deccan, Handia was the point from where the armies crossed the Narmada river while passing through that region. The British considered these strategic forts very useful during the Pindari campaign. This treaty was followed by another one in June 1817 by which Sindhia had to cede Ajmer to the British and Islam Nagar to Bhopal State. He also agreed to accept a British resident at Gwalior and relinquished his supremacy over the states of Rajputana. After 1819 Daulat Rao Sindhia led an uneventful political life and died on 21st March 1827.

After the death of Daulat Rao, his widow Baiza Bai adopted an eleven-year old boy Jankoji Rao Sindhia on 17th June 1827 and herself acted as Regent up to 1832. She was an ambitious woman and was anxious to retain power even after Jankoji had attained majority. This led to a conflict between herself and the supporters of Jankoji. The climax came when in October 1836 Jankoji fled from his place and took refuge in the Residency at Gwalior. This was followed by a revolt of Gwalior army against Baiza Bai, who had to retire in favour of Jankoji. Though Jankoji remained loyal to the British till his death in 1843, he was a weak and incompetent ruler resulting in anarchy in the State. After him his minor widow Tara Bai adopted an 8 year old boy Jayaji Rao who now ascended the throne of Gwalior and was looked after by his maternal uncle

Mama Saheb. The young widow Tarabai became a tool in the hands of Dada Khasgiwala. His rival Mama Saheb had the support of the Gwalior army of 40,000 which craved for the revival of the past military glory. Dada Khasgiwala did not like the dominance of the British any more and soon he appointed those persons who were ousted at the instance of the British Resident and expelled those who did not like his anti-British policy. Naturally the British wanted the removal of Dada Khasgiwala which was not complied, and ultimately the British forces attacked the Gwalior army in 1843 and defeated it at the battle of Maharajpur. The Sindhia had to bear the expenses incurred by the British in the battle of Maharajpur. In the arrangement that followed, the Sindhia had to cede permanently the revenue of some districts for the expenses of the British troops within the Gwalior State. The fort of Gwalior was also occupied by the British troops and kept under a British Commander. The 40,000 strong Sindhia army was reduced to 9000 men. Out of these, not more than 3,000 infantry with 12 field guns and not more than 200 gunners with only 200 other guns. The glorious Gwalior Contingent was a matter of past and there remained only a fraction of it. From 1844 to 1853, during the minority of Jayaji Rao, the administration of Gwalior State was conducted by the Regency Council controlled by the British administration. In 1853 when Jayaji Rao became major he was given powers to rule with the assistance of his pro-British Chief Minister Dinkar Rao Rajwade.

Bhopal State

Bhopal State was founded by Dost Mohammad Khan in the early 18th century. Nazar Mohammad Khan was the ruler of Bhopal State from 1816 to 1819 and was married to Qudasia Begum, who was very influential. Nazar Mohammad Khan, scared by the growing power of the Marathas, followed the policy of helping the British against the Marathas. This made him favourite of the British who helped to bring him out of Sindhia's control. By the treaty of 1818 the British authorities gave him the Sindhia's fort of Islamnagar which was near Bhopal and was in early days capital of Bhopal

State. He was also given five *parganas* from the Vinchurkar family. A British Resident was posted at Sehore near Bhopal with a force of 1,000 men, the cost of which was to be borne by the Bhopal State. After the death of Nazar Mohammad in 1819, it was decided that Munir Mohammad Khan should succeed him under the regency of Qudasia Begum and he should marry Sikandar Begum, the only daughter of Nazar Mohammad. In 1827 Munir Mohammad Khan, due to his differences with Qudasia Begum, had to retire in favour of his younger brother Jahangir Mohammad Khan. Qudasia Begum delayed the marriage between Jahangir Mohammad Khan and Sikandar Begum, but ultimately the marriage took place in 1835. When Jahangir Mohammad died in 1844, his minor daughter Shahjahan Begum became the ruler of Bhopal under the regency of her mother Sikandar Begum. In 1855 Shahjahan Begum was married to Baqi Mohammad Khan, but the regency of Sikandar Begum continued by the Company's Government as a reward for her unflinching support to the British.

Dhar and Dewas States

Dhar[5] was an important State in Malwa ruled by Ramchandra Rao Pawar II. When the British troops entered Malwa in 1817, Dhar was the only possession that remained with Ramchandra Rao Pawar II and the whole revenues of the principality did not amount to more than thirty-five thousand rupees.[6] Ramchandra Rao entered into a treaty with the East India Company's Government in January 1819. By the intervention of the British, Badnawar, Berchha, Kukshi, Nalchha and other *parganas*, which Dhar had been dispossessed by the Sindhia and Holkar prior to 1818, were restored to Dhar.[7] The British were to protect Dhar State against external aggression and in return the Raja of Dhar agreed to cede the tributes of Banswara and Dungarpur to the British.

In 1832 one Achyut Rao, with the support of the Bhils attacked Dhar but was compelled to return by the British intervention. In 1833 Ramchandra Rao Pawar II died and was succeeded by an adopted son of 11, Yashwant Rao II. Since he was selected through the influence of his uncle, the Raja of Dewas Anandrao Pawar, close relations developed between the two states. Yashwat Rao Pawar died of cholera in 1857, when the great uprising broke. He was succeeded by his adopted son Anand Rao III, aged thirteen.

Earlier the Pawars of Dewas played an important role in Maratha expansion in Malwa. Unfortunately between 1806 and 1818 they lost huge chunks of their territory to the adjoining powerful states. In the words of John Malcolm, the Resident of Indore, 'with territories situated in the most distracted part of Central India, and unable to maintain any force, they have alternately been plundered and oppressed, not only by the governments of Sindhia and Holkar, but by the Pindary chiefs and indeed every freebooter of the day. A detail of their history during the last twenty-five years leave an impression of wonder at their being in existence, o having an inhabited village in their country.'[8] In 1818 there were two branches of Dewas, Senior and Junior and their relations were most cordial. Raja Rukmangad Rao ruled Dewas Senior from 1827 and Raja Haibat Rao ruled Dewas Junior from 1840.

Other States

Jaora: It was a small State, which came into being in 1818 when by the treaty of Mandsaur, Ghafur Khan Pindari received the State of Jaora from the British as a reward for betraying Holkar, his master. Ghafur Khan died in 1825 and was succeeded by Ghaus Mohammad Khan, an infant of two years under a Regency. He got ruling power in 1842. He was pro-British and sided with the British during the great uprising of 1857 and sent information about the movements of the insurgents to the Resident.

Sitamau: It was also a small state ruled by Raja Raj Sinh of Rathore clan who had ascended the throne in 1802. During the initial years of the reign of Raj Sinh, the menace of Marathas had increased. In the year 1820 A.D., by the intervention of the Resident Sir John Malcolm, decision was taken to pay yearly tax of Rs 60,000 to the Sindhias under the British domain. Following this, the rule of Raj Sinh over Sitamau was finally accepted and as peace returned to Sitamau, Raj Sinh shifted his capital back to Sitamau from Laduna. He was an able ruler and ruled from 1802 to 1867.[9]

Rajgarh: During the settlement of Malwa by Sir John Malcolm, many villages were made over to the Sindhia in lieu of his claims for tribute from Rajgarh, and now only the British government had the right to interfere in the affairs of the State. Rawat Moti Singh succeeded to the throne in 1831 and ruled up to 1880. Since his administration was not efficient, the British took up the management from 1846 to 1856. Jan Ali Khan, an employee and favourite of the British, was appointed as the Manager of the State.

Narsinggarh: In 1818 through the mediation of the British administration, an agreement was reached between Sobhag Singh, the Raja of Narsinggarh on the one hand and the rulers of Indore, Dewas and Gwalior, which defined his territories. In 1827 Hanwant Singh succeeded Sobhag Singh and ruled till his death in 1873.

Ratlam: When the British entered Malwa, the small state of Ratlam was ruled by Parbat Singh of Rathore clan of Rajputs. In 1819 he entered into an agreement with the Brtish acknowledging their paramountcy. After his death in 1825 Balwant Singh succeeded him and ruled up to 1857.

Sailana: This was a petty Rajput state situated near Ratlam and was politically dominated by the Sindhia. By the settlement of 1819, Sailana state was made independent of the Sindhia's control and Laxman Singh, the ruler of Sailana agreed to pay an annual tribute to Sindhia under British guarantee. Laxman Singh died in 1826 and was succeeded by his son Ratan Singh who too died after a year. There after Ratan Singh's uncle Nahar Singh ruled Sailana from 1827 to 1850 and was succeeded by Dule Singh. As Dule Singh was minor there was a Minority Administration up to 1857.

Amjhera: It was a petty state near Dhar state and was under the domination of the Sindhia government and a small detachment of the Sindhia government was kept in this state. The ruler of Amjhera had to pay an annual tribute to Sindhia but he was not regular in payments. The troops of Amjhera state were dominated by the Arab soldiers. To do away with the turbulent Arab soldiers the Company's Government advanced money to the ruler of Amjhera and asked him to pay arrears to the Arab soldiers and disband them. It also guaranteed to the Sindhia the punctual payment of a tribute of Rs. 35,000 per annum by the ruler of Amjhera. In return, the Sindhia had to withdraw his troops from Amjhera and terminate his political sovereignty over the State. During the eruption of insurgency, Amjhera was ruled by Bakhtawar Singh, who unfurled the flag of revolt in 1857.

Jhabua: It was a small Rajput state situated far west of Malwa and governed the territory of the Bhils and Bhilalas. By the Company's intervention it was freed from the control of the Holkar state. The state employed a large force of Arab mercenaries. The British administration pressed him to reduce their number and in 1836 the Company crushed the mutinous Arab soldiers and established peace in Jhabua. Gopal Singh ruled Jhabua from 1840 to 1895.

Barwani: It was ruled by Jaswant Singh (1839-1880) and its population mainly consisted of the Bhils. Ali Rajpur state, also inhabited by Bhils and Bhilalas, was ruled by Jaswant Singh from 1818 to 1862. When he was minor, Makranis were powerful under their leader Muzaffar Makrani till 1836 when Jaswant Singh attained majority.

Foreign Mercenaries

During the period in question, foreign mercenaries were employed in different states in India. Their groups emerged after the fall of the Mughal empire and during the unsettled conditions of the Indian states. In Malwa almost every state kept foreign mercenaries who came from Afghanistan, Makran (Baluchistan) and Arabia. These mercenaries took part in armed conflicts and were motivated to take part in the hostilities by desire for private gain. They fought for money or other material gains. Since they were professional soldiers they joined any party who paid them better salaries and were even prone to change sides without any scruples. In some states they became so powerful as to raise arms against their employers, as has been the case of Dhar and Ali Rajpur states. It was mostly done for payment of their arrears. Some of the mercenaries established themselves as rulers in different parts of India in early eighteenth century, notable among them were Nawabs of Loharu and Nawabs of Bhopal.

When the Company first established its supremacy in Malwa in 1818, its policy was to reduce the strength of the these mercenaries, particularly Arab soldiers, employed in the States. During the great uprising of 1857 these mercenaries took active part in the struggle along with the rebels.

Agents to the Governor-General

After the defeat of the Marathas in north India in 1818, a British Political Residency was established at Indore. Between 1818 and 1857 there were several Agents to the Governor-General with their Headquarters at Indore. Under the Agent to the Governor-General, were posted a number of Political Agents and Residents who were directly attached to the States and exercised control over them. Sir John Malcolm was the first Agent to the Governor-General for the affairs of Malwa. He established British military stations at Mhow, Sardarpur, Mahidpur, Neemuch and other places.

Sir Robert Hamilton worked as Agent to the Governor-General from 1844 to 1859 with a short break from April to December 1857 when he went on leave to England. During his absence, Colonel H.M. Durand became the Officiating Agent to the Governor-General. 'An engineer and soldier, he singularly lacked insight into the Indian mind. His anti-Indian feeling earned for him a bad name among the people of Malwa. Unfortunately there was no love lost between Sir Robert Hamilton and Colonel Durand and they carried on their personal quarrel to such an extent that it adversely affected the interests of the ruling chiefs and people of Malwa.'[10]

Cantonments

The condition of Malwa in 1818 was such that the British had to establish some cantonments to keep an eye on the states of Malwa. For Indore state cantonment was established at Mhow and for Gwalior state, at Gwalior and Mahidpur were chosen and to control the states of Nimar and Jhabua, cantonment was stationed at Bhopawar. Besides, Malwa Bhil Core was established at Indore and it was entire constituted by the recruitment from Bhil tribe. It was also meant to control the Bhils of Jhabua and Nimar, who were in the habit of looting the caravans and travelers. Expenditure of the troops kept in these cantonments was provided by the state concerned e.g. expendiure of Mhow cantonment was borne by the Holkar state, while the Gwalior Contonment troops and Mahidpur troops were supported by the Gwalior state. Bhopawar cantonment was maintained by the money provided by the States of Niamr and Jhabua. The Cantonment for Bhopal state was stationed at Sihore and its expenses were borne by the Bhopal State. This shows the sagacity and diplomacy of the British who could maintain a good army at the expense of the surrounding native States. These armies had officers of British origin while the soldiers were Indians.

Reference :

1. Popularly known as Robert the Bruce (1724-1329) He became one of Scotland's greatest kings, as well as one of the most famous warriors of his generation, eventually leading Scotland during the Wars of Scottish independence against the Kingdom of England.
2. S. N. Sen, *Eighty Fifty Seven*, Third reprint, July 1995, pp. 380-81.
3. K. L. Shrivastava, *The Revolt of 1857 in Central India-Malwa*, 1966, pp. 1-2.
4. Shrivastava, op. cit., p. 6
5. Forty-seven kilometers west of Indore.
6. John Malcolm, A Memoir of Central India, Vol. I, 1824, p. 110
7. Shrivastava, op. cit., p. 12.
8. Johm Malcolm, op. cit., p. 113.

9. Vazir Beg, the *vakil* of Sitamau State was stationed at Indore and during the uprising he regularly sent letters in local dialect *Malwi* informing about the events to the Diwan of Sitamau. Fortunatly, his letters were kept safe in Sitamau State archives and later they were published by Shri Natnagar Shodh Sansthan established by the erstwhile Sitamau State, under the title *"Malwa ke mahan vidrohkaleen abhilekh"* edited by Dr. Raghubir Sinh. These letters are a mine of information about the insurgency from an eye witness.
10. Shrivastava, op. cit., p. 18

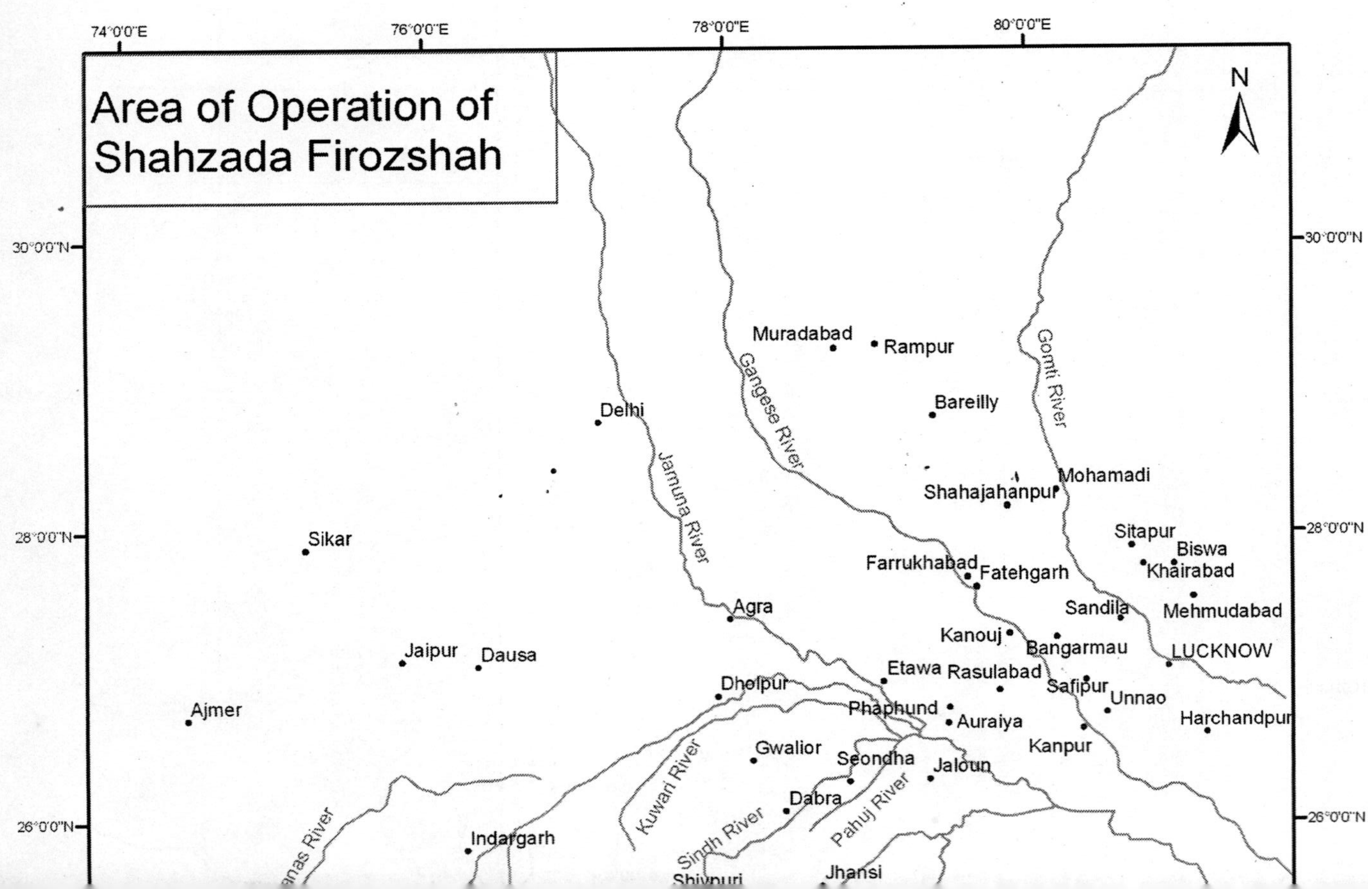

Area of Operation of
Shahzada Firozshah
N
74°0'0"E
76°0'0"E
78°0'0"E
80°0'0"E
30°0'0"N
28°0'0"N
26°0'0"N
Muradabad
Rampur
Bareilly
Delhi
Gangese River
Gomti River
Jamuna River
Mohamadi
Shahajahanpur
Sitapur
Biswa
Khairabad
Mehmudabad
Sikar
Farrukhabad
Fatehgarh
Sandila
Agra
Kanouj
Bangarmau
LUCKNOW
Jaipur
Dausa
Etawa
Rasulabad
Safipur
Unnao
Dholpur
Phaphund
Auraiya
Harchandpur
Ajmer
Gwalior
Seondha
Kanpur
Jaloun
Kuwari River
Dabra
Sindh River
Pahuj River
Indargarh
Jhansi

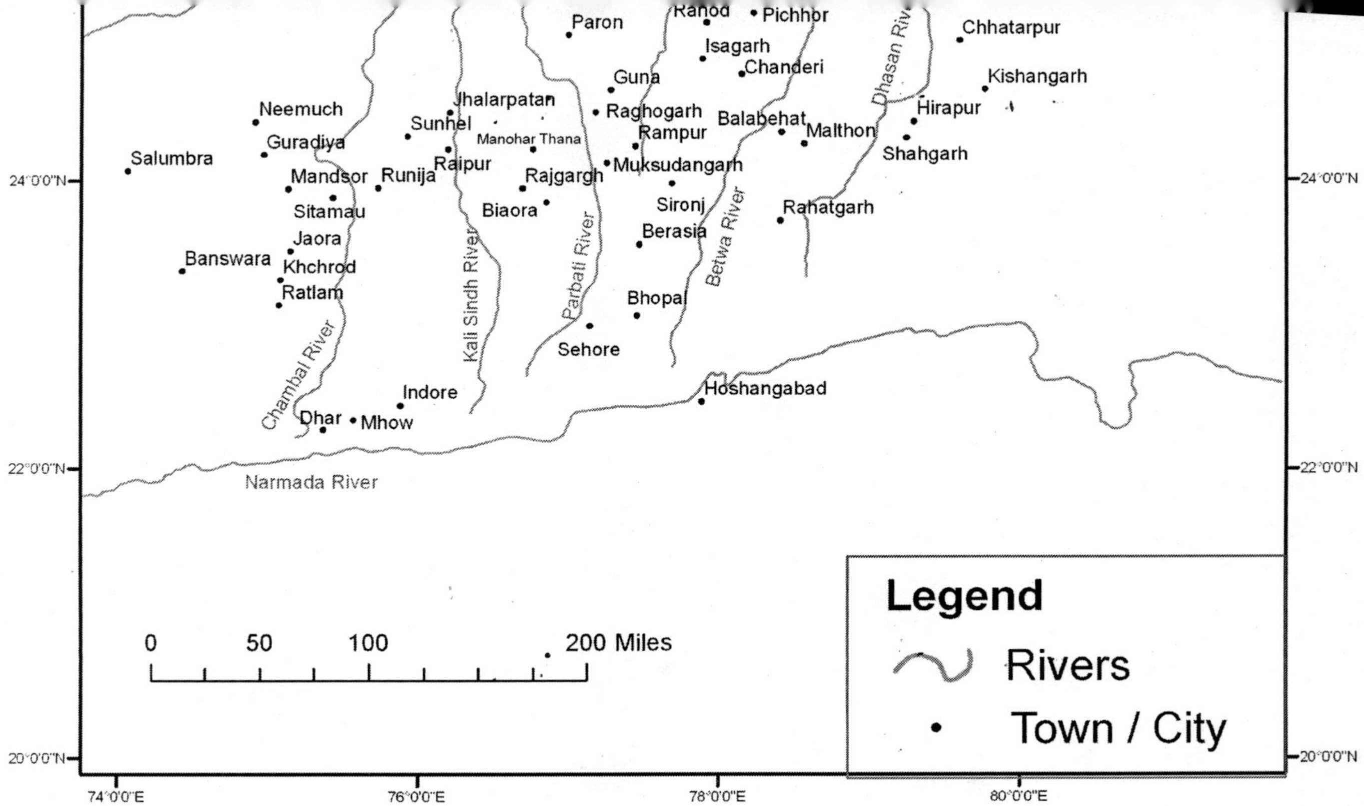
Paron
Ranod
Pichhor
Chhatarpur
Isagarh
Chanderi
Guna
Kishangarh
Dhasan River
Neemuch
Jhalarpatan
Raghogarh
Balabehat
Hirapur
Sunhel
Rampur
Malthon
Guradiya
Manohar Thana
Shahgarh
Salumbra
Raipur
Muksudangarh
Mandsor
Runija
Rajgargh
Sironj
Rahatgarh
Sitamau
Biaora
Betwa River
Jaora
Berasia
Parbati River
Banswara
Khchrod
Kali Sindh River
Ratlam
Bhopal
Chambal River
Sehore
Indore
Hoshangabad
Dhar
Mhow
Narmada River
24°0'0"N
22°0'0"N
20°0'0"N
74°0'0"E
76°0'0"E
78°0'0"E
80°0'0"E
0
50
100
200 Miles
Legend
Rivers
Town / City

Chapter - 2
Firoz Shah In Malwa

Uprising in Malwa and adjoining region

The uprising in Malwa began from Neemuch[1], where on the 4th June 1857 the Sepoys of the British cantonment of Neemuch took up arms and just a few days latter, on the 8th June the Sepoys of Nasirabad[2] Cantonment followed suit. On the 10th of June Mahidpur[3] contingent also took up arms to be followed by the Gwalior Contingent on the 14th June. A fortnight latter, a part of Holkar's army at Indore rose on the 1st July 1857 under the leadership of Saadat Khan, Maulavi Abdus Samad and Waris Muhammad Khan a scion of Bhopal ruling family. Sadaat Khan was a military officer in the army of the Holkar king of Indore State and was the local leader of repute. Abdus Samad was a Persian teacher. Waris Mohammad Khan belonged to the family of the Nawabs of Bhopal and was claimant of the Bhopal throne, with the result that the Sikandar Begum, the regent of Bhopal state was annoyed with him and confiscated his jagir. Waris Mohammad Khan had to leave Bhopal and he came to Indore and became active during the insurgency. He wanted to use the rebel sepoys against the Bhopal state for his own purpose. The Indore events gave impetus to the insurrection at the adjoining cantonments of Mhow,[4] Sardarpur[5] and Mahidpur. The sepoys of the British cantonment of Mhow rose under Murad Ali Khan. Thus within no time, Gwalior, Mhow,

Mahidpur, Bhopawar[6], Indore and Dhar were engulfed by the fire of insurgency.[7]

Dhar mercenaries marched to Bhopawar and Sardarpur, and burned the military posts there and by the end of July, they occupied the fort of Dhar. The Raja of Amjhera, Bakhtawarsingh, with his Arab mercenaries took up arms and raided Bhopawar and Sardarpur cantonments and made the British officers flee towards Jhabua to save their lives.

Eastern portion of Malwa was under Nawab Sikandar Begum of Bhopal with a contingent under British command at Sehore[8]. The Begum was pro-British but was facing opposition from Waris Mohammad Khan and the Nawabs of Garhi Ambapani.[9]Fazil Mohammad Khan and Adil Mohammad Khan. As mentioned earlier, Waris Mohammad Khan had joined hands with Saadat Khan at Indore. As regards Ambapani Nawabs, they had occupied the fort of Rahatgarh[10], which was then under British control, but was managed by the Ambapani Nawabs till the year 1807 when the Sindhia ruler of Gwalior occupied it. Later in 1826 it came under the supervision of the British. Situated on the banks of Bina river, this fort was of immense strategic importance. As will be shown, Adil Mohammad Khan and Fazil Mohammad Khan played important role during the uprising in Bundelkhand. Though Fazil Mohammad Khan was killed at Rahatgarh during the siege of Sir Hugh Rose but Adil Mohammad Khan was active even after the suppression of the uprising.

Indore Insurgents leave for Delhi

The insurgents of Indore and Mhow left Indore for Gwalior and Agra under the leadership of Saadat Khan, Bhagirath Silawat and Waris Mahommad Khan on the 4th of July 1857. They were accompanied by commandant Vanshgopal, *jamadar* Sher Khan, teacher Maulvi Abdul Samad, Nanhen Khan, gunner Mohammad Ali, Rahamtulla Khan of Mahidpur and a military officer Durga Prasad. They took away with them cash and kind amounting to about 9 lacs of rupees and all the guns, elephants and carriages that they could carry. The rebel force consisted of 23rd Mhow Regiment Native Infantry, 3 troops of Cavalry and 7 guns and 2 Companies of Foot, and 1 Rissalah of Holkar's troops and several other followers from the civil population, making a total of some thousands.[11] On the 14th July the insurgents left Biaora for Gwalior via Guna. Passing through Raghogarh, Piplia, Badrawsas and Kolaras, Sipri (Shivpuri) they reached Morar on the 30th July and on the 1st of August, 1857, they encamped at Gwalior.

Emergence of Firoz Shah in Malwa

The arrival of the insurgents at Morar coincided with an important event in Malwa. A youngman named Firoz Shah entered Malwa and with his personality, organising apacity and declared object, collected a huge following around himself within a month. His rise and growing power worried the Malwa states and the British administration also took it with concern. His emergence opened a new chapter in the history of insurgency in Malwa and later in north India. Very soon his name was included in the list of great insurgent leaders of the country.

In 1855 Firoz Shah left Delhi to undertake the pilgrimage to Mecca. He arrived back in India in May 1857 landing at Bombay[12] and made his way northwards in order to take part in the struggle against the British "hurrying to the front of what he considered was a war for independence".[13] Aged about 20 he was of a good disposition and had always borne the character of *Talib-al-ilm*, or a seeker of knowledge and had learnt Arabic and other general languages.[14] After alighting at Bombay, Firoz Shah is next found in Malwa.

The earliest contemporary documentary reference about the emergence of Firoz Shah in Malwa is found in a letter dated 14 August 1857 written from Nahargarh[15], by Paharsingh Qanungo to Hulasrai, Diwan of Sitamau, stating that a Shahzada has come from the side of Mecca along with 10-20 persons. Coming to Khachrod[16], he had collected a crowd of one or two hundred. The government (Sindhia) ousted the persons who had joined him and asked the

Shahazada to leave that place. It was heard that the Shahzada had come to Sitamau.[17]

A Marathi letter of 24th August 1857 also informs that a *Faqir* came to Sitamau and said that he had come from Mecca and having stopped there a few days, went towards Jaora, and wrote to the Nawab (of Jaora) that he was a Shahzada. He had been robbed on the road and was anxious to meet him. The Nawab gave an audience to him and made a present of Rs.50 and furnishing him with few swords, sent him away. He went to Khachrod and put up with Jama Masjid and had interview with several people of the place, who represented to him that his remaining there might lead to trouble. He left and went to *Parnajee Daba* where a few miscreants gathered around him. On hearing this, the Suba [of Sindhia Govt.] sent the Kotwal and had him turned out of the place. He then went to Khachrod and stopped there for some days on account of rain. 25 or 30 persons collected around him. He gave out that all who desire to aid the faith (*Deen)* come to him. There after he proceeded with them to Mandsaur[18]. The Mewatis etc. who were out of employment at Mandsaur erected standard of Islam and with beating drums went to receive him into the town.[19]

The events that followed have been given almost identical in a Marathi letter forwarded by the Indore Prime Minister Ramchandra Rao to the officiating AGG Durand. It said that at about 9 A.M. on the 26th of August 1857, the Shahzada alighted at the *Dargah* of Doodan Sayyad with four or five attendants. When the *Kotwal* heard of this he went there with 25 or 30 followers and desired him to go away. The Shahzada said that he would go away after the Muharram, The *Kotwal* said, his orders were not to allow strangers to remain in the town. The Shahzada reported that he had orders to remain there. The *Kotwal* perceiving the refractory manner of the Shahzada, sent word to the *Tahsildar*. When Dajuba Bhuskute, *Tahsildar*, Malhar Rao Gulwute, belonging to Baba Sahib, Ramrao Tatea, on the part of the *Suba*, came to the Shahzada with fifty or a hundred men, the Shahzada made a signal and two or three unemployed Mewatis, appeared. High words passed and swords were drawn. Four *sawars* were killed. The *Ghole* of the *Lashkar* Bhairogarh, and the Suba and also the Mandsaur *Sebandies* combined and took the Shahzada to the Palace and placed him on the *Masnad*; and erecting the Royal standard, proclaimed the assumption of the Government. The Shahzada sent for the businessmen and *Sahookars,* and gave them assurances of safety and protection and they presented *Nazars*. All the records and documents found in the Palace were torn and burnt. Four of the *Kamdars* were confined. It was supposed that after the Moharram the insurgents will go towards Neemuch[20] and Rampura[21]. Nana Saheb, *Suba* of Mandsaur was at Bhairogarh. The *Naib Suba* Ganpat Rao Baba made his escape.[22]

The Indore Prime Minister Ramchandra Rao pointed out that "insurrection, raised by the person calling himself a 'Shahzada' had already acquired a formidable appearance, and is likely to lead to extensive disasters in Malwa if not crushed at once. The Jaora and Ratlam rebels will no doubt flock to the standard of revolt, and Musalmans, and others from all parts of the country, will readily gather round this nucleus of disorder and devastation. It is said that ten thousand rebels have already collected at Mandsaur."[23]

A letter from the Nawab of Jaora dt. 27th August, informs that the whole force of Maharaja Sindhia including Cavalry, Infantry and Artillery joined by *Vilaytees*, Mewatis and Hindus had set up the Shahzada and apprehended all the *Ahalkars* who from mere force and fear had been compelled to show outward allegiance. Presents were taken from the *Sahukars*. The whole Force amounted to about 15,000 men. The Shahzada had commenced enlisting new men at the following rate- Infantry 20 Rs. Cavalry 40 Rs. and had also issued *Parwanas* in every place saying that all should unite with him or else they would meet with punishment. The Nawab also sent a copy of a *Parwana* of Firoz Shah which said that the Shahzada has taken his seat on the throne of Mandsaur on the fourth Moharrum and 30 Rs. to a *Jamadar*, 20 Rs. to a *Duffadar* and 23 Rs. to a *Nishanburdar* and 15 Rs. to a Sepoy have been fixed.[24]

Who was Firoz Shah?

Firoz Shah was a grandson of the Mughal Emperor Bahadur Shah II, as he himself declares it in his Azamgarh proclamation of 25th August 1858.[25] Against this clear evidence about his lineage, some authorities hold different views. Zambaur genealogy[26], Beale[27] and Thompson[28] say that Firoz Shah was a son of Bahadur Shah II while the genealogy of the Mughal dynasty given in Royal Ark[29] and Ferdinand Justi Iranisches Namenbuch[30] make no reference to Firoz Shah as a son of Bahadur Shah II.

G.W. Forrest calls him "Firoz Shah, of the Delhi royal family".[31] In a letter to Secret Committee written by the Agent to Governor General, Central India, Firoz Shah has been described as a descendant from the Imperial family of Taimur, and a pensioner from Banaras.[32] R.C. Mazumdar also[33] calls him 'a direct descendant of the Mughal Emperors of Delhi'

Some historians[34] hold that Firoz Shah who took an active role in the uprising was the son of Nizam Bakht, the grandson of the Mughal Emperor Shah Alam II (1759-1806) and the great grand daughter of the Mughal Emperor Alamgir II (1754-1759) Abadi Begum. This is corroborated by genealogy given in the website of Royal Ark[35] which gives the detailed genealogy of the Mughal dynasty and mentions almost every member of the Mughal dynasty even after 1857. But all these versions may be disregarded against the evidence of Azamgarh proclamation mentioned earlier.

Muinuddin's version

Muinuddin Hasan[36], an eye witness to the great uprising writes, with other things, about the rise of Firozshah, in his memoirs written in 1878. He has a strange story to tell. He says that during *haj*, a fifty year old *Kashmiri* of the same name (i.e. Firoz Shah) was with him and accompanied Firoz Shah in his return journey. When Firoz Shah joined the rebels of Neemuch contingent, the soldiers, due to his princely origin, honoured him and took him with them leaving behind Firoz Shah *Kashmiri*. After the departure of the

Neemuch contingent and Mirza Firoz Shah, Firoz Shah *Kashmiri* declared himself as Shahzada.[37]

Moinuddin Hasan wrote his reminiscences in 1878 on the behest of Charles Metcalf and according to the wishes of Moinuddin Hasan, Metcalf published it in 1892 after his death in 1885. It seems that Moinuddin could not get away with the rumour that Shahzada Firoz Shah was an imposter. Looking to other evidences, Moinuddin's view is untenable and can not be accepted.

His early activities in Malwa

We have at our disposal three local Urdu chronicles, which, though of latter period, provide some detailed information about the early activities of Shahzada Firoz Shah in Malwa. They are *Tarikh-e-Malwa* of 1290 A.H. i.e. 1874 AD,[38] *Baghawat-e-Malwa*[39] bearing no date and *Tarikh-e-Jaora* of 1947[40]. These corroborate the main events mentioned above, but also give some minute details, which seem to be quite authentic and interesting too.

According to *Tarikh-e-Malwa*, Firoz Shah first stepped into a *musafirkhana* and declaring himself as the Shahzada of Delhi, sought a meeting with the Maharaja Holkar which was not accepted but was presented rupees fifty. Others also gave him some money and he left Indore and reached Jaora.[41]

Baghawat-e-Malwa[42] gives a detailed description of the events from his arrival at Jaora to his enthronement at Mandsaur. According to it a short stature man came to the the *sarai* of Jaora along with two servants seated on a mare. After two-three days he sent a message to the grandson of Nawab of Jaora that his name was Humayun[43] and he belonged to the family of Taimur and was the son of Khurram, a resident of Benaras.[44] He had come with a decision to go to *Haj* but due to shortage of funds he was not able to proceed. Nawab of Jaora called for this man. This man praised the British government before the Nawab and said that they were receiving subsistence by the courtesy of the Government while the Emperor of Delhi had written them off. Advised by the Nawab to proceed to *Haj*, he left Jaora and halted at Parnakhedi[45], about three *kos*[46] from Khachrod. There also he declared himself as a Prince and earned reverence from the populace. Some miscreants joined him and provoked him to collect a group, which he did. He then went to Khachrod and collected 5-7 persons. When he was one *kos* north of Parnakheri, the *thanadar* Bakar Hussain of Barawda[47] wrote in detail to the Nawab, who forwarded this letter in original to Nana Saheb Krishnarao Anantrao, the *Subadar* of Mandsaur, who was then at Khachrod. Nana Saheb immediately sent the *Kotwal* of Khachrod to drive out Humayun. The *Kotwal* threatened him that if he does not leave his area, he will be imprisoned. Firozshah left Khachrod and related the entire episode to the Mewatis.[48] On their advice he went to Mandsaur, where he could expect a good number of *Vilayatis*. He then went to Afzalpur[49] and some Mewatis and *Vilayatis* joined him. Sheikh Mohammad Ali, the *thanadar* of Sindhia government also helped him and joined him. Now the *Kamavizdar* of Mandsaur sent Ibrahim Khan *Vilayati Zamadar*, Kamaruddin Khan Mewati *Jamadar* and Sheikh Rahim Bux Moharrir to Afzalpur to drive out the Shahzada. Leaving Afzalpur, the Shahzada sat in the nearby *Dargah* of Sheikh Karanji.[50] Now the Mandsaur Mewatis invited the Shahzada to come to Mandsaur. On his arrival all the Mewatis, moving *chanwar* and *morchal*, brought him to Mandsaur and placed him in the mosque of Madarpur. After two days Dajiba, the *Kamavizdar* of Mandsaur ordered the Shahzada to leave Mandsaur. Since *Muharram* had commenced, Mirza Humayn, the Shahzada sought permission to stay up to *Muharram*. But his Mewati followers defied the orders of the *Kamavizdar* and vowed to die for the Shahzada, whom, they called their *murshid*. Next day, Chand Khan Mewati of Nayapura, with his associates seated Mirza Humayun on a horse and brought him to the 'Dargah' of Dudhan Shahid.[51] two miles from Mandsaur on the Neemuch road. People started gathering there and the situation became riotous. Now the Kamavisdar sent Kotwal Devi Prasad, a Kashmiri, to drive out the Shahzada. The *Kotwal* found the situation serious and found all the people, Hindus and Muslims in revolt. The *Kotwal* reported this situation to *Kamavizdar*, who accompanied by Deviprasad *Kotwal* and Madhavrao Pandit proceeded with 150 *Vilayatis* and Indian sepoys and sent a message to Humayun to leave that place otherwise his head would be severed. Shahzada, on his turn, abused the *Kamavizdar* and drove the messenger. When the messenger reported back the incidence, the *Kamavizdar* Dajiba himself went to Shahzada. The Shahzada, flowing his *nishan*, invoked the *Vilayati* sepoys of the Kamavizdar to come under his *Muhammadi* flag or be prepared to fight. The *Vilayati* sepoys immediately joined the Shahzada and left Deviprasad *Kotwal,* Dajiba *Kamavizdar* and Madhavrao Pandit in lurch. The *Kamavizdar* fled towards the town on his horse. Unfortunately, the horse stopped suddenly and the *Vilayatis* attacked him by sword and shot a fire on Madhavrao Pandit, injuring his hand. Both of these fell down. *Kotwal* Devi Prasad took shelter in a mosque and to save his life offered to accept Islam and his live was spared. The *Kotwal* and the *Kamavizdar* were imprisoned.

Baghawat-e-Malwa continues that the insurgents went back to Dudhan Shahid hill and on 22nd August 1857 (Muharram 4, 1274-AH), brought Mirza Humayun to the Tahsil Office and placed him the same day on the throne.[52] He was honoured by a salute of 9 gun-fires. Next day the sepoys demanded their 6 months[53] balance. After five days some intelligent persons contacted Amir Beg, (the grandson of Mirza Chaman Beg, the erstwhile *suba* of Mandsaur during Madhoji Sindhia) and forcibly brought him in the court and made him to sit on the *masnad* to work for his master, the Shahzada. To pay the balance of the sepoys, Amir Beg with the concurrence of the Qazi and prominent persons of the town, called for the businessmen through the Mewatis and demanded money. About 4 lac[54] rupees were collected and were distributed to all.

Firoz Shah also sent a *parwana* to one Rasul Khan Jamadar stating, "this day, the fourth of Mohurrum, I, Shahzada Humayoon Shah, have been placed on the Musnud at Mundisore and the standard of the Prophet has been planted. The following rates of pay being fixed, you are requested to repair to this place without delay. Rates- per *Jamadar*- 30 Rs., per *Duffadar*- 23 Rs., per *Nishanburdar*- 20 Rs., Per Sepoy- 15 Rs."[55]

Wazir Beg also writes that Mirza Amir Beg[56] was appointed as *Naib Peshkar* and the *Peshkars* were Qaziji, Munshi Nuruddin, Rahim Bux and Sheikh Ali Arshad. According to Wazir Beg, Qaziji was a good man but other three were identical.[57]

Baghawat-e-Malwa further states that Sheikh Ali Arshad *Sarishtedar* the Suba of Mandsaur was forcibly brought before the Shahzada. The Sarishtedar, Sheikh Nuruddin and Qazi Bahaulla were asked to help in the administration. Munshi Ghulam Muhiuddin, who was earlier *Muharrir* in the Jaora court and was ousted on charges of bribery, took over the work of *Munshi* and writer. Ghulam Muhiuddin and Maulvi Jamaluddin also joined the administration. When the news of Mandsaur events reached Jaora, the Nawab Jaora sent Mir Jafar Ali to bring information of Mandsaur. Jafar Ali met the Shahzada, who asked Mir Jafar Ali to convey the Nawab that his arrival would be welcomed. Jafar Ali was given a *pagari*. Munshi Ghulam Muhiddin handed over a letter for the Nawab asking the Nawab to present himself before the Shahzada at the earliest.

Jaora Nawab

The Jaora Nawab Ghaus Mohammad Khan sent the copy of the letter of Mirza Humayun to the top British officer and prepared to crush the insurgents. There after Raj Khan and Mastukhan planned to capture or kill the Shahzada. They also took into confidence the Mandsaur people viz. Mirza Amirbeg, Qazi Bahaullah, Mirza Bundubeg, Khudayarkhan Jamadar, Shahrasul Khan Jamadar, Munshi Nuruddin, Sheikh Ali Arshad, Sherandaz Khan, Samand Khan *Risaldar*, Kale Khan, Madari Khan, Ali Khan, Kabir Khan, Mohammad Khan, Umar Khan, Amir Khan, Johar Khan, Ahmad Khan, Ahmad Khan and Bholu Khan. On the tenth Muharram (i.e. 31st August) nothing could be done due to crowd and next day the Shahzada had some inkling of the plot against him and he reprimanded Mastu Khan, the person behind the plot, and the plot fizzled out. Next day Mastu Khan and Ali Arshad returned to Jaora and submitted the report to the Nawab.

On the 29th August 1857 the Nawab of Jaora sent a letter to the British authorities stating that Shahzada came to Mandsaur and murdered many Maratha writers of that place and plundered the village and he himself declared that he was a Shahzada and the King of Delhi had sent him to Malwa to drive all the Europeans. He added that Firoz Shah had sent many letters to every place stating that whosoever will come to him, will be given good pay such as Rs.15 to Sepoys and Rs. 35 to 40 to *Sawars*. Firoz Shah wanted to go towards Neemuch to drive European troops and then to Mahidpur and Mhow. Some Mohammedan *Harkaras* were visiting every place. Nearly two months ago that "*Badmash*" with some Mewati sepoys traveled through Badnagar, Khachrod, Jaora and other places, and by force he has taken money from the *Sahookars* of these places for expense, saying that the King of Delhi sent him to drive Europeans from Mandsaur. The Jaora Nawab felt that though the insurgent troops may be more than 10 to 15,000 men, they were not fit for one fire of any company of artillery.[58]

Meanwhile, Ratlam ruler Raja Balwant Singh died on the 29th August and the Jaora Nawab went to Ratlam for condolence. Taking advantage of Nawab's absence, his nephew Abdul Sattar Khan, with some of his followers, went to Mandsaur to join Firoz Shah. Firoz Shah welcomed him with the title of Nawab and a robe of honour and salute of five guns and was appointed him the *Sipahsalar* of the army. This hurt the *Mewatis* who pressurised Firoz Shah to bestow the title of Nawab to Chand Khan Mewati. Both now became rivals and its result was seen in the battle of Neemuch.[59]

Giving the mood and perception of the Mewatis, Tarikh-i-Malwa says that the leaders of the Mewatis thought that they have committed mistake by going against the British Government and the Sindhia Government. If they are pardoned by the British authorities and by the Malwa Subedar, Baba Aptia, they will join the Sindhia. They submitted this proposition before the Nawab of Jaora, who sent his emissary Mirza Rahim Beg and Daraj Khan Jamadar to Nana Saheb at Khachrod. On getting satisfactory reply, they both went to Mandsaur. The informers of Firoz Shah apprised him about the intentions of Mirza Rahim Beg and Daraj Khan. Firoz Shah ordered to capture both of them but they had already fled. Incidentally one Kasim Khan of Firoz Shah's side tried to apprehended Mirza Rahim Beg in a village but in vain.[60]

Firoz Shah's preparations

Shahzada Firoz Shah now collected all his adherents and took oath from them on Quran Sharif that no body will betray him. On the advise of Ghulam Mahiuddin he fixed the salaries of his followers as follows: Rs. 30/- to a *jamadar*, Rs. 20/- to a *dafedar*, Rs. 20/- to a matchlock man and Rs. 15/- to foot soldier. He sent circulars to different states for recruitment of cavalryman on Rs. 40/- pay, responding to which numerous Mewatis and Vilaytees leaving their jobs joined the Shahzada.[61]

The Shahzada of Mandsaur declared that whatever he had done was for the sake of religion (*deen*). It was proper that the Hindus and Musalmans who care for their religion must slaughter Europeans and their followers.[62] Firoz Shah also spread his wings beyond Mandsaur and went to Mahidpur in late August and appointed one *Mirza*, son of a former *Subedar* of Mahidpur, as the head of the rebels.[63]

A letter of 11th September 1857 from Nahargarh written by Pahar Singh Qanungo to Hulasrai, Diwan of Sitamau reveals that a force of 4000 had started from Ujjain. Due to rains it could come only upto Khachrod. The force was so scattered that some portion of it was at Jaora, some at Bardavda and some at Dhodhar. The letter further stated that Baba Saheb from Bhairavgarh and Nana Saheb from Khachrod had informed that Alexendar had started with a force from Lashkar. Further, the insurgents at Mandsuar were facing dissension. The Vilayatis had been placed above the Mewatis, Shahzada was sitting apart and the Sebandis were demanding 15 days salary. The Shahzada was facing financial trouble so rupees twenty thousand had been collected from the *Sahukars* and had been distributed to the soldiers. Mewatis had sent their families to the villages of Narayangarh Malhargarh. The Shahzada had unnecessarily created problem. The delay on the part of the British in suppressing the uprising was due to rains.[64]

The entire force of Maharaja Sindhia including Cavalry, Infantry and Artillery joined by *Vilayatis*, Mewatis and Hindus, had set up the Shahzada and apprehended all the *Ahalkars,* who from mere force and fear had been compelled to show outward allegiance. Gifts were taken from the *Sahukars*. The whole Force amounted to about 5,000 men. The Shahzada had commenced enlisting new men at the following rate- Infantry 20 Rs., Cavalry 40 Rs. and had also issued letters in every place to this intent, that all should unite with him or else they would meet with punishment. Nawab of Jaora also received an order to present himself, or else it will not be good for him in the end. 'No one looks to fidelity, and every individual intends going to Mandsaur.'[65]

Sitamau, Mandsaur and Khachrod

No sooner Firoz shah established himself firmly at Mandsaur, than he started taking action to collect funds for his further plans. He first sent his forces towards Sitamau, which soon reached Bilahri, two *kos* from Sitamau. The Raja of Sitamau, immediately sought provisions from the Nawab of Jaora, who sent Thakur Harisal with provisions and advised the Raja of Sitamau to proceed to Neemuch, in case, the conditions becomes out of control. The Mandsaur force, consisting of about 2000 soldiers with four guns, proceeded further and Sitamau was only one kos away from it. The Raja was asked to present himself before the Shahzada with one lac rupees, ten horses and one elephant and pay all the installments of the revenue, otherwise he will have face destruction by Shahzada's forces. The Raja then sent Bhopal Singh to Mandsaur to meet the Shahzada, who compelled Bhopal Singh to pay rupees eight thousand *hundi* to the Shahzada.[66]

Here at Mandsaur, military activities were at climax. Daily two-three hundred persons joined his army. *Mahajans* and businessmen of Mandsaur were harassed and the contingents of the Shahzada were going here and there. The well wishers of the Sindhia planned that when the forces of the Shahzada are out of Mandsaur, they would call the Sindhia forces and apprehend the Shahzada. Kedar Rao, with his three hundred cavalry was at Mandsaur at the service of the Shahzada, but, in fact he was faithful to Sindhia. The Shahzada was advised to send his forces to capture the supplies and material, thought to be left by the British during their campaigns. When his forces left Mandsaur, the followers of Sindhia planned to let the gates of Mandsaur open in the night, to allow Sindhia forces could enter Mandsaur. Laxman Singh Jamadar left open the Govindi Khandi gate of Mandsaur for the whole night. The Maratha forces under the leadership of the brother of Baba Saheb left Bahadurgarh for Mandsaur. Unfortunately, their forces were late and at the day break they were about 5 kilometers from Mandsaur and they had to turn their backs. Laxman Singh Jamadar with 80 persons was ousted for his betrayal. The returning Maratha force of Baji had skirmishes with some Makranis and then with Kasim Khan Jamadar with 500 Vilaytis and was defeated. Baji fled to Jaora and then to Khachrod. His defeat led the people believe that the Vilaytees can not be defeated and people started thinking of joining the Shahzada's forces.[67]

The atmosphere was so charged that the Sindhia contingent of Khachrod changed its mind and decided to kill Nana Saheb Subedar, whom they thought, was responsible for their destruction. They caught hold of Burhan Ali, the town Qazi, Maulvi Abdul Ghani and Ramzan Shah and proceeded with them to Mandsaur. Nana Saheb now fled from Khachrod to Mhow and met Col. Durand and sought his help. Col. Durand expressed his inability because his absence from Mhow would encourage the Dhar insurgents to occupy Mhow or even Indore. Nana Saheb, then, proceeded to Gwalior for help. Kedar Rao, the cavalry in charge, along with his three hundred cavalry joined the Shahzada. Mirza

Jan Beg, the officer of Risaldar cavalry also took arms. He unfurled the flag of revolt at Khachrod and collected around four thousand persons, of which 50 to 60 persons held *Nishan* and were intent on looting. These insurgents sent letters to Jaora and Ratlam and instigated the inhabitants of those places to take up arms. But Ratlam did not pay heed to the appeals of Jan Beg. At Mandsaur, Sattar Khan and his associates wrote letters to Hindus and Muslims for support.[68]

Situation around

Situation in adjoining areas was far from satisfactory. H.M. Durand, writing in the biography of his father Henry Marion Durand, the erstwhile Agent for the Government General sums up the situation aptly.[69] "To the north-east the outlook was even more threatening. It seemed only too probable that the Nana's forces, broken by Havelock about Cawnpore, might strike southward into Bundelcund, and gathering to themselves the Banda and Gwalior mutineers, pour down upon Central India, where there was nothing to stay their advance but the small column at Mhow. The Nana's agent, Tantia Topee, was known to be intriguing at Jhansee; and throughout the great stretch of Mahratta country from Gwalior southward, the advent of the "Peishwa" was eagerly awaited. Meanwhile, immediately to the east of Mhow, a body of foreign mercenaries, "Velayutees," menaced Nimar; while immediately to the west a strong force of Afghans and others rose and occupied Dhar and Amjhera. From this position they communicated by their left with the Mundesore army, and threatened with their right the Bombay road below Mhow."

He continues, "All this time the little force at Mhow was chafing in helpless idleness. It could not attempt to enter on a campaign during the rains. Its strength lay in cavalry and artillery, and until the "black soil" was dry, there was no possibility of using these arms with effect. The roads themselves were, in most parts around Indore, execrably bad at this season, and off the roads there was no firm ground whereon to deploy and act. The infantry by itself was too weak to do much; and, moreover, the exposure of the men in the open, when carts, baggage, and commissariat stores could not follow, was to ensure the ruin of the force from wet bivouacs and want of supplies. Swayed partly by these considerations, and partly by others of a political nature, my father decided to keep the column stationary at Mhow until the rains should cease, and the surface of the country should become sufficiently hard to admit of rapid and effective movement. In this course he was supported by the Bombay Government, who feared for the security of their frontier, and objected to the employment of the column at any distance from Mhow."

Uprising Predominantly Muslim !

It is not difficult to assess that Firoz Shah's rise as an insurgent leader was unexpected and quick. Starting from an insignificant following, he gathered around him a huge following, which was the result of the charged atmosphere prevalent in the entire country. His rise and the incidences attached to his activities have been also viewed from another angle. Ralph H. Thorpe[70] is of the view that the events between July and November 1857 were significant not only because of the important strategic considerations, but even more so because of the predominantly Muslim character of the uprising. All accounts stress the part played by the mercenary elements but inadequate attention is given to the fact that the events of 1857-58 made more favourable, rather than created, the conditions in which these elements were able to exercise predominant control. Only a few enclaves of Muslim rule remained such as Bhopal, Tonk and Jaora, and the mercenaries, described variously as Pathans, Arabs, Vilayatis, Afghans, Rohillas and Makranis, though were of supreme importance in political conflicts, had to accept a subordinate position to their Maratha and Rajput employers. It is in this context that the *jihadi* enthusiasm , and the attempt to set up a Muslim state at Mandsaur must be studied, not merely as an expression of revolt against the British. A study of the Muslim leaders shows the importance of pre-existing inter-dynastic disputes in determining the choice of revolt or acquiescence to British rule. At Indore the major influence was concentrated in the hands of Nawab Waris Muhammad Khan, an unsuccessful claimant to the regency of Bhopal. Other collaterals of the Bhopal line actively leading the insurgents were the Ambapani Nawabs. At Tonk the Nawab proclaimed that a holy war against the English was unjustified, but his uncle had to be arrested for pro-rebel sympathies. Again, the Nawab of Jaora was extremely co-operative with the British, but his relative Abdul Sattar Khan joined Firoz Shah, and remained in the field until February 1859.

Thorpe adds that as against Delhi, where the Hindus and Muslims looked to Bahadur Shah as their leader, here at Mandsaur, a state, Muslim in outlook was being coming up. While at Delhi the *jihadi* contingents were regarded as an embarrassment threatening Hindu-Muslim co-operation while at Mandsaur an assertion of the Ghazi attributes of the Mughal Emperor can be seen in periodic new proclamation of the jihad and in "The Kotwal, a Brahmin was made a Mussalman of ... an illustration of ... the intolerance of the leaders of the movement." An estimate of the rebel strength makes reference to almost exclusively Muslim support.[71]

An idea of this support may be had from the composition of force of Firoz Shah, which consisted of 5000 Mewatis, 500 Afghans, 200 Bhils, 400 Makranis, 3000 miscellaneous and 1000 Cavalry.[72] Moreover, we find more than once that the Afghans and Makranis and other foreign mercenaries joining Firoz Shah went out raising the standard of Islam.[73] This does not seem to be unnatural, because there were concentrations of underemployed mercenaries in most of the small states. Various Arab and Rohilla groups were expelled from Hyderabad in 1853, and others were thrown out of work by a reduction in the size of armies under the Subordinate Treaty system.

Implications

Mandsaur, which was under Sindhia, now came under the control of Firoz Shah and his influence was felt all over Malwa. The establishment of Firoz Shah's headquarters at Mandsaur was bound to affect the British strategy of the British in Malwa area. The communication of the British with Bombay was threatened and they were unable to start a military campaign against Firoz Shah and his allies. The impending rainy season gave enough opportunity to Firoz Shah to strengthen his position around Mandsaur and the success of his allies at other places enhanced his power and influence. His prestige was greatly enhanced attracting the mercenaries and other rebellious elements with the result that by September a huge army was at his disposal. The Jaora Nawab was of the opinion that 'the insurgent troops may be more than 10 to 15,000 men.....'[74]

As Showers puts it, the temporary success of the rebel force was daily attracting supporters to the Shahzada's standard, and was producing a disastrous effect throughout the surrounding district of the British superintendence. Several of the chief towns, on receiving the Shahzada's call to allegiance, ejected the British authorities and declared for him. Some places around Neemuch viz. Jawad, Ratangarh, Singoli, all rose in open rebellion.[75] On the 30th of August the troops of Nawab of Jaora were mutinous and threatening. The Muslims commenced plundering in city of Ratlam.[76] About ten thousand insurgents had collected at Mandsaur.[77] According to Col. G.B. Malleson, it was estimated in September that some fifteen thousand men with sixteen or eighteen guns, had rallied round his standard, and this estimate was subsequently found to have been below the actual number.[78]

British situation

The insurrection erupting on 1st July at Indore gradually engulfed most of Malwa and by second week of August 1857 situation deteriorated to such an extent that Colonel Durand, Agent to the

Governor-General, had to sum up his review of the insurrection in Central India on 13 August 1857, in these words: "The means of coercion at our disposal are extremely inadequate to restoration of order, and to the stay of anarchy wherever that exists. The Gwalior contingent has wholly gone from our colours and is now with its well-equipped artillery, in Scindhia's hands, and, of course, at his disposal. It may be against us; it can never ask (sic) for us. The Malwa contingent has lost all its cavalry, a body of 800 good horse, and the infantry so misbehaved at Indore that it is impossible not to hold the whole body in suspicion......The Bhopal contingent after its disgraceful and treacherous behaviour at Indore, is now in open mutiny at Sehore[79]. The Bheel Corps is in course of reassembling . . . . At Nagode . . . there is not a gun, there is not a sabre, there is not a musket which can be called in aid of the maintenance of order and British supremacy."[80]

George W. Forrest also has same words about the prevalent situation-- Every hand was now against the English—from Neemmuch to Saugor, from Gwalior to Mhow—and the force at Durand's disposal was extremely inadequate to the restoration of order and the say of anarchy. The Gwalior Contingent had become our most powerful foe; the Bhopal Contingent was in open mutiny and no trust could be put in the Malwa Contingent. Holkar's force, which had supplied the troops who had attacked and burnt the Residency consisted of 30 guns of various caliber, about 1400 Horse and five battalions of disciplined Infantry and Holkar's capital contained a turbulent population ready to burn and slay. Durand's force was sufficient to disarm Holkar's force at Indore and maintain order in the city. But he could not at the same time disarm Holkar's troops stationed in separate cantonments. He was weak in Infantry and the rain had rendered the country impassable. He, therefore, wisely determined to leave Indore alone for the present and to make preparations for operations against the enemy who were openly defying our power and spreading rebellion over the whole State of Malwa.[81]

A poem on Firoz Shah, 1860

Shahzada Firoz Shah's exploits in Malwa inspired some local poets to write about the condition and reaction prevalent in days. One such composition of 85 lines in *Malwi* dialect has come to light recently. The poem commences with the onslaughts of Shahzada Firoz Shah followed by the oppressive activities of the insurgents. It describes as to how the Makranis, Iranis and Vilaytis were being cut by the English. Then the poet prays the Lord *Ganpati* to relieve the people of these atrocities.

Later half of the poem deals with the businessmen of Mandsaur for whom the composer uses most abusive language. Probably he had some personal vengeance against them.[82] The poem is an indication of popular feelings against the atrocities committed by the insurgents. As would be seen, Shahzada Firoz Shah had later warned the insurgents in his Proclamation not to indulge in the murders and atrocities.

Tarikh-e-Malwa also mentions about the complaints of the inhabitants of Mandsaur to the British authorities as to how the people had to suffer the atrocities inflicted by the Vilaytis, who molested ladies and tortured people, particularly Bohra Muslims.[83] These were known as Daudi Bohras and belonged to Shia sect, but were different from other Shias. They were amongst prominent businessmen in Malwa and were found almost in every towns of Malwa. Since they were ardent Shias, they were despised by the Vilayti mercenaries.

Shahzada Firoz Shah was aware of these developments and must have been in close touch with Saadat Khan and Waris Khan, the leaders of Indore uprising and was quick to plan his next move, which involved, joining hands with the Indore and Mhow insurgents at Gwalior. Very soon he found himself at the top of rebel forces proceeding to Delhi and even after his defeats he maintained a considerable following amongst the insurgents. Though he was not a ruler of any jagir or State, nor was he a military officer of any State, as was the case with other insurgent leaders, still he began to be considered an important person who effected the course of the insurgency. He carved his place with the principle insurgent leaders of the country viz. Rani Laxmibai, Tatya Tope, Nana Saheb Peshwa, Khan Bahadur Khan, Maulvi Ahmadulla Shah and others.

Reference :

1. Fifty kilometers north of Mandsaur in M.P.
2. Twenty kilometers south of Ajmer.
3. Forty eight kilometers north of Ujjain.
4. Twenty three kilometers south-west of Indore,
5. Forty one kilometers west of Dhar in M.P.
6. Near Sardarpur. Distt. Dhar, M.P.
7. For a detailed description of day to day events see the letters of Vazir Beg, the Vaqil of Sitamau placed at Indore published in Raghubir Sinh, *Malwa ke Mahan Vidrohkaleen Abhilekh,* 1986
8. Thirty seven kms. west of Bhopal in M.P.
9. Thirty eight kilometers east of Raisen in M.P., between Dehgaon and Ghairatganj.
10. *M.P. Gazetteers, Sagar District,* 1970 (Hindi), p. 524. Rahatgarh is 23 kilometers west of Sagar in M.P.
11. Shrivas[illegible] op. cit., pp. 131-132.
12. S.A.A[illegible] and Bhargava, Freedom Struggle in Uttar Pradesh,1957-61, Vol. II, [illegible]5.
13. E. Thompson, *The Other Side of the Medal*, London, 1930, p. 103-04.
14. Wazir Khan's (a close associate of Firoz Shah) deposition, 3-3-1859, Political Proceedings 30-12-1859, No. 311, letter no. 54, dt. 9-3-1859. See Appendix 1. In March 1859 Wazir Khan mentions his age as 22, so in mid August 1857, he must be about 20 years.
15. 21 kilometers from Sitamau and Mandsaur in M.P.
16. Twenty-five kilometers north-east of Ratlam in M.P.
17. Letter dated *Bhadrapad badi* 10, *Samvat* 1914 (i.e.14th August 1857) written by Paharsingh, the *Qanungo* of Nahargarh to Hulasrai, the *Kamdar* of Sitamau state, Preserved in Shri Natnagar Shodh Sansthan, Sitamau, Basta no. 115, file no. 43. Sitamau is situated thirty-two kilometers south-east of Mandsaur.
18. Eighty-five kilometers north of Ratlam on Ratlam-Neemach road in M.P.
19. Foreign Department, Secret Consultations 30-10-1857, S.No. 291, Translation of Marathi letter dt. 24-8-1857
20. Fifty kilometers north of Mandsaur on Mandsaur Chittorgarh road.
21. Forty five kilometers east of Neemach, now on the western bank of Gandhisagar dam.
22. Translation of news report from Mandsaur of the 26th August 1857, Tuesday, Received at Indore, 30th August 1857 sent by Ramchandra Rao Martand,

offg. Minister, Holkar Darbar to Col. H.M. Durand, Offg. Agent Governor General for Central India, Camp Mhow, dated Palace Indore, 30th August 1857. Foreign Department, Secret Consultations, 30th Oct. 1857, No. 284, F.S.U.P. III, pp. 148-50.

23. Letter from Ramchandra Rao Martand, Offg. Minister, Holkar's Darbar, to Colonel H.M. Durand, Offg. Agent Governor General for Central India, Camp Mhow, dated Palace Indore, 30th August 1857, Foreign Secret Consultations, 30th October, 1857, No. 284. F.S.U.P. III p. 148
24. Letter from Lt. Col. H.M. Durand, Offg. Agent Governor General, Central India, to G.F. Edmonstone, Secretary to the Government of India, Fort William, dated Indore Residency, Camp Mhow, the 1st of September 1857, Foreign Secret Consultations, 30th October 1857, No. 313. F.S.U.P., III, pp. 155-156.
25. Quoted in Charles Ball, *The History of the Indian Mutiny*, Vol. II, 1858-59, pp. 630-32.
26. Zambaur, table V and footnote 43 *"combatys contre les Anglais 1857-8, disparait"*
27. Thomas William Beale, *An Oriental Biographical Dictionary*, new edition revised and enlarged by H.G. Keene, India reprint, 1996. 38
28. E. Thompson, *The Making of the Indian Princes*, London, 1930, p. 282.
29. website: http://www.royalark.net/India4/delhi9.htm gives the names of twenty sons of Bahadurshah II but Firoz Shah does not figure in this list. (website visited on 4th May 2012)
30. pp. 472-5 (1895)
31. G.W. Forrest (ed.), *The Indian Mutiny 1857-58*, LPP reprint 2003, Introduction,, p. 69
32. Dispatch to Secret Committee, no. 21, AGG CI letter dt. 7-9-1857, n. 84
33. R.C. Mazumdar, *The Sepoy Mutiny ad the revolt of* 1857, 1963, p. 91
34. Raghubir Sinh, *Malwa ke Mahan Vidrohkaleen Abhilekh,* 1986, Introduction. Also Sen, p. 310. and S.A.A. Rizvi and Bhargava, *The Freedom Struggle in Uttar Pradesh,* 1957-61, Vol. II, p. 655
35. website: http://www.royalark.net/India4/delhi9.htm (website visited on 4th May 2012) According to it Jahandar Shah were seven brothers and one of them was Muhammad Azim who had eight sons and one daughter. His fourth son was Muhammad Humayun, who had a son named Muhammad Ali Shah and and a daughter Zamiunnisa. Muhammad Ali Shah had three sons- Karim bkht Kallu and Muhammad Shujat Afshar. Shujat had four sons: Khuda Baksh, Hidayat, Kamruddin and Noor Baksha. Noor Baksh's son was Nizam Bakht and according to genealogy, while Bahadurshah II was of the fourth generation after Jahandarshah, Noorbaksha was also of the fourth generation after the cousin of Jahandarshah. Thus Bahadurshah II and Noorbaksha were cousins and Nizam Bakht, son of Noorbaksha was the nephew of Bahadurshah II.

    To make the things easier this may be put like this: Emperor Muazzam> son Muhammad Azim> son Muhammad Humayun Bakht Bahadur> son Mirza

Muhammad Ali Shah> son Muhammad Shujat Afshar> son Noorbaksh> son Nizam bakht.

Other branch of Emperor Muazzam was as follows: Emperor Muazzam> son Emperor Jahandar Shah> son Empedror Alambir II> son Emperor Shahalam II> son Emperor Akbar II> son Bahadur Shah.

36. During the great uprising at Delhi Moinuddin Hasan was working as a Kotwal of Pahadganj Thana of Delhi, appointed by the Emperor of Delhi. He had saved the life of Sir T.J. Metcalf and after the suppression of the uprising, on the request of Metcalf, he wrote his memoirs in 1878 with the title *"Khadang-e-Gadar"*, with the condition that these would be published after his death. He died in 1885 and the English translation was completed in 1892 and was published in 1898 from England.

    Its Hindi translation by Abdul Haq was published in 1999 with the title *"Gadar-1857"* by the University of Delhi, Delhi.

37. Moinuddin Hasan, *Gadar-1857*, Hindi Translation by Abdul Haq, 1999, Delhi, pp. 123-24

38. *Tarikh-e-Malwa* by Munshi Syyed Karim Ali, Meer Munshi, Residency, Indore, published by Ratan Prakash Mudranalaya, Ratlam. A copy of this huge work is preserved in the Library of Shri Natnagar Shodh Sansthan, Sitamau. The Sansthan has got it translated into Hindi by Maulvi Yusuf Mohammad khan. This work is dated Hijri 1290 i.e. about 1874 AD.

39. *Baghawat-e-Malwa* by Qazi Abdul Quddus Faruqi Depalpuri. A copy of this work is with Mohammad Idris Khan, Mandigate, Mandsaur, M.P. from whom my friend K. C. Pandey (Dashpur Shodh Sansthan, Nai Aabadi, Mandsaur, MP) so kindly got it translated into Hindi for me. This work does not bear any date.

40. *Tarikh-e-Jaora* by Ashfaq Ahmad Jahidi. A copy of this work is preserved in the library of Shri Natnagar Shodh Samsthan, Sitamau, Distt. Malwa and relevant portion of this work were translated for me by Amanulla Khan, Laduna, Sitamau. This work is dated January 1947. Since this work is quite recent, it has been used by me sparingly.

41. *Tarikh-e-Malwa,* p. 990

42. *Bagawat-e-Malwa*, pp. 70-80.

43. As regards the title of Humayun, it is clear that Firoz Shah initially bore the title of Mirza Humayun and this fact is corroborated by British records, Foreign department, Secret Consultations, 30th Oct. 1857, no. 290. But he was later popularly known as Shahzada Firoz Shah.

44. In a letter to Secret Committee written by the Agent to Governor General, Central India, Firoz Shah has been described as a descendant from the Imperial family of Taimur, and a pensioner from Banaras. Dispatch to Secret Committee, no. 21, AGG CI letter dt. 7-9-1857, no. 84.

45. *Tarikh-e-Malwa*, p. 991 has also Parnakhedi.

46. A *kos* is equal to about three kilometers.

47. Probably Barauda, eighteen kilometers south-east of Jaora in M.P.

48. According to *Tarikh-e-Malwa*, pp. 990-991, he, thereafter, along with his attendant Karim Bakhsh reached Dewas region. Karanjeet Singh kept him in

his residence. During rains Firoz Shah stayed at Mandu and then went to Khachrod and stayed in the *chouki* of the Mewatees.

49. Thirty kilometers south-east of Mandsaur and fifteen kilometers south-west of Sitamau in M.P.
50. *Tarikh-e-Malwa*, p. 991 also has Sheikh Karanji.
51. Shrivastava, op. cit., p. 145 writes it Dudan Saiyid and says that he came there at about 9 a.m. on the 26th August 1857 on the basis of Inward Vol. 80, News Report from Mandsaur, dated 26th Aug 1857, from Offg. Minister Indore Darbar to Offg. A.G.G. for C.I. In the light of the date of the events that followed, this date is erroneous. It seems that Shrivastava has picked up the date of the letter written by Offg. Minister Indore and has assigned it to the event, while the letter must have been written after the incidence, i.e. arrival of Firoz Shah at Dudhan Saiyid *dargah*. *Tarikh-e-Jaora* also says *Dudhan Shahid*.
52. *Tarikh-e-Jaora*, p. 62 has 2nd August
53. *Tarikh-e—Malwa*, p. 992 has 3 months
54. *Tarikh-e—Malwa*, p. 992 has 1 lac
55. Foreign Department, Secret Consultations, 30th October. 1857, No. 290
56. It seems that the descendants of Mirza Amir Beg resided at Mandsaur for a long time. Some relevant information is given in Narayanrao Deshmukh's article *'Mirza Amir Beg-Krantikari Rajya ka Pradhan,* published in *Pratham Swatantrata Sangram mein Mandsaur Jile ka Yogdan*, research seminar, 14th November 1987, published by District Archaeological Association, Mandsaur. This article gives the following information— The present Kalakhet was earlier known as *Mirzaji ka bagh* i.e. Garden of Mirzaji. Out of this *bagh*, Mirza Naim Beg son of Mirza Abdul Rahim Beg sold some land to the Government in 1958, where the present Balaganj Middle School was built. According to the survey no. 1339 and 1345 there were *dargahs*, a pucca house and a *baori*. Probably this family migrated to Ujjain. Some descendants still reside at Ujjain and there is one Mirza Naim Beg *Marg* . Mirza Naim Beg died at Mirzawadi, Ujjain on 8th January 1958.
57. Raghubir Sinh, op. cit., p. 106, letter no. 22, dated 2nd September 1857.
58. Foreign Department, Secret Consultations 30-10-1857, No. 297. p. 4346, *Urgee* from the Nawab of Jaora dt. 29-8-1857 forwarded by Ramchandra Martand, Minister Indore to Durand, AGG Indore.
59. *Tarikh-e-Jaora*, p. 66.
60. *Tarikh-e-Malwa,* pp. 994-95.
61. *Tarikh-e-Malwa,* pp. 994-95.
62. Entry in the *Holkar Darbar Baranishi*, 1857. No. 4789- Proclamation to the members of Indore Darbar, Luniya (ed.), *Phases of Freedom Struggle in Madhya Bharat*- 1857, 1957, pp. 127-128.

    Though this entry does not have any date, according to the editor, it may belong to 7th August 1857.
63. Inward Vol. 80, Letter No. 73, dated Indore Palace 1st Sept. 1857, from Rao Ramchandra Rao, Offg. Minister, Indore Darbar, to Capt. Hutchinson,

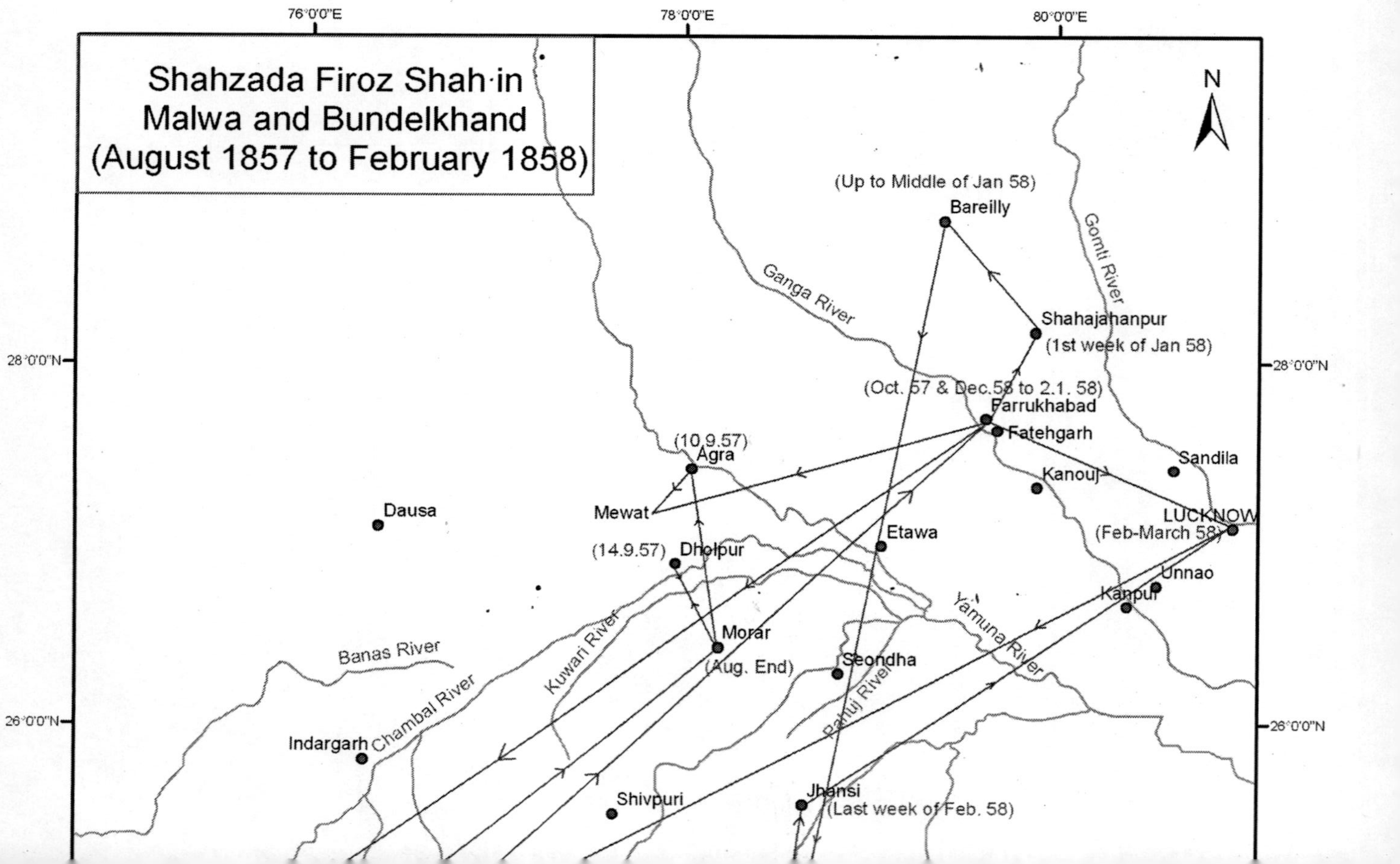
Shahzada Firoz Shah in
Malwa and Bundelkhand
(August 1857 to February 1858)
N
76°0'0"E
78°0'0"E
80°0'0"E
28°0'0"N
26°0'0"N
(Up to Middle of Jan 58)
Bareilly
Gomti River
Ganga River
Shahajahanpur
(1st week of Jan 58)
(Oct. 57 & Dec.58 to 2.1. 58)
Farrukhabad
Fatehgarh
Sandila
Kanouj
LUCKNOW
(Feb-March 58)
(10.9.57)
Agra
Mewat
Dausa
Etawa
(14.9.57)
Dholpur
Unnao
Kanpur
Morar
(Aug. End)
Banas River
Kuwari River
Yamuna River
Seondha
Pahuj River
Chambal River
Indargarh
Shivpuri
Jhansi
(Last week of Feb. 58)

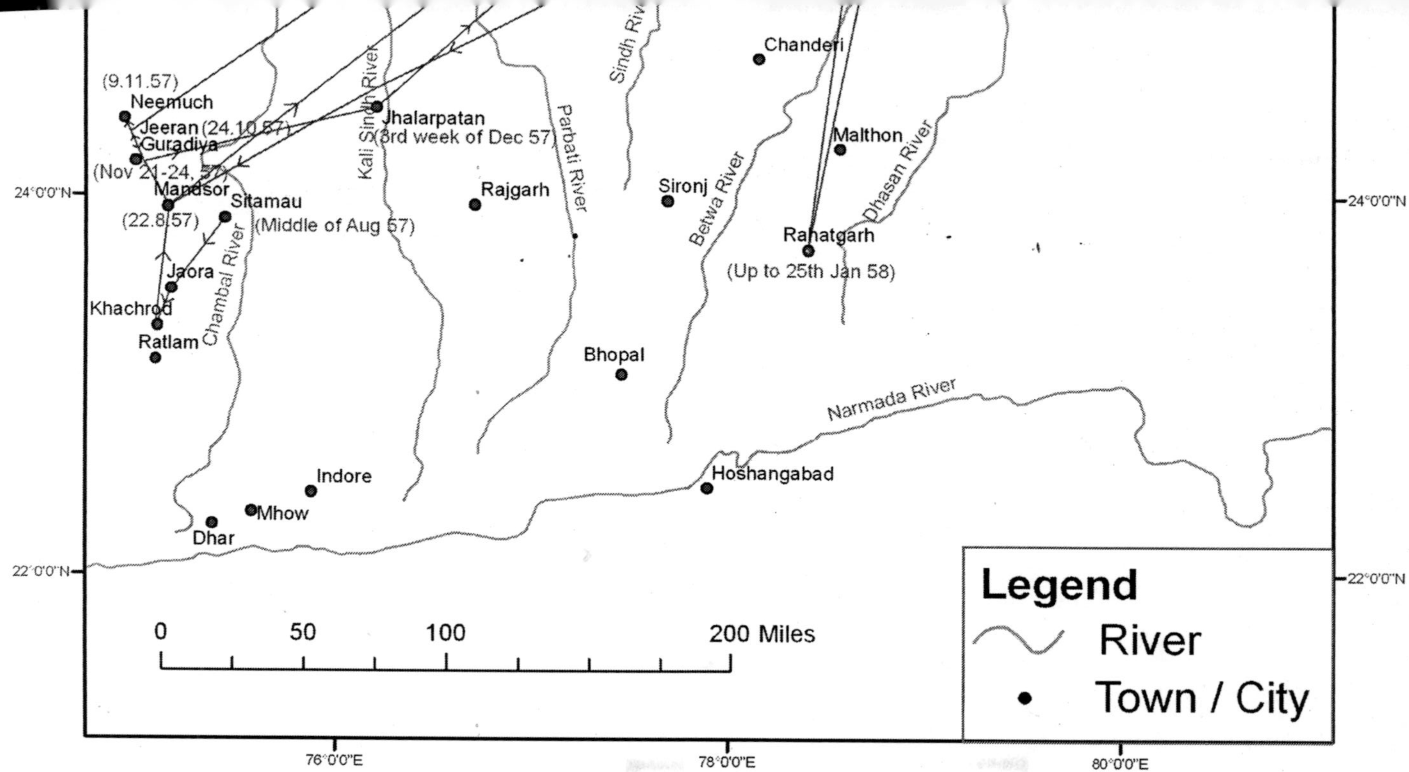
(9.11.57)
Neemuch
Jeeran (24.10.57)
Guradiya
(Nov 21-24, 57)
Mandsor
(22.8.57)
Sitamau
(Middle of Aug 57)
Jaora
Khachrod
Ratlam
Chambal River
Kali Sindh River
Jhalarpatan
(3rd week of Dec 57)
Rajgarh
Parbati River
Sindh River
Chanderi
Sironj
Betwa River
Malthon
Dhasan River
Rahatgarh
(Up to 25th Jan 58)
Bhopal
Narmada River
Hoshangabad
Indore
Mhow
Dhar
24°0'0"N
22°0'0"N
0
50
100
200 Miles
Legend
River
Town / City
76°0'0"E
78°0'0"E
80°0'0"E

Map 2

Commdt. at Mhow. (quoted in Shrivastava, p. 147, fn 5. But K.L.Shrivastava probably on the basis of the letter of 1st Sept. infers that Firoz Shah went to Mahidpur in early Sept, which is not correct.)

64. Letter dated Bhadrapad Badi 8, Samvat 1914 (i.e. 11th September 1857) written from Nahargarh by Paharsingh, Qanungo to Hulasrai, Diwan of Sitamau. Shri Natnagar Shodh Sansthan, Sitamau, Basta no. 115, file no. 43
65. Letter from Lt. Colonel H.M. Durand, Offg. Agent to Governor General, C. India, to G.F. Edmonstone, Secretary to the Govt. of India, Fort William, dated Indore Residency, Camp Mhow, the 1st Sept. 1857. Foreign Department, Secret Consultations, 30th October 1857, No. 313. F.S.U.P., III, p. 155-157.
66. *Tarikh-e-Malwa*, p. 995.
67. *Tarikh-e-Malwa*, p. 996.
68. Ibid, pp. 996-997
69. H.M. Durand, *The Life of Major-General Sir Henry Marion Durand*, London, 1883, pp.225-26
70. Ralphe H. Thorpe, *Bengal Past and Present*, July-December 1969, Vol. LXXXVIII Part II No. 166, pp. 137-138.
71. Thorpe, p. 139
72. Letter from Lieutenant H.M. Durand, Offg. Agent Governor General for Central India, to G.F. Edmonstone, Secretary to the Government of India, Fort William, dated Indore Residency, Camp Mhow, the 28th September 1857, F.S.U.P. III, p. 153.
73. Secret Proceedings 30-10-1857, S.No. 291, p.4342, Translation of Marathi letter dt. 28-8-1857 and From Agent, No. 25 dt. 11-8-1857, N. 84 dt. 7-9-1857, No. 66 dt. 1-9-1857, N 63 dt. 1-9-1857, N. 117 dt. 15-9-1857.
74. Foreign Department, Secret proceedings 30-10-1857, No.. 297. p. 4346, *Urgee* from the Nawab of Jaora dt. 29-8-1857
75. C.L. Showers, *A Missing Chapter of Indian Mutiny*,1888, p. 122. Jawad- 15 kms. north of Neemuch, Ratangarh- 40 kms north-east of Neemuch and Singoli 60 kms north-east of Neemuch.
76. Parliamentary Papers XLIV 1857-58 part I p. 223. Further Papers 4. Durand to Governor .General. 30th August 1857, forwarded by Ramchandra Bahadur Martand, Minister Indore to AGG, Indore.
77. Letter from Ramchandra Rao Martand, Offg. Minister, Holkar's Darbar, to Colonel H.M. Durand, Offg. Agent Governor General for Central India, Camp Mhow, dated Palace Indore, 30th August 1857, Foreign Secret Consultations, 30th October, 1857, No. 284. F.S.U.P. III p. 148
78. G.B. Malleson, *History of the Indian Mutiny*, 1857-59, Vol. III, London, 1888, p. 66.
79. Thirty-seven kilometers west of Bhopal.
80. Foreign Deptt. Secret Consultations, Nos. 87-89, 29th January, 1858
81. George W. Forrest: *The Indian Mutiny*, 1857-58, Vol IV C, 'Introduction', p. 69.
82. The poem along with its English summary is given in Appendix 4.
83. *Tarikh-e-Malwa*, pp. 116-117.

Chapter - 3
Morar, Jeeran & Guradia

Firoz Shah had been attempting to secure the support of different rebel military contingents in Malwa and was planning to march towards Delhi with their support. He knew that on 4th July 1857 Saadat Khan, the insurgent leader of Indore had left Indore for Gwalior and Delhi with a large army consisting of rebel contingents and other mercenaries. The rains had set in but this did not deter the insurgents. They all proceeded towards Delhi by Bombay Agra Road via Dewas, Biaora, Rajgarh, Shajapur, Kolaras and Seepri (Shivpuri) and their first important halt was to be at Morar cantonment of Gwalior State.

Jayaji Sindhia, the ruler of Gwalior state, was loyal to the British not so much out of natural sympathy as of necessity. Thirteen years ago his army was badly battered by the British army in the battle of Maharajpur and he had to sign an humiliating treaty which he was deprived with some of his territories and had to reduce his army. Despite the reduction in size the Gwalior army was still a formidable force due to its discipline and training received by the French military commanders. Early in 1857 in a visit to Calcutta, he was impressed by the enormity of British power. He was told by the British authorities that as soon as the British control disappeared, the Jat, the Bundela and the Rajput would simultaneously rise against the Marathas. This led Jayaji Sindhia and his prime minister Dinkar Rao to espouse the cause of the British during this critical juncture.

The Gwalior contingent

Sindhia's force at Morar cantonment had already revolted at Gwalior on the 14th June 1857. In fact the Gwalior contingent was at the centre of the revolt in the Gwalior territory. Looking to the quality and capacity of this force, a short background of the Gwalior contingent may be given here. It was created in 1844 after the disbanding of a major part of Sindhia's army after its defeat in the battle of Mahrajpur. Originally the Gwalior contingent consisted of a regiment of 400 cavalry and 200 Maratha horse, 52 *golandaz*, 2 nine pound guns and 2 twenty-four pound guns, a howitzer and an infantry regiment of 600 men. The rates of salaries paid to its sepoys was quite high. 30 Chanderi rupees per month were given to cavalryman and 7 Chanderi rupees per month to an infantryman. These salaries were higher than those of Bengal Army. From time to time, as the need arose, the strength of the contingent was increased. By 1857, the size of the cavalry and infantry had grown from 600 each to 1,158 and 6,412 respectively. The number of its gunners increased from 52 to 74 and that of guns from 4 to 26. Sizable section of the sepoys and officers of the contingent were Muslims. The artillery was predominantly manned by the *poorbeas*, who were mainly Brahmans and Thakurs from eastern part of Awadh and the adjoining districts of Bihar. Though the Gwalior contingent was raised, trained and officered by the British and financed by Sindhia, it was not under the control of Sindhia. 'The contingent consisted of exactly the same elements as the Bengal Army and were liable to be inspired by the same feelings as the sepoys in the British employment. They shared their fears and suspicions and were as much moved by the story of the greased cartridge and adulterated food as other people in Oudh and North-Western Provinces.'[1] In addition to the Gwalior contingent, there were present in the Gwalior territory in 1857 three other troops- Sindhia's regular troops, Baiza Bai's troops and irregular troops of the chiefs under Sindhia.[2]

On the night of the 14th June 1857 the whole lot of sepoys came out of their barracks shouting and began to set fire to the bungalows and shoot the officers and Europeans indiscriminately. The Political Agent and a few others with some of the ladies found an asylum in the Phulbagh palace and were later escorted to Agra. As regards, Jayaji Rao, the ruler of Gwalior, he was prepared to pay for their withdrawal, but Major Charters Macpherson, the Political Agent at Gwalior, advised otherwise. He advised the Sindhia ruler that he should pretend to take the insurgent into his service and keep them at Gwalior as long as possible. This was in the interest of the British, because, the trained army of Gwalior could have played havoc against the British, if it leaves Gwalior and joins the insurgents in adjoining areas. Accordingly, the Sindhia continued to pay their salary and gave them hope that he would lead them against the British. Any now he was successful in retaining the rebel sepoys till September, 1857. Thus, as S.N. puts it, "Sindhia had rendered a great service to his friends. A formidable body of well-trained and well-armed rebels, whose intervention could at different times decide the fate of Agra, Delhi and Kanpur, sat idle in their lines at Morar, when the British were slowly restoring their authority over North India."[3]

Before the arrival of Mhow and Indore contingents, the Gwalior rebel contingent was busy consulting amongst themselves about their further move. It appeared that there was a difference of opinion between various sections of the insurgents, some favouring the cause of Nana Saheb, while others of Bahadur Shah II. The *Poorbeas*, mostly high-caste Hindus, pleaded for the contingent to move away to Kanpur, which was located closer to the region from where they hailed. As against this, the elements from the 'North', mostly Muslims recruited from the Doab region as well as those hailing from Gwalior itself (among whom naturally would also, be included a large number of Marathas) were insisting that it would be better to go to Agra, and from there, to Delhi. These differences were apparently so pronounced that Sindhia, instigated by the English officers, tried to use one section of sepoys against the other. He went to the extent of offering bribes to the officers of the contingent and 'their priests' for instigating the sepoys to continue to press their respective views vehemently. This problem tended to become particularly serious after the arrival of the insurgents from Indore and Mhow at Morar on 31st July. They were on their way to Agra and were very eager to persuade the contingent to accompany them. This was bound to aggravate differences between the *Poorbeas* and the rest. And then, around the same time, arrived at Gwalior sepoys of 6th infantry regiment, who were dispersed from Kanpur after Nana Sahib's flight from there on 15th July. These fugitives from Kanpur started spreading a very defeatist view within the contingent's ranks. They reportedly argued that the leaders' plan to engage the British forces were impracticable and advised them to give up all such ideas. This defeatist view was ultimately rejected by the leaders as well as the sepoys.[4]

The plan of the insurgents of Mhow and Indore was to join hands with the Gwalior insurgents and then jointly march towards Agra. Five companies of the 6th regiment, stationed at Lalitpur, were also marching towards Gwalior. On the 30st July 1857, the Indore rebels came to Morar.[5] Their strength was one Regiment of Mhow 700, Regular Sepoys 400, Sowars 200, and guns of Indore 7 and 1000 *'Ghazis'*. With the addition of Gwalior contingent the combined force at Morar Cantonment had the strength of 574 cavalry and 3000 sepoys of Sindhia contingent, 400 hundred sepoys of Holkar Batallion, 1000 *Ghazi* Mewati, seven guns of Holkar, 700 sepoys of 23rd Batallion of Mhow and 120 sepoys of Bengal Light Infantry.[6] This force was unable to decide its further course and deliberation between themselves went on. They spent about a month at Gwalior and created suspense amongst the people at large and also were a matter of concern for the Sindhia government. Sepoys of the Gwalior contingent were passing time and had no plan to move further because they were being paid their salary by the Sindhia government. The attitude of this formidable force of Gwalior contingent killed all the hopes of Mhow and Indore insurgents, who had planned to move to Delhi along with this powerful and well trained Gwalior contingent. But three weeks passed on without any activity.

Firoz Shah in Morar

By the end of August Shahzada Firoz Shah, covering a distance of about 265 miles, joined the Morar gathering with his own contingent which must be of considerable size. With Saadat Khan's concurrence Firoz Shah was accepted as their Chief Commander and Saadat Khan as his ADC and a salute of 22 guns was given to Firoz Shah. Now it is not difficult to imagine the influence of Firoz Shah. He earned the respect and allegiance of the insurgence collected at Gwalior. Though he might have been benefitted by his lineage, but later on he succeeded by his own capability and it seems, the insurgents were impressed by his fast success in and his organising capacity in Malwa. It is to be remembered, as the events show, he had never met Saadat klhan and his associates before Morar, because Firoz Shah became active in Malwa, after Saadat Khan had left Indore. The respect and attention he earned in Morar by the insurgent leaders quickly spread in north India. The young man of around 20, who was an unknown figure before two months, attained the category of top insurgent leaders of the country. The credit may be given to his brilliant personality and courage.

No sooner Firoz Shah was accepted as a leader of the insurgents, than Saadat Khan wrote a letter to the Sindhia Maharaja requesting him to honour Firoz Shah befitting to his title and adorn him with the royal dress wore by an Emperor. The Sindhia Maharaja immediately tore this letter.[7] The *Vakil* of Gwalior informed the Political Assistant about this incidence adding that the reply of his master to Saadat Khan was that the Raja of Gwalior had been several times deceived by forged princes as Raja, therefore, it was necessary to wait till the arrival of the Delhi king who was ready to go to Mecca with all the Royal family in course of two months, then the *salam* and *nazrana* will be paid at once. At this answer the mutineers were displeased and made arrangements to put the forged prince upon a throne and proclaimed him the King of Gwalior and then plunder the Lashkar."[8]

While Firoz Shah was away from Malwa and was planning to proceed to Delhi with Saadat Khan, the insurgents in Malwa were quite active in asserting their authority on the adjoining territories. In the mornong of 29th August 1857 many of the Mohammedans as well as some of the Hindus of the infantry regiment spoke of joining Firoz Shah's standard after doing away with the British at Mahidpur. [9] Further south they plundered Bhopawar and Sardarpur, and then marched on Dhar occupying it on the 31st August.[10]

To Dholpur

Indore and Mhow insurgents ultimately could not pursue the Gwalior contingent troops to accompany them to proceed to Delhi. Its reason was clear, The Sindhia ruler, advised by the British administration, promised the Gwalior contingent to pay their full salary and this resulted in making the Gwalior contingent indifferent towards the cause of the insurgents. This condition prevailed for about four months and the British were saved from the problems which could be created if the Gwalior contingent had become active and had joined the Indore and Mhow insurgents. The British could now get time to improve their condition.

The inactivity and non cooperation of the Gwalior contingent was extremely detrimental to the cause of the insurgent troops of Indore and Mhow who wanted to proceed to Delhi. They were deprived of an efficient and powerful army. If they had succeeded in soliciting the support of the Gwalior Contingent, their chances of success would have been enhanced many fold. The cunningness and diplomacy of the British thus rendered the insurgent army and leaders weak to a considerable degree. The non cooperation of the Gwalior contingent not only delayed the departure due to deliberations, but also disheartened the Indore and Mhow insurgents.

From Gwalior, the Indore and Mhow insurgents along with Firoz Shah and other insurgent leaders proceeded to Agra. On the 3rd September 1857 they pushed forward 5000 men and on the 4th crossed the Chambal to rescue the *ghaut* and the fort of Dholpur. This sudden advance was undertaken because they had the news that an English force was moving on Dholpur. The insurgents, therefore, even considered it necessary to their circumstances.[11]

On the 8th September the luggage was sent to other side of the river, but due to heavy rains the insurgents had to wait. Their entire luggage could only cross the river till 14th September. On reaching Dholpur, Amabapani Nawab Waris Mohammad Khan wrote to Rana Bhagwantsingh[12] of Dholpur to welcome Firoz Shah in the camp but the Rana did not agree to it. Though the Rana had only 700 cavalry, he was undaunted. The Rana also refused Waris Khan's demand of Rupees one lac. But Waris Mohammad Khan any how exacted that amount from the Rana and disbursed the pay of his force. In Dholpur camp the number of insurgents swelled to 2000 by now and they also occupied 8 guns of the Rana of Dholpur. The insurgents declared Firoz Shah as the ruler of Dholpur and remained at Dholpur till 18th of Septebmer.[13] A *parwana* was sent by Firoz Shah to the Raja of Dholpur that the Raja should give the charge of the fort to the two companies sent by Firoz Shah. The result of this parwana is not known properly, but then we find Firoz Shah coming to Morar Cantt., where he was received with a salute of 21 guns and every honour was paid to him. Fifty sawars were sent to bring his baggage from Dholpur. He was treated with greatest respect and consideration by the insurgents.

Bhagirath Silawat of Indore had, in the meanwhile, gone to Delhi and had arrived there. Another thing, which needs to be mentioned, was that a misunderstanding had taken place between Waris Mohammad Khan and Saadat Khan. While the former wanted to go to Delhi, the latter to the Nana Saheb to Bithoor, near Kanpur. Further, the Hindus and Muslims were quarrelling amongst themselves, the former wished to join the Nana Saheb of Bithoor and the latter the king of Delhi.[14]

In the meantime the followers of Firoz Shah in Malwa were active around Mandsaur. This is evident from a letter of Wazir

Beg, the *vaqil* of Sitamau State at Indore, written on 14th September 1857 wherein he says that it was heard that 25 thousand persons had gathered at Mandsaur and the effluent section of Mandsaur had called for the mercenaries on the condition that if the town was not plundered, they would be given one fourth of the amount. The effluent section of the town paid rupees 25 thousand to the new regime and were opposed the extra demand.[15] This shows that Firoz Shah had made suitable administrative and military arrangements at Mandsaur to work efficiently in his absence. In fact, Mandsaur was the base camp of Firoz Shah, where he could come back and resume his command and activities.

It was reported on 20th September that Alexander (Assistant to Sir John Malcolm, the Resident of Indore) had entered in Bherogarh with a force and had started from Khachrod but his progress was slow due to rains.[16]

The number of insurgent army in Malwa, in the close of September 1857, consisted of 1200 Afghans and 3800 Mewatis, 17 guns on wheels, 3 guns on ground. As per another estimate the strength of the insurgents was as under:

Mewatis	5000	
Afghans		500
Makranis	400	
Bhils	200	
Miscellaneous	3000	
Cavalry	1000	
Total	10,100	

According to this estimate, in the insurgent army at Malwa, 16 guns were serviceable but the insurgents were short of ammunition and were making great exertions to manufacture powder and shot. It was also reported that money was scarce and the pay had been reduced from 15 rupees to 7 rupees a month for Sepoys.[17]

Further, on the 3rd October, 1200 insurgents with 3 guns went to Sitamau and demanded tributes and *nazar* of 1.5 lacs of rupees from the chief who was obliged to meet the demands.[18] Obviously in the absence of Firoz Shah, they were directed by his associates stationed at Mandsaur. This shows that despite the absence of Firoz Shah from his headquarters at Mandsaur, the insurgents were quite active.

Defeat at Agra

As has been said, the insurgents under the leadership of Firoz Shah and Sadaat Khan did not get any support from the Raja of Dholpur and without wasting time they left Dholpur on 5th October and proceeded to Agra.[19] Daily they busied themselves in manufacturing bombs, gun powder and ammunitions. They always kept their guns ready to fire lest they may not be caught unaware by their enemies and advanced rapidly. Looking to the rapid campaign of the insurgents the British thought it prudent to act fast and a force was sent against the insurgents under Colonel Greatheart accompanied by Captain Maxwell's contingent. On the 10th October 1857 the insurgents under Saadat Khan and Firoz Shah had to face the British force under Captain Maxwell at Manowat, 6 miles from Agra. The battle lasted for two hours and about one thousand five hundred insurgents were killed and their entire luggage along with the guns was captured amounting to rupees ten lacs. The insurgents, after the defeat, scattered here and there.[20]

This defeat dealt a severe blow to the insurgents and ultimately they had to stop their march and Saadat Khan and Firoz Shah decided not to proceed further. Saadat Khan went to Alwar and stayed there for some time and Firoz Shah, according to Wazir Khan's deposition,[21] separated from the greater part of the Mhow-Indore insurgents, went to Mewat with about 10-12 followers and remained there for sometime. It may be mentioned that Wazir Khan, after the reoccupation of Delhi by the British Force had come to Farrukhabad.

In Farrukhabad

On arrival of the Jodhpur Legions in Mewat, Firoz Shah accompanied them to Farrukhabad, where the Awadh insurgents had placed Nawab Tafajjul Hussain Khan on the throne. Needless to say that he must be well aware of the developments at Farrukhabad, where the Awadh insurgents had placed Nawab Tafajjul Hussain on the throne. Farrukhabad, prior to the outbreak of 1857, had a chequered past. Muhammad Khan Bangash at his death in 1743, held Frrukhabad and other adjoining areas. For some time Farrukhabad domains were formally annexed by Awadh, but were recovered in 1750 by Ahmad Khan, another son of Bangash. After Ahmad Khan's death in 1771 his territory then became tributary to Oudh. In 1777 British troops were stationed at Fatehgarh as part of the brigade which guarded Awadh, and from 1780 to 1785 a British Resident was posted here. In 1801 the Awadh government ceded to the British its land in the District, together with the tribute paid by the Nawab of Farrukhabad, and the latter gave up his sovereign rights in 1802.[22] This state of affairs continued till the eruption of 1857 uprising.

On 14th May 1857 the news of the outbreak at Meerut reached Fatehgarh close to Farrukhabad. The 10th Native Infantry stationed at Fatehgarh showed symptoms of a mutinous spirit on May 29, but it was not till June 3 that a body of Awadh insurgents crossed the Ganges, and arranged for a rising on the following day. The European officials and residents abandoned Fategarh the same evening; but several of them returned a few days later and remained till June 18, when another outbreak occurred, and the rebels placed the Nawab of Farrukhabad on the throne. The 41st rebel Native Infantry, from Sitapur, marched into Fatehgarh, and the Europeans began to strengthen the fort. On June 25 the rebels attacked their position, which became untenable by July 4. The fort was then mined, and its defenders escaped in boats and the Europeans were compelled to flee from Fatehgarh. The Nawab governed the District unopposed till October 23, when he was defeated by the British at

Kanauj. The troops, however, passed on, and the Nawab, with Bakht Khan of Bareilly, continued in the enjoyment of power until Christmas.[23]

Though Firoz Shah and Farrukhabad Nawab knew each other with regard to their rebel activities at their respective bases, this was probably the first meeting between Firoz Shah and Farrukhabad Nawab Tafajjul Hussain Khan. It seems that Firoz Shah became popular with the insurgent sepoys of Farrukhabad to such an extent that when Firoz Shah was about to leave Farrukhabad, the rebelled 41st Native Infantry prevented him from going and placed him at their head.[24] Firoz Shah had to stay for more time at Farrukhabad but the circumstances prevailing at far off Mandsaur were preventing him to stay at Farrukhabad.

Back to Mandsaur

While at Farrukhabad, Firoz Shah was in close touch with his followers at Mandsaur and the critical situation which suddenly arose in Mandsaur area, did not allow him to stay at Farrukhabad for long and he hastened towards Mandsaur. With his band of followers he rushed towards south-west to cover a distance of about 400 miles, one of his longest dash, and reached there in time. Since we find him in the battle of Jeeran[25] (24th October) it may be surmised that leaving Farrukhabad, Firoz Shah might have reached Mandsaur in the middle of October, because we find him writing a letter from Mandsaur to the Nawab of Jaora for supply of some items immediately.[26] He wrote to Jaora Nawab, "You have been since long putting off your attendance here, but now I must tell you in plain terms that if you are willing to come to me you must make haste and let it be impressed upon your mind that you will be the most deserving of my favor and consideration. While on the contrary that is in case of your refusing to attend, I will myself be soon there, and then obedience and supplication on your part will do you no good. Should you take the advice of one like myself who is the well wisher of the people in general and of the Mahommedans in particular, it would be better for you that previous to your waiting on me you should send without failure 60 or 70 *maunds* of gunpowder and 12 or 18 *maunds* of lead along with the bearer of this Shooka [Rooka], as I am to move to some place I require these materials and your supplying them to me will in some measure ingratiate you to me. If you are a well wisher of the Islam and of the house of the Sultan you will do as desired." As a post script it was added that on the very receipt of this *Parwana* and without delay either to day or tomorrow should be sent :

Some money in cash according to your ability.
60 or 70 maunds of Gunpowder
12 or 18 maunds of lead.
Some Golden tea Cups
A few pair of plates.
-do- of China cups.
-do of large plates.
1 or 2 pairs of Chandeliers.
2 Candle Sticks.
2 or 3 Carpets.
2 pairs of fine shawls white or green.

The Nawab of Jaora sent a copy of this letter to Col. Durand, Off. AGG for Central India.

Revolt at Dhar

Meanwhile, the Pawar ruler of Dhar had opposed the forces of the British Government in the open field, and when beaten in the field, the Dhar troops held out the fort of Dhar. The leaders of the Dhar troops were in communication with the Mandsaur insurgents and pressed Firoz Shah to relieve the besieged fort of Dhar by the rapid advance of a reinforcement of 4000 men and 10 guns. The insurgents, who had occupied the fort of Dhar for more than a week (22-31 October 1857), now attacked the Mahidpur contingent under Major Timnis. Sheikh Rahmatulla unfurled the green flag and his people joined the insurgents. Since Diwan Ramchandra Rao Bapuji and Rani Jeejabai of Dhar and her brother Bhim Rao

Bhosle were unfriendly towards the British Government, charges were framed against Bhim Rao and *Diwan* Ramchandra Rao and the administration of Dhar State was taken over by the British Government.[27]

In October itself, the Firoz Shah's troops, who had previously occupied Dhar and Amjhera, advanced to the Bombay road and threatened to interrupt Durand's communications with Bombay, to command the line of the Narmada river along the Bombay frontier, and to attack Neemuch. They also sent a pressing invitation to Holkar's troops to join them.[28] But ultimately they were defeated by Major Orr.

With the commencement of October, the rainy season came to a close and the Mhow contingent was ready for an advance. Durand also called up some of the Hyderabad Contingent Cavalry from south of Narmada river. He had now to decide his first target. Though it was the need of the hour to first disarm the insurgents of Indore, their strong position dissuaded Durand to try to disarm them. Instead, he finally decided to move towards Mandsaur via Dhar. On the 22nd of October the British force of about 1500 men arrived before the fort of Dhar and occupied it on 1st November 1857.[29]

In the meantime events had proceeded fast at Mandsaur-Neemuch leading to the battle of Jeeran.

Battle of Jeeran 24th Oct. 1857

On 22nd October 1857 a body of 400 insurgents was dispatched from Mandsaur to intercept a convoy of ammunition which was erroneously reported to have left Jaora for Neemuch, and which they expected to fall in with at Kungeti, on the Neemuch road. Being disappointed of their booty they made an unpremeditated raid on the adjoining village of Jeeran, about 10 miles from Neemuch. Jeeran was within the assigned district under British superintendence. When the authentic intelligence of the march of the insurgents to Jeeran was received by the British Officers at Neemuch, the Superintendent, without consulting Showers called upon the Officer Commanding, Captain Simpson to march a force to drive the rebels out. As the plan of attack was matured by the Officer Commanding without seeking any co-operation from Showers in his official capacity, Showers inferred that the a arrangements made were enough for this enterprise. Two advanced parties of the 2nd cavalry, under Captain Tucker and Lieutenant Blair respectively, were sent on the night of 23rd October by different roads, the main column following at half-past 5 A.M. On 24th October the party under Captain Tucker fell in with the insurgents near Jeeran at daylight . He advanced with a few men towards the insurgents, and charged right through them, paying with his life for the daring act. In the *melee*, Captain Lawrie, of the 21st Native Infantry was wounded severely in the breast with a lance. His horse was shot under him; and one trooper, with Captain Tucker, was killed in the charge. The body of Captain Tucker was carried off by the rebels, but afterwards recovered by the men of his own troop severed from the head, which had been retained by his murderers. [30]

While this was in progress, the main contingent from Neemuch, under Captain Simpson, arrived before the walls of Jeeran, and found the insurgents assembled on the brow of a hill, about 200 yards in front of the town. Captain Banister was then dispatched with a squadron to the other side of the town and the action proceeded, and raged for some time. The infantry in vain attempted to dislodge the insurgents from their position; and Captain Reade, commanding a detachment of the 83rd regiment, was killed, and Captain Soppit, of the 12th native infantry, dangerously wounded. Both infantry detachments seeing their commanders fall, made a retrograde movement, and the insurgents, emboldened by it, rushed upon them, but Captain Simpson recaptured the mortar, and dispersed the insurgents, who fled to the fort. In this charge, Captain Simpson was severely wounded in the head, and his two lieutenants were also disabled. At the end of the day a report reached Captain Bannister, who succeeded Captain Simpson in command of the column, that a large force of the insurgents was advancing on Neemuch from another direction. For this reason, as well as on account of the great natural strength of the place, Captain Bannister determined upon returning to protect Neemuch, which he reached with the remains of his column the same night, taking with him the body of Captain Reade.[31]

Jeeran had to be left in the possession of the insurgents and the British force had to return to cantonments the same night. The heads of Captain Reade and Captain Tucker were cut off by the insurgents and carried away and placed over the gates at Mandsaur.[32] While the defeat at Jeeran was very much depressing for the British side, it provided great confidence amongst the insurgents. It was the first victory of the insurgents after their success in subduing Mandsaur under Shahzada Firoz Shah in the last week of August 1857. The Insurgent troops, besieging the fort of Neemuch, were now full of hopes to take it from the British garrison.

Showers' Reaction

Brigadier Showers took this reverse seriously because he considered it as a prelude to an attack on Neemuch. He sent an urgent message the next morning to Colonel Durand, at Mhow, and also reported the matter to Brigadier-General Lawrence, and communicated them his views about the probable consequences. He requested General Lawrence to adopt precautionary measures in view of the attack that might now be anticipated. But General Lawrence treated Showers' apprehension as without sufficient foundation. Colonel Durand, on the other hand, took Showers' communication and apprehension seriously and replied to Showers on 29th October 1857 that he was sorry to learn about the reverse at Jeeran, which may embolden the Mandsaur insurgents to move against Neemuch before the British side was ready to advance to Neemuch. Concurring with Showers, he believed that the reverse at Jeeran might induce the insurgents to attack Neemuch, Durand expressed his intention to march to Mandsaur as soon as the work of Mhow Column in his immediate vicinity was over. Contrary to Showers' views, Captain Lloyd, the Superintendent, who had called for and accompanied the expedition, had reported the result of the Jeeran affair to Brigadier-General Lawrence as a "victory", basing his views upon the evacuation the place by the insurgents. The fact was that having been left in possession of Jeeran, the insurgents had returned the following day to Mundsaur to carry back their spoil and the trophies.[33]

To have an overview of the situation AGG Durand planned to visit Badnagar via Ratlam, Khachrod and Mahidpur and proceeded to Mandsaur via Sitamau. It was reported that there was general order to the military to kill and plunder Mandsaur and at the Camp site of AGG, the Mewatis were killing the travelers.[34]

Insurgents Approaching Neemuch

The effect produced by the Jeeran incidence changed the whole aspect of affairs at Neemuch which was then a British stronghold between the Rajput State of Mewar and Malwa. It was 120 miles south of Nasirabad and 25 miles north of Mandsaur. Originally the Jawad-Neemuch districts had formed an integral portion of the Udaipur territories. Later Jawad-Neemuch districts were occupied by and finally ceded to the Marathas. In 1843 these districts were assigned over to the British government from Gwalior Darbar for the punctual payment of the Gwalior Contingent force consisting of 72nd Native infantry, 7th Regiment of the Gwalior contingent and a wing of the 1st Bengal Cavalry. The contingent at Nasirabad rose in arms on the 28th May 1857 igniting the uprising at the Neemuch on the 3rd June. No officers lost their lives, and through the help of some loyal Indians they managed to escape to Udaipur.

The insurgents of Neemuch contacted some Mewar officers viz. Bakhtawarsingh and Khoobchand, who were posted at Neemuch, to occupy Neemuch under Mewar. There request was turned down on the plea that they can do it without the permission of Mewar government.[35]

The insurgents of Neemuch, after plundering the bungalows, the Treasury, and the rich people of the town, left for Agra and Delhi to serve under the Delhi Emperor as was done by the other insurgent bands. Neemuch was soon afterwards occupied by British contingents from Mewar, Kota and Bundi. When the insurgency had flared up under Shahzada Firozshah, the British troops at Neemuch were anxiously keeping an eye over the developments at Mandsaur. The Superintendent at Neemuch conveyed to Showers the rumour of a threatening inroad of the insurgents in force into the district, and similar rumours prevailed almost daily, causing the bazaar to be deserted in panic.[36]

As *Tarikh-e-Malwa* puts it, Hirasingh Jamadar, meanwhile, had come to Mandsaur along with his two hundred followers and had joined Firoz Shah. On the behest of Hirasingh, Mahidpur platoon and artillery were summoned. On November 5th, 1857 five thousand Mewatis, Vilaytis and Makranis and local people fully armed proceeded to Neemuch. They had with them two guns named Fatah Lashkar and Kala Pahad and two small guns. But the force did not possess proper magazine and had only coal and salt on the name of gun powder. The other officers of this force were Maulvi Jamaluddin, Shamand Khan Risaldar and Chand Khan Mewati, Abdul Sattar Khan and Noorkhan. Soon 7000 foot soldiers, two hundred gunners and 500 cavalry were collected accompanied by 1000-1500 persons with batons. The total was around 10,000. Leaving Mandsaur, this force reached Malhargarh and then to Jamunia.[37]

According to British accounts, the insurgent force collected for the purpose, was understood to consist of some 66 Afghans or Vilaytis, 4000 Mewatis and 350 horsemen of various races, with seven guns. Thus the threatened danger was obviously of a serious character. For several days, no perceptible movement on the part of the insurgents appeared to substantiate the rumour; but at length on Sunday, the 8th of November, a spy arrived at the British camp at about 3 P.M., and announced that the insurgents, who had been for a day or two encamped at Malhargarh, about 12 miles from Neemuch, were advancing in great force and their advanced guard of cavalry was already within three miles of the town. As no time was to be lost in an effort to check their approach, a detachment of the 2nd light cavalry, consisting of a hundred men under Captain Bannister, moved out, and proceeded along the Mandsaur-road.

By the time they had marched about two miles, the insurgents were drawn in a commanding position on a hill. They had three guns, and numbered at least 3500 men. With such an immense disparity of numbers, and advantage of position, the British decided not to attack them.[38]

The fort of Neemuch was a small square, measuring externally 170 yards, with a quadrangular bastion at each angle; the walls, 18 and half feet high, by 8 feet thick at the base, had on the inner face open casemates, which were chiefly converted into barracks. The eastern and western bastions were built solid, to allow heavy ordnance or mortars being placed upon them; the southern and northern were hollow, but bomb-proof; and in the former of the two the magazine was contained. The gateway of the fortification was in the north-eastern curtain, protected by a drawbridge and deep ditch; and in front of it, at a short distance, was a mound or embankment to mask the gate, called the Victoria mound, upon which a 24-pounder gun was mounted. On the bastions were placed on 8-inch mortar, two 9-pounders, two French 6-pounders, and a couple of guns taken from the insurgents at Nimbahera. The stock of ammunition was limited; and as there were no loopholes in the parapet of the curtain, about 1000 sand-bags were made, and arranged to supply the deficiency.[39]

Externally, on three sides of the fort, and extending for about 1500 yards, was a tolerably deep trench, the excavated soil forming an embankment towards the fort; and on the fourth side was a wide *nullah*, which had been dammed up. Upon the space between the trench and the walls of the fortification, the political agent Captain Showers had his bungalow and compound, the latter being well stocked with trees and outhouses. The garrison within the fort consisted of about 327 fighting-men. There were also in the fort, for protection, two ladies with their families, several sergeants' wives with their children, forty-one sick of the various corps, and some native servants; making altogether a total of 778 persons. Besides these there were all the gun horses, with about twenty others belonging to the officers, and several commissariat bullocks. For this number of persons and cattle there was but an indifferent supply of provisions; and the water supply for the whole was only to be obtained from two wells in the fort, each about ten feet in diameter, and containing about twelve feet of water.[40]

On approach of the insurgents, the regular Cavalry, consisting of about 250 sabers, was ordered out to meet them. The officer in executive command, Captain Bannister, called upon Showers before mounting, in company with the Superintendent Captain Lloyd, to seek his co-operation with his body-guard of Mewar troops. Showers joined him with 300 Horse. They met the insurgents advancing beyond a *nullah* forming the rear defense of the British Cantonments. On the approach of the British contingent Firoz Shah formed line in open single files so as to display as extended in front as possible, and showed many flaunting flags. His numbers appeared about 2,000, of which 100 were horse; of the foot, between 500 and 600 were undisciplined vilayatis and the remainder were armed rabble who had come, probably, in the hope of plunder.[41]

On forming up, the enemy opened fire from three guns. Showers proposed to Captain Bannister a combined charge on the enemy's position. but Captain Bannister declined on the ground of restrictive orders from the officer in command, who, being on the sick list, was unable to take the field. After observing the enemy for about an hour, he retreated upon the fort. The insurgents then breaking again into column of route continued their march towards Neemuch. Observing this, Showers advanced the Mewar detachment to oppose a check to the enemy's entry. The movement had the desired effect and the the insurgents halted bringing theirs guns to the front, and opened fire again. He stood held in check till nightfall, when he camped on the open ground on the same spot. The Mewar detachment was then withdrawn from the field, a strong picket being left at the bridge. Showers in his dispatch of the day's operations commented on an officer in the field acting under general restrictive orders from a commandant not in the field.[42]

Firoz Shah was still camping on the open ground. Looking to the situation, Showers proceeded to the fort and strongly urged the officer commanding to move out the troops to attack Firoz Shah at daybreak. But the Officer Commanding decided not to attack the insurgents, but to occupy the fort with Infantry. After some time the Officer commanding marched straight away from Neemuch, in disregard of Showers' official remonstrance against his doing so.[43]

On 9th November Firoz Shah sent a letter to his Commander-in-Chief Maulvi Jamaluddin, 6 *Risaldars* of the Mewatis and 2 *Risaldars* of Makaranis and all he Makranees and *Vilayati sardars* stating that, 'On the strength of each *Shooka [?]* and the representations of spies, well-wishers and *Elakadars*, I am convinced of the dubious character of the forces of Rapoora, sent by the ill-natured or disaffected Kotharee. It is now advisable that they should be sent to me and although they might have pledged their faith by *Kooran* or the Ganga they are not to be trusted. Summud Khan *Risaldar* spoke to me that the *Kotharis* were not to be trusted. Should it be not possible to send the whole force, tell the principal leader to come to me with a detachment and then watch whether he is willing to come or not. Should he be willing to come send him with a proper escort, if not believe in their infidelity and so arrange that they may not be able to do you harm and see them placed in such position that no other recourse may be left to them, but to die or fight the enemy. Secure his guns and use his ammunition in killing the enemy. Be always on your guard with regard to this force and act in such a ay that it may do us no harm and the life and property of these men may be in danger. The proverb "Make the enemy to deal with a serpent" should be the principle of your action, for should the serpent bite the enemy or the enemy kill the serpent in both cases we are to gain out object. We will destroy one of the two enemies. Should an action have taken place and it be in your power, secure the guns and ammunition. On the contrary should these doubts be proved to be real kill the man, for its is proper to kill the enemy when it is in our power to do so. You are all wise, do as you may think proper'.[44]

Neemuch Fort Besieged- 9th Nov. 1857

The success of the insurgent force in marching unopposed to Neemuch and sit down before the fort, was daily attracting supporters to Firoz Shah's standard, and producing a disastrous effect throughout the surrounding district of the British superintendence. Several of the chief towns, on receiving the Shahzada's call to allegiance, ejected the British authorities and declared for him. Jawad, Ratangarh, Singoli, all rose in open rebellion. On the 3rd morning of the siege i.e. on the 11th November, Showers was advancing with a handful troop towards the fort from Kasoonda, a village within sight of Neemuch.[45]

Advancing from the south, he swept rapidly down upon the villages of Bugana and Nixonganj.[46] Taken completely by surprise, the insurgents fled in a panic. Many were cut up, some burnt alive in huts that were fired. When they had increased to about 50 in number, Showers urged the Lieutenant commanding the troop to charge them. But instead of doing so he inclined away, the men firing with their carbines. All this time the insurgents were increasing rapidly till they amounted to about equal in strength with the British troop, and, emboldened by the inaction of the troop, they began to advance towards the troop. The next moment the insurgents were upon the British force. Jackson and Showers were only saved by being splendidly mounted. Retiring upon Nimbahera, both of them encamped securely under its walls.[47]

The British garrison in the fort was running short of small arm ammunition. The insurgents on their part were preparing ladders for escalading the Fort. An attempt at escalade was made a few days afterwards, and successfully repulsed by the fire of the garrison without any of the insurgents' ladder party getting within 50 yards of the walls, or any loss sustained by the garrison.[48]

On Wednesday, the 18th of November, the tenth day of the siege, an attempt was made from the fort to dispatch a messenger to the Mhow force, which was supposed to be then at Mandsaur to request for replenishment of the supplies but the poor messenger was taken by the insurgents.[49]

On the night of the 20th November at about four on the following morning, a sepoy of the 12th regiment reported, that the insurgents were advancing towards the north-east curtain. The alarm was sounded. Almost at the same moment, a heavy fire of musketry opened upon the insurgents from the southern bastion, and from the curtain on both its flanks. The effect of the fire was such that the attacking division was driven off. Another portion of the insurgent force was bringing a gun as near as possible to the southern bastion to try the effect of shot at close quarters on the wall. After repeated efforts to advance, the insurgents retired from the ground dispirited and thoroughly checked, leaving behind them their scaling-ladders, and, one of their consecrated Muslim standards. The acquisition of the standard became an object of intense desire among the officers in the fort, and several volunteered to bring it in. But Captain Simpson refused to risk his Europeans for the purpose. At length, a *havaldar*, Teeka Singh, and the Biloch, Mulam Khan, offered to descend from the southern bastion and bring in the coveted prize, and they were permitted to make the attempt. The two brave men descended, under cover of the fire from the walls, and seizing the standard, quickly returned with it. Mulam Khan was made a *havaldar* on the bastion at once, and Teeka Singh was promoted to *jamadar*.[50]

The number of insurgents had greatly increased by the unexpected advantage they had obtained in getting possession of the Cantonment unopposed. The ammunition of the beleaguered force was running low, and there appeared no prospect of any supply being thrown in. The surrounding district under the British, having almost wholly declared openly for Firoz Shah, no supplies of any kind could be thrown in. In consequence of the rapid growth of the movement and increase in numbers of the investing force of the insurgents, the situation of the garrison had become most critical.[51]

On the night of 21st, considerable noise was heard in the rebel camp towards the residency and in Showers' compound, and a desperate attempt to recover the captured standard was expected; but, to the great relief of the garrison, about five o'clock in the morning of the 22nd, it became apparent that the insurgents were moving off. Meanwhile a message had arrived from the Shahzada at Mandsaur, ordering all the insurgents to return to Mandsaur to assist in repelling the attack made upon Mandsaur by the Mhow column.[52] Immediately the insurgents stopped their activities in Neemuch and returned post haste towards Mandsaur to save it from the Mhow column which had arrived in the vicinity of Mandsaur and intended to head towards Neemuch for the relief of the British contingent. Thus Neemuch and its little garrison was saved.[53]

Arjun Singh Sahiwala, an officer of the state of Mewar was also present during the siege along with Showers. He gives some minor but interesting incidences during the siege.[54]

Showers' annoyance

Two incidents of the siege of Neemuch seemed to Showers, in view of the loss of prestige, to call for public enquiry. "First, that a band of undisciplined rabble should have been suffered to enter and burn the Station, and shut the garrison up in the Fort, without their being attacked by the British Troops, And second, the Officer Commanding the Regular Cavalry marching away from the vicinity of the beleaguered fort, instead of remaining to co-operate for the relief of the garrison.[55]

Battle of Guradia- 21-24 Nov. 1857

While the Mandsaur insurgents were engaged in Neemuch, the British Forces, accompanied by Col. H.M. Durand commanded by Brigadier Stuart, commanding Malwa Field Force, reinforced by the troops of Major Orr, Commandant of Hyderabad Field Force and supported in the rear by the Allied Forces of the Indian States of Ratlam, Sailana, Jaora and Sitamau, encamped four miles south of Mandsaur on the 21st November 1857.[56]

A fierce battle was fought at Guradia near Mandsaur, a detailed description of which was sent by Brigadier C.S. Stuart to his superiors.[57]

According to it, on the morning of the 21st November, the force, accompanied by the field force, Hyderabad Contingent arrived within three miles and-a-half of Mandsaur about 9 A.M., and as Stuart had no good information about the roads or the area in the immediate vicinity of the town, neither he knew the fords of the river Shivna, which it was necessary to cross before reaching the town. He determined upon encamping until a good reconnaissance had been effected. The insurgents at Mandsaur, hearing of his approach, had posted pickets entirely covering the country and mustered in some force outside the walls of the town, and appeared inclined to attack him. Stewart, however, contented himself with reinforcing the pickets, and leaving the whole charge of the front to Major Robertson, 25th Regiment Native Infantry, the field officer of the day, returned to camp. About 3 p.m. Stuart received intimation that the insurgents were advancing in force, and threatening both the flanks and center. Stuart, accordingly moved out to meet them. The insurgents advanced steadily, with banners flying, and appeared in great numbers. They were charged by Lieutenant Dew and Major Orr and the were driven back with great loss. The insurgents were pursued for some distance, in fact, until they nearly reached the walls of the town, and nothing further occurred that day.

As has been mentioned earlier, this impending danger on the security of Mandsaur made the insurgents to raise the siege of Neemuch and proceed to Mandsaur with their force. On the 22nd November Shahzada Firoz Shah, accompanied by his force, proceeded to defend Mandsaur and to join his associates stationed at Mandsaur. Stuart had already received intelligence from the Government General's Agent about Firoz Shah's move and determined to frustrate this by intercepting him.

Early on the morning of the 22nd instant, Stuart moved forward his force in order of battle. His advance was unopposed, and reaching the village of Kalgipur near Mandsaur, made a flank movement to the left and crossed the Bakri ford of the river Shivna, about 1,400 yards to the south-west of the town of Mandsaur. He then encamped facing the west of the town, his flanks well protected by the two branches of the river, and his line running at right angles. It was reported that Cavalry were seen on the left, and Major Orr taking the Hyderabad Contingent under Captain Abbott and Captain Murray, saw about 300 horse, supposed to be under Heera Sing, keeping at too great a distance to allow of being attacked. Reinforcements of Cavalry were sent for, and whilst the left wing under Captain Gall and Lieutenant Clerk was moving up, intelligence was brought to Major Orr that Heera Sing's baggage had just left the village of Guradia, on the Neemuch road. It seemed that the object of Heera Singh's party was to draw the British Cavalry away from his baggage. The British troop galloped off in pursuit and caught up the insurgents about two miles south of Peeplia, 10 miles north of Mandsaur on Mandsaur Neemuch road, and, after cutting up about 200 of them, halted at a *nullah*, a mile to the south of that village. On perceiving it strongly occupied by the insurgents, they then returned to camp.

Feeling assured that the infantry seen in Peeplia formed the advance guard of the insurgents, Stewart moved at 8 o'clock A.M. on the 23rd instant by his left, and crossed the northern branch of the river Shivna and halted his column, and collected all his baggage on the reverse flank, then moving on to his proposed camp on the Neemuch and Mandsaur Road, to oppose the insurgents coming from either direction. On coming on to the ground he strongly reinforced his rear-guard, and proceeded to meet the insurgents. After a short advance, he found the enemy occupying a very strong position, with their right in and beyond the village of Guradia, their right center covered by a *nullah* and lines of date trees, their battery of six guns on a rising ground, with a large mud hut protecting their gunners, and their left stretched along the ridge running east from the village. The insurgent infantry, with banners flying, moved down to meet the British troop through the intermediate fields of high *jowarry*, and their guns opened fire. Stuart immediately halted his line, and replied to the fire with Captains Hungerford's and Woolcombe's batteries. After a few rounds he permitted Captain Hungerford to move his half battery to a position on our right front, from which he could enfilade the insurgents. After an advance of about 300 yards, firing was resumed, which was very effective. A most gallant charge was then made on the guns of the insurgents by Lieutenant Martin, who found, however, that the position was still very strongly held by the insurgent infantry. Severely wounded he was compelled to retire. Captain Hungerford's half battery was again advanced to within 100 yards, and after a round or two of grape, the guns of the insurgents were at once again charged and captured. The insurgents had to flee in great numbers into the village to their right. The 3rd Regiment of Cavalry, Hyderabad Contingent, under Major S. Orr, was just at this moment rapidly advanced and swept down upon them in their retreat, and killed great numbers. Having halted within about 300 yards of the village.

"The men of the 86th and 25th Regiments dashed forward in the most gallant manner, and, having entered the village, commenced to drive all before them. They soon met, however, with very warm opposition, the enemy having taken possession in great force of many houses, from which a most harassing fire was kept upon our men. Under these circumstances, and as, moreover, I could get no satisfactory accounts of what was passing in my rear which I knew from the firing I heard, as also from the pressing applications I had received for reinforcements had been warmly engaged, I recalled the Infantry, and posted strong pickets all round the village, and moved the remainder of the men a short distance off to where the baggage had been passed up from the rear. I then learnt that, during the afternoon, when we were hotly engaged in the front, a strong body of the enemy from Mundesore attacked our rear, and endeavoured to carry off the siege train, baggage etc. They were, however, most gallantly repulsed on every occasion. In one of these attacks, I regret to say that Lieutenant

Redmayne, Her Majesty's 14th Light Dragoons, was killed, whilst most bravely leading his men against the enemy. Notwithstanding the many attempts made by the enemy to press upon and harass our rear, it gives me great satisfaction to be able to state that not a particle of baggage was lost, nor a follower injured, on this occasion." Para on the 24th instant Stewart arranged with Captain Hungerford, Commandant of Artillery, that the village of Guradia in which the rebels had taken refuge, should be well shelled and again assaulted by the Infantry. Accordingly, he moved up to it about noon, and found that the insurgents were as he had left them the preceding evening. After a heavy fire of three hours, the detachments under command of Major Keane and Major Robertson again stormed the village and killing great numbers of the insurgents they themselves also suffered severely. At sunset the troops were withdrawn intending to move against the fort of Mandsaur the next day.

On the morning of the 25th instant, it was learnt that the insurgents had, during the night, completely evacuated Mandsaur, and were scattered in flight in various directions, having lost about 1,500 of their number. Stewart accordingly removed his camp to Mandsaur, and engaged himself in dismantling the forts, destroying the guns, etc., before leaving Mandsaur. By the successful operations of the Malwa field force, and field force Hyderabad Contingent, in the vicinity of Mandsaur, the Neemuch garrison was been relieved from the assault with which it was threatened.

Brigadier Stuart sent to his superiors, the names of those British Officers, who won his commendation and were recommended for reward. They were-

- Colonel Durand, Officiating Agent to the Governor General for Central India
- Major Boileau, Field Engineer and his assistants, Lt Prendergast and Gordon;
- Captain Mayne, Intelligence Department
- Captain Coley, Major of Brigade

- Lieutenant Macdonald, Deputy Assistant Quartermaster-General
- Lieutenant Thain, Sub-Assistant Commissary-General
- Surgeon Mackenzie, Staff Surgeon
- Captain Gall, commanding left wing of Her Majesty's 14th Light Dragoon
- Major Orr, 3rd Regiment Cavalry, Hyderabad Contingent
- Captain Hungerford, Commandant of Artillery, Malwa field force
- Captain Woolcombe, commanding No. 4 light field battery
- Captain Brown, and the officers and men of the B Company, Madras Sappers and Miners
- Major Keane, Her Majesty's 86th Regiment.
- Major Robertson and the officers and men of the 25th Regiment, Native Infantry.
- Assistant Surgeon Butler, of the Artillery.

The Guradia reverse was a serious blow to Firoz Shah, who, after his victory at Jeeran, was in high spirits hoping to succeed against Neemuch. Now having his forces scattered, he had not only to gather his troops but also had to find out another suitable base to continue his struggle. Despite his reverse this young warrior did not loose hope and proceeded to selvage his strength and resources to prepare for further struggle.

After Guradia

On 25th November 1857 Nana Saheb Apte, the *Sar Suba* informed the Resident that Firoz Shah has fled towards Nahargarh and the town of Neemuch was empty. Next day the Resident entered Neemuch and wrote to Muhtsham Uddaula, the Jaora Nawab to send provisions for the army immediately. There upon Jaora Nawab sent thirty camel loads of provisions to Neemuch along with his friend Miyan Valayat Shah and the Commissariat Waterman and next day sent twenty five camel loads of provisions for the British contingent.[58]

A correspondent from Chandwasa[59] reported that nearly a thousand men were killed in British side including both (natives and Europeans). On the side of the insurgents twenty-five-hundred *Vilayatis* and *Mewatis* were killed and the rest fled away. The *Vilayatis* fled from Mandsaur by Aora, Kerlaya, Gagsigardya *ghats*, etc. From morning to sun-set about two to four thousand *Vilayatis* must have fled with their families. This report was received from the village of Badaliya, and troopers have been sent from this place to the *ghats* for search. The *Sondhiyas* and others of the villages of the aforesaid *taluqa-* namely, Asawati, Ranayra, Vanle Gangasi, Agar etc, had gone to loot the fugitive *Vilayatis*. It was heard that the fugitives included Firozshah, Hirasingh, Jorawar Singh of Khajuri and others.[60] The remnants of Shahzada force with Shahzada, were however, on the 27th November 1857, near Rampura (Mandsaur) until they were taken prisoners. The Bitah chief with his own troops and Bheels said to have affected their escape.[61] The Resident also sent his forces to search out the fugitives, who were apprehended and brought daily in hundreds and after brief enquiry were finished off.[62]

It was latter learnt that he had gone towards Nahargarh and they were reported in the forests of Dungarpur, Pratapgarh and Banswada in eastern Rajputana, and Firoz Shah fled towards Kota.[63]

At Mandsaur, which was now fully under the control of the British, 'a general parade of troops was ordered for the evening. The troops assembled and formed three sides of a square, three guns occupying the fourth. By-and-by twenty six prisoners were brought up, three of whom were the *subedar* major, the *subedar*, and *jamadar* of the Mahidpur artillery; these three were tied to the guns and blown into atoms. The twenty and three others were then blindfolded and shot by musketry!'[64]

Despite the control of the British on Mandsaur, the Resident Colonel Durand was not satisfied with the state of affairs and he, in November 1857 wrote about Mandsaur affairs, "It is extremely difficult to convey by words the state of affairs both in the city and the neighbouring district. Sindhia's authorities are powerless and their influence gone, and the present conjuncture is very much analogous to the state of affairs when our power first became supreme in Malwa and the country had to be braced up and recovered from the Pindaree and Maharatta wars and troubles."[65]

In another incidence, Major Orr apprehended and made prisoners on the morning of the 4th December, a body of horsemen lately in the service of the Sindhia, amounting in all 113, under command of an Indian officer named Kedar Rao Paigga. Thirty seven of them were charged with treason to the British Govt. with having entered the service of Firoz Shah with having taken pay from him, with having been in arms opposing the troops of the British Government at Jeeran and Neemuch. These prisoners were tried by a European General Court Martial composed of 5 Officers. The charge was fully proved against 53 of them and they were sentenced by the Court to be shot to death by musketry. This was carried out in the morning of 7th December 1857 in the presence of whole of the troops at Camp Mandsaur. The other 58 persons were handed over to the Political Agent Western Malwa for investigation.[66] Rest of the prisoners were sent on the 8th December under proper escort to Neemuch with the view of their being tried at that place.[67] Many insurgent fugitives, mainly Vilaytis were apprehended in different villages and were handed over to the British authorities.

After the debacle of Guradia, Firoz Shah, though a fugitive now, on 15th December sent his representative Rahim Bax to Sitamau to extract money. Some businessmen of Sitamau state sent him back giving him some money.[68]

On 16th December 1857 again four persons viz. Anwar Khan Jamadar, Munshi Gulam Mohodi Khan, Rahim Bax and Lala Sohadmal were hanged in front of Mandi gate. Moreover, Muslim soldiers were searched out and were apprehended.[69] It was ordered that if any *ghazi* was found, he should be apprehended. Following this order, twelve persons were captured and rest were being traced.[70]

At the close of the third week of December 1857 Firoz Shah went to Jhalrapatan (close to Jhalawad) region where he encountered the force of that place killing many on both sides, but Firoz Shah escaped safely.[71] As would be seen, from Jhalrapatan he went to Farrukhabad and then to Shajahanpur and Bareilly and thereafter to Rahatgarh in Saugor District. Defeat would not deter this undaunted young man and he would explore all possibilities to achieve his goal. His commitment led other insurgent leaders to help him again and again. Now the area of operation of Firoz Shah shifted to Ruhelkhand and Awadh where he joined hands with the insurgent leaders like Nawab of Farrukhabad Tafajjul Hussain, Begum Hazrat Mahal of Lucknow, Maulwi Ahmadulla Shah, Nana Sahab Peshwa, Rana Beni Madhav Singh of Shankarpur and Nawab Khan Bahadur khan of Bareilly. It is note worthy that despite his younger age he was accepted as an important leader by these insurgent leaders. It was only because of his ability to face the complex situations and his organizing capacity.

Resident Hamilton and Jaora Nawab

In the meantime Sir Robert Hamilton took charge of Indore Residency from Col. Durand on the 16th December 1857. Durand, while leaving, wrote a letter of thanks to Jaora Nawab, expressing his pleasure for Nawab's role and his timely help in suppressing the rebellion. Robert Hamilton sought opinion of the Jaora Nawab for the disposal of the prisoners held at Mandsaur and Jaora Jails because of the fact that the Nawab knows the roles of different prisoners. The Nawab proposed the following categories for the punishment to the prisoners:

1. The persons who fought with the government forces at Jeeran and Mandsaur, should be killed, hanged or imprisoned for life.
2. The persons who went to Mandsaur for employment and having no employment, apprehended while fleeing during the battles, should be given imprisonment from one to three years.
3. The rebel Mahidpur cavalry should be challenged to Central India Agency.
4. The persons who joined the British at Mandsaur but fled at Neemuch should be imprisoned for seven years.

5. The cavalry, which fled to save their life and did not went to Delhi or Mandsaur should be left on bail.
6. Butchers, *Kanjar, Chheepa* etc. should be fined according to their position and be left on bail.
7. Persons who are murderers should be hanged.
8. Persons who have been apprehended from other areas should be sent to their masters.
9. Those Thakurs and *Zamindars* who have helped the rebels should be fined for his one year revenue.

It is not known how far these recommendations of the Nawab of Jaora were accepted and followed by the Resident, but these recommendations are a proof of importance given to the Nawab by the British.

Reference :

1. Sen, op. cit., p. 288.
2. Iqtidar Alam Khan, 'The Gwalior Contingent in 1857-58. The Organization and Ideology of the Sepoy Rebels' in *Facets of the Great Revolt 1857*, 2008 edited by Shireen Moosvi
3. Sen, op. cit., p. 289
4. Iqtidar Alam Khan, op.cit., p. 64.
5. Letter, dated Gwalior, 31st July 1857 from H.H. Sindhia's Vakil to Major S.C. Charters Macpherson, P.A., Gwalior (Agra). Morar was a suburb of Gwalior.
6. Foreign Department, Secret Consultations 43-45 dt. 26-3-1858, Jan Ali Khan's statement, p. 17.
7. Foreign Department, Secret Proceedings. no. 364, letter no. 104, dt. 22-09-187, letter dt. 23-09-1857.
   Also Foreign Department, Political Proceedings, 30-12-1859 (N.I-312).. S. no. 364, 365 dt. 22-9-1857, AGG to Govt. of India, enclosing a copy of the letter dt. 3-9-1857 from a post office clerk.
8. Foreign Department, Secret Proceedings, dt. 27-11-1857, Part I. No. 172 Jugal Kishore to PA Gwalior
9. Foreign Department, Secret Proceedings 30-10-1857, S.N. 293. p. 4344. letters dated 29-8-1857, Camp Mahidpur from Major Commanding Malwa Contingent to AGG CI.
10. Revolt in Central India, 1857-59, compiled in the Intelligence Branch, Division of the Chief of the Staff, Army Head Quarters India, Shimla, 1908, p. 75.
11. Foreign Department, Secret Consultations. 697 dt. 18-12-1857, set. SM 224 dt. 7-9-1857, from PA Gwalior to Govt. of India. 7-9-1857

12. *The Imperial Gazetteer of India*, Vol. XI, 1908, p. 324.
13. Foreign Department, Secret Proceedings 27-1-1857, No. 313, dt. 2-11-1857, para 13, Secret. Proceedings 27-11-1857, Part 1. No. 87, Maratha news report from Gwalior 28-9-1857.
14. Foreign Department, Secret Proceedings. 30-12-1857, S. No. 426 – Maratha News dt. 28-9-1857
15. Raghubir Sinh, op. cit., p. 111, letter no. 23, dated 14th September 1857.
16. Letter dt. *Asoj Sudi* 2, *Samvat* 1914 (i.e. 20 September 1857, from Paharsingh, Qanungu to Hulasrai, Sitmau, Bsta no. 115, file no. 60, letter no. 14.
17. Letter from Lt. Col. H.M. Durand, Offg. Agent Governor General for Central India, to G.F. Edmonstone, Secy. to the Govt. of India, Fort William, dated Indore Residency, Camp Mhow, the 28th of September, 1857. Foreign Department, Secret Consultations, 30th October 1857, No. 375. National archives, New Delhi. F.S.U.P., III, 153-154
18. *Revolt in Central India*, an official History, p.13. and AGG's letter 17-10-1857
19. T. H. Thornton, *General Sir Richard Meade and the Feudatory States of Central and South India*, p. 43.
20. Thomas Lowe, *Central India during the rebellion of 1857-58*, p. 61.
21. See Wazir Khan's disposition in Appendix 1.
22. *The Imperial Gazetteer of India*, Vol. XII, New edition, pp. 65.
23. *Ibid*, pp. 65-66.
24. Foreign Department, Political Proceedings, Deposition of Wazeer Khan, 30-12-1859, No. 311, letter no. 54, dt. 9-3-1859. Wazeer Khan puts it in September, while actually it was in October 1857. Text of Wazir Khan's deposition is given in Appendix 1.
25. Fifteen kilometers south of Neemuch and thirty kilometers north of Mandsaur in M.P.
26. Foreign Department, Secret Consultations. 255-b of 27-11-1857 letter no. 195 dt. 19-10-57 AGG Central India to Govt. of India.
27. Foreign Department, Political Consultations, 239-43 dt. 6-8-1858-B letter no. 6 A dt. 3-11-1857 from Col. Durand AGG, Indore.
28. G.B. Malleson, Op. Cit., Vol III, p. 67.
29. H.M. Durand, op. cit., pp. 230-32
30. C. L. Showers, *A Missing Chapter of the Indian Mutiny*, 1888, pp. 114-115.
31. Chalres Ball. *History of Indian Mutiny*, Vol. I, p. 213.
32. Showers, p. 116. Placing of the heads of two British officers over the gates of Mandsaur is still remembered by the local people.
33. Showers, op. cit.. pp. 117-118.
34. Raghubirsinh. op. cit., p. 123. letter no. 26, dt. 7th November 1857.
35. Arjunsingh Sahiwala. *Jeevan Charit*, reprint. *samvat* 1967 i.e. 1910 AD, part one, p. 56.
36. Showers. op. cit., p. 119
37. *Tarikh-e-Malwa*, p. 999
38. Ball. op. cit.. Vol. I, pp. 213-14.

39. Ibid, p. 214
40. Ibid.
41. Showers, op. cit., p. 119.
42. Ibid, p. 120.
43. Ibid, p. 121
44. Foreign Department, Secret Consultations, 29th January 1858, No. 116.
45. Showers, op. cit., pp. 122-23.
46. Both in Neemuch district, M.P.
47. Showers, op. cit., pp. 123-126
48. Ibid, p. 126
49. Ball, Vol. I, op. cit., p. 215
50. Ibid.
51. Showers, op. cit., pp. 127-129
52. Ball, I, p. 215-16
53. *Tarikh-e-Malwa*, op. cit., pp. 999-1000 has given a summary of the encounter.
54. Arjunsingh Sahiwala, *Jeevan Charit*, reprint, samvat 1967 i.e. 1910 AD, Part I, p. 65-68.
55. Showers, pp. 129-130
56. Issue Vol. 91, Letter No. 251, Gen. No. 887, dated Mandsaur, the 25th Nov. 1857, from H.M. Durand, Offg. A.G.G. for C.I. to G.F. Edmonstone Esqr., Secy. Government of India.
    Also so H.M. Durand, *The Life of Major-General Sir Henry Marion Durand*, London, 1883, pp. 230-32
57. Report of Brigadier C.S. Stuart, Commanding Malwa Field Force to the Adjutant-General of the Bombay Army from his camp Mandsaur, dt. 27th November 1857. G. W. Forrest (ed.), *The Indian Mutiny 1857-58, Jhansi*, Calpee, Gwalior, Reprint 20003, Appendix E, pp. lxvii-lxxiii. It may be mentioned that in the title of this document the name of the Brigadier is written as Stewart, while, at the close of the report, his signature is given as Stuart. Since, as will be seen later, Sir Hugh Rose's report has Stewart, we may take it as Stuart instead of Stewart. For another interesting and graphic description of the battle, also see Thomas Lowe, *Central India during the Rebellion of 1857-58*, London, 1860, pp. 105-129
58. *Tarikh-e-Jaora*, p. 81
59. Forty five kilometers east of Mandsaur. Now on the eastern bank of Gandhi Sagar Dam.
60. B. N. Luniya, Lunia, B.N. (ed.) *Freedom Movement in Madhya Bharat,* 1956, No. 324, letter no. 4875, pp. 588-590
61. Foreign Department, Secret Consultations. 180 dt. 18-12-1857, dt. 5-12-1857, AGG, Central India to the Govt. of India.
62. *Tarikh-e-Jaora*, p. 81
63. A.Q. Qazi, Faruqi Depalpuri, *Tarikhi-e-Jaora* (Urdu), 1947, p. 81
64. Thomas Lowe, *Central India during the Rebellion of 1857-58*, London, 1960, p. 126. *Tarikh-e-Malwa* pp. 1013-1015 has also described the battle of Guradia in detail.

65. Issue Vol. 91, Letter no. 257, dated 27th Nov. 1857, from Col. Durand to G.F. Edmonstone, Secretary to Govt. of India.
66. Foreign Department, Secret Consultations, letter no. 255 dt. 7-12-1857, Camp Mandsore, From Maj. Orrs, Commanding Hyderabad Contingent, addressed to AGG Central India.
67. Foreign Department, Secret Consultations, 156-57 dt. 22-1-1858, letter no. 257 dt. 13-12-1857 , Camp Peeplia, from AGG to Govt. of India.
68. Basta 115, Bundle 44, letter of Allabux from Mandsaur to Lala Hulasrai dated *Paush Badi* 14, *Samvat* 1914 *Vikram*, i.e. 15th December 1857. Raghubirsinh, p. 144, fn 3.
69. Basta 115, bundle 44, Letter dt. Paush badi 15 samvat 1914 (16th December 1857) , Basta 115, bundle 44, Shri Natnagar Shodh Samsthan, Sitamau.
70. Basta 115, bundle 44, Letter of Allbux from Mandsaur to Lala Hulasrai, Diwan of Sitamau state, dated *Paush sudi* 3, *Samvat* 1914 (19th December 1857)
71. Raghubirsinh, op. cit., pp. 166-67, letter no. 39, dated 23rd December 1857.

Chapter - 4
Rahatgarh, Jhansi and Bareilly Proclamation

In Farrukhabad

After the disaster of Guradia followed by a quick visit to Jhalrapatan in Rajputana, Firoz Shah went to Farrukhabad covering a long distance of about 300 miles. The details of his flight are not known, but it shows the swiftness and vigilance with which he completed his journey. As has been seen, after his defeat at Agra on 10th Oct. 1857, Firoz Shah had visited Farrukhabad and was not a new comer there. He had cordial relations with the Nawab of Farrukhabad and was popular with the rebel troops there.

This visit of Firoz Shah is corroborated by an official narrative of occurrences, which said that during the rule of the Nawab of Farrukhabad, some notable persons had stayed at Fatehgarh. Amongst them were Bakht Khan from Delhi, Walidad Khan and Raja of Mainpuri, Princes Kushak Sultan and Firoz Shah, who remained at Fatehgarh till 2nd January 1858, when they fled with the Nawab at the approach of the British forces after the battle of Khudaganj.[1] The British force under Sir Collin Campbell occupied the Fatehgarh fort on 3rd January 1858. The Nawab of Farrukhabad, together with Firoz Shah and Ismail Khan, came to Shahjahanpur with a small force, and remained there for a few days, and then proceeded to Barreily in Ruhelkhand.[2]

Firoz Shah remained at Bareilly for a few days only and went to Bundelkhand to muster support of the Bundelkhand rulers, as indicated in a letter of 11th January 1858 written to Firoz Shah by Raja Mardan Singh of Banpur, a close associate of Rani of Jhansi and Raja Bakhat Bali of Shahgarh.[3] Mardan Singh wrote to Firoz Shah that both (he and Bakhatbali, the Raja of Shahgarh) of them would do their utmost. He also informed Firoz Shah that most of the rulers and *Jagirdars* of Bundelkhand had changed their sides and had started helping the Christians and their Indian associates. Mardan Singh suggested that looking to the condition, it is necessary that Firoz Shah should himself write to the rulers of Orchha, Charkhari and others and there after he himself along with Bakhatbali would join him and punish those who do not obey and pay respect to Firoz Shah.[4] It seems that Mardan Singh wrote this letter to Firoz Shah from the fort of Rahatgarh[5], where he was staying with Bakhatbali of Shahgarh, Fazil Mohammad and Adil Mohammad, who were the principle leaders of insurgency in Bundelkhand. Thus Rahatgarh, owing to its strength, provisions and strategic position, had become the centre of insurgency.

Leaving Bareilly, Shahzada Firoz Shah wanted to reach Rahatgarh to join the insurgent leaders who had gathered there. Rahatgarh was about 330 miles away from Bareilly and he had not more than two weeks at his disposal, because Sir Hugh Rose had left Mhow with his second brigade on the 6th January 1858 towards Sagar via Sehore and of course Rahatgarh, which was on way to Sagar and was expected to reach there at the end of January. As would be seen Rahatgarh fort had by now become the rendezvous for the insurgent leaders of Bundelkhand, who wanted to make this strong fort as a base for their future activities. Very soon, Rahatgarh fort was soon to become the center of fierce battle between Sir Hugh Rose and the insurgent leaders of Bundelkhand.

Rahatgarh fort: Centre of Insurgency

Standing on a two and half kilometer long plateau covered with dense forest on the left bank of Bina river the fort of Rahatgarh had a deep reservoir and had good arrangement of storing grain. It was situated in the western boundary of Saugor District under the British. The fort was under Ambapani Nawabs Adil Mohammad Khan and his brother Fazil Mohammad Khan. They were related to the Nawab family of Bhopal and were holding the *jagirs* of Ambapani in the north-east region of Bhopal state. Both these brothers were not in good terms with the Bhopal ruling family and indulged in instigating the *sardars* of Bhopal against the Nawab Sikandar Begum of Bhopal with the result that the Begum confiscated their *jagir* of Ambapani. Ambapani brothers did not keep silence and created disturbance in the eastern part of Bhopal State and also sided with the Bundela chiefs during the Bundela revolt of 1842.

During the upheaval of 1857, disaffection was brewing in the sepoys of 31st Native Infantry of Saugor and 52nd Native Infantry of Jabalpur and within no time the 31st Native Infantry of Saugor revolted on 1st July under Sheikh Zaman with the result that the families of European Officers of Saugor cantonment had to take shelter in the mud fort of Saugor, which had a very small garrison of sixty-eight European gunners. The neighbouring stronghold of Garhakota was in the hands of insurgents and the Bundela chiefs disturbed the neighbouring districts. Adil Mohammad Khan and Fazil Mohammad Khan attacked the fort of Rahatgarh with their associates on 26th July 1857 along with two thousand insurgents, mostly Pathans and Ruhelas and Pindaries and occupied it on 28th July 1857. Surrounding *zamindars* and the Pathans of Rahatgarh were also helping the Nawabs. South of Sagar, disaffection prevailed in 52nd Battalion of Jabalpur Cantonment. The execution of a dispossessed Gond Raja Shankar Shah and his son Raghunath Shah on 18th September 1857 drove the 52nd Native Infantry of Jabalpur to rebellion followed by a widespread uprising in the entire Saugor-Nerbudda Territories. The situation, in short, was very critical for the British and they had to rely upon the contingents of other military stations e.g. Kalpi, Raipur and Mhow etc.

With the spread of insurgency in the Saugor and Nerbudda Territories in Central India, the Rahatgarh fort became the main center of insurgency in that part of country and insurgent leaders like Bakhatbali of Shahgarh and Mardansingh of Banpur also joined Ambapani Nawabs at Rahatgarh, to be followed by Firoz Shah who came there at the end of January 1858. These leaders were associated with each other since quite a long time.

Bakhatbali, the Raja of Shahgarh had his own grievances leading him to jump in the struggle against the British. The Shahgarh territory was the remnant of the Garhakota[6] state; its remaining parts had fallen either into the hands of the Peshwa's representatives at Saugor or those of Sindhia. Bakhatbali wanted to occupy Garhakota, which, during Bakhatbali's father Arjun Singh, was under an alliance, occupied by Sindhia leaving Shahgarh with Arjunsingh. Arjunsingh's son and successor Bakhatbali wanted Garhakota from Sindhia with the assistance of the British and to earn the goodwill of the British he in 1842 imprisoned the main rebel of 1842 and handed him over to the British. But it was of no avail.

Raja Mardansingh of Banpur had also his grievances against the British. The forefathers of the Mardan Singh had once held the fortress of Chanderi and the districts dependent on it. His father Mur Pahlad was obliged to cede two third of his former state to the Sindhia. He was henceforth styled as the Raja of Banpur after the name of a town in his share. In 1843, Mardan Singh succeeded his father as Raja of Banpur on his death. In 1844 Sindhia ceded his share of Chanderi to the British Government. Mardan Singh entertained the hope of recovering the entire state of Chanderi in the event of the overthrow of the British Supremacy.[7] Incidentally both of them met at Jhansi where they had been to express condolence on the death of the Jhansi ruler Ganghadhar Rao, the husband of Rani Laxmi Bai. There, impressed by Tatya Tope, Bakhatbali and Mardansingh decided to take up arms against the British and after their return to their respective capitals, they revolted openly.

Sir Hugh Rose

At this critical juncture Sir Hugh Rose was appointed Commander of the Central India Field Force in December 1857 to operate in Malwa, Bundelkhand, Rajputana and Central India in co-operation with the Rajputana Field Force and Saugor and Narmada Field Force, while the Commander-in-Chief was engaged in Oudh and North-Western Provinces. Sir Hugh Rose assumed charge of his new office on 7th December 1857. His experience was not limited to the army alone. He had made his mark in diplomacy as well. His promotion in the army was remarkably rapid. He began his military career an ensign in 1820 and rose in twenty years to the rank of a Lieutenant-Colonel. He distinguished himself in Syria during the Turco-Egyptian War and was later appointed Consul General there. In 1851 he became Secretary to the British embassy at Constantinople and was attached to the Headquarters of the French army as Queen's Commissioner during the Crimean War. In September 1857 Sir Hugh came to Bombay to assume the command of the Poona division. Shortly after he had arrived at Mhow, disquieting news reached Sir Hugh from Sagar. He, therefore, decided to march from Mhow to Sagar via Sehore and Bhopal and commenced his journey on 6th January 1858 from Mhow with his second brigade. The force reached Sehore on 16th January 1858 and proceeded towards Rahatgarh which had become a rebel-stronghold.

Siege of Rahatgarh fort

Hugh Rose's arrival to Rahatgarh followed by the siege and evacuation of Rahatgarh by the insurgents forms a good description in the letter written by him to his higher-ups on 7th February 1858 from Saugor Camp.[8] The following description of the siege of Rahatgarh is based entirely on the above letter.

As Sir Hugh Rose approached Rahatgarh, he received information of the assemblage of Rebels at Udaipur[9] in Sindhia's territory and in order to ensure the safety of the Siege Train, he brought it up by a night march to my Force, and adopted precautions against any surprise attack of the insurgents.

On 24th January, going through a pass over a range of hills, the Officer Commanding the leading flankers, took by mistake the right instead of the left road, in consequence crossing the River Beena by the wrong ford, got into a skirmish with the insurgents posted in the suburbs of Rahatgarh. To extricate the flankers from a position so unfavorable to Cavalry, Hugh Rose helped to bring them in their proper position.

Next day he made with Major Boileau, and Captain Forbes, a complete reconnaissance of eighteen miles of the whole Country round the rock of Rahatgarh. The reconnaissance confirmed in all essentials the information on which he had formed his plan of attack. Sir Robert Hamilton had placed at his disposal 600 or 700 Troops of all Arms of the Regiment of Bhopal; and Hugh Rose asked him to invest the South-West of the Fort and to take the village of Puttan, which they did after firing a few shots.

The next day [26th January] as soon as the Officers Commanding the Artillery and Engineers had reported that they were ready for the siege, Hugh Rose attacked the Fort from the left, at the South-West end of the rock, under cover of a feint from the right, against the Town, from which all possible advantage was to be derived. The pretense against the Town drove the insurgents out of it into the Fort, and enabled Brigadier Stuart, to take possession of the *Idgah*, opposite the North face commanding the Town and within range of the main gate of the Fort. He skillfully placed Captain Lightfoot's Battery and Mortars. These Batteries formed an effective fire on the line of defenses and buildings of the Fort.

From the Town attack Hugh Rose directed a Detachment of the 3rd Europeans and 24th Native Infantry, with two Companies of the 24th Native Infantry in reserve, and under cover of houses and trees and of a heavy fire from the Idgah Battery to take a low massive tower close to the main gate. On the 28th instant at 8 a.m. the two 18-Pounders and the 8-inch Howitzer commenced their fire against the outer wall of the East curtain of the Fort and it was evident that a practicable breach would be soon made.

The insurgents coming in force out of the thick jungle, crossed the River Bina and attacked the right rear of the British camp. Another large body of them appeared at the same time on the opposite bank. The two bodies amounted to 1,500 or 2,000 men, many of them were Sepoys and Vilaytis.

Brigadier Stuart, advancing from the Idgah with a few rounds of artillery, compelled the insurgents to retire on the other side of the River into the jungle. After nightfall, the insurgents made a feeble and unsuccessful attack on the left of the Camp from the Saugor Road. The insurgents who had come from their fortified Camp Nariavali[10] and from the Fort of Khurai[11], failed completely in their attempt to surprise the British Camp and relieve Rahatgarh.

About 4 o'clock a.m. the insurgents attempted to make a sortie from the main gate. Twenty-five out of fifty of the insurgents who had attempted to force their way were cut. Colonel Liddell entered by the uncompleted breach and took possession of the Fort. The main body of insurgents fled by an ancient sally port and a hole dug under the parapet to the South-West, from which the ropes were hanging, by which they had let themselves down. The insurgents, crossing a ford over the Beena to the South-West, passed into the jungle.

Unfortunately, Nawab Fazil Muhammad Khan of Ambapani, along with his staff, was captured. Hugh Rose handed over eighty prisoners to Sir Robert Hamilton, of whom twenty-four were executed, and forty-eight were handed over to the Civil Authorities. At the sunset of 29th January, Fazil Mohammad Khan and the Nawab Kamdar Khan, a pensioner of the British Government and a son of the great Pindaree Chief, taken by Sir John Malcolm, were hung over the gate of the Fort. The next day seventeen insurgents were executed.

Shazadah Firoz Shah was not in the Fort, "as was proved by an unopened letter from the Rajah of Banpoor to his address found in the Fort by an Officer of the 3rd Europeans, he had left it the day of our arrival. In this letter, which is curious, the Rajah gives him the title of "King," and deplores that may Native Chiefs do not venerate his Kingly authority as they ought to do, but have the bad taste to prefer the rule of the "Kafir and infidels."

In the Fort were found great stores of salt and grain sufficient for a year's consumption, a few Camels, Cattle and several Horses, two of them belonging to Mahomed Fazil Khan, one with a silver bridle and another to Shahzada Firoz Shah, a mould for casting cannon, and shot, and an immense mass of correspondence in local dialect and English accounts.

The fall of Rahatgarh fort and the defeat of the principle insurgent leaders of Bundelkhand was a great blow to the insurgent leaders who had gathered there with considerable troops and high hopes. They lost immense quantity of resources behind them and had no place around to fall back upon. Probably they were confident to hold the fort against Hugh Rose and had not make any arrangement as a stand by. The only place of rescue for them was Jhansi where Rani of Jhansi had raised the standard of revolt against the British. But army under Hugh Rose was also proceeding towards this stronghold of the insurgents and was soon to reach there.

Firoz Shah had left the fort on "the day of our arrival", i.e. on the 24th or 25th January 1858. The events which followed, show that from Rahatgrh, Firoz Shah and Adil Mohammad khan went to the heart of Bundelkhand and finally proceeded to Jhansi, which was now the hot bed of insurgency.

Condition at Jhansi

Political condition at Jhansi had also changed drastically after the death of its ruler Gangadhar Rao, who, before breathing his last, had adopted a boy as his successor. But the British Government, despite repeated petitions of the dowager Rani Laxmi Bai, did not agree to the new arrangement and declared the annexation of the Jhansi territory on 13th March 1854. Rani had not yet reconciled herself to the decision of the British Government and still hoped for justice. She also appealed to the Court of Directors at London, but in vain. After annexation, the British authorities introduced such measures which further hurt her feelings. The Rani had a number of grievances against the British administration, but she had to reconcile herself to her fate. Then came the eruption of the great uprising of 1857 which starting from Meerut stepped in Jhansi. On 6th June the Europeans of Jhansi city were put to sword by the insurgents. The events that followed led the Rani to unfurl the flag of revolt against the British. It is interesting to note that Karl Marx had, as early as 14th August 1857, foreseen it and had written 'With respect to Jhansi in Bundelkhand, we may remark that it is fortified and may thus become another centre of armed rebellion.'[12] Soon she took over the administration of her territory and prepared herself against the attacks of her neighbouring states- Orchha and Datia. She appealed for assistance against the aggressors and they were finally repulsed.

In spite of the best efforts for friendly relations with the British, the Rani failed to get response to her appeals. Sir Hugh Rose was already on his way to Jhansi and the Governor General Lord Canning gave instructions to Sir Robert Hamilton that in case the Rani fell into the hands of the British force, she must be tried. "It was only when the Rani felt convinced", remarks Dr. R.C. Majumdar "that the British Government held her responsible for the mutiny and massacre of Englishmen at Jhansi, and that she would have to face a trial on this charge, that she decided to fight- preferring an honourable death in the battle field to a hangman's rope."[13] The decision of Rani to fight made Jhansi an important centre of insurgency and insurgent leaders flocked to Jhansi from surrounding areas. With stalwarts like Tatya Tope and Banda Nawab Ali Bahadur II, Rani of Jhansi had made Jhansi the hot bed of insurgency. This trio worked in close association throughout the insurgency and formed the central leadership in Central India.

Ramchandra Pandurang, alias Tatya Tope was a personal adherent of Nana Saheb Peshwa and was extremely loyal to him. 'Tatya Tope had obviously inherited the natural instinct of his race for guerilla tactics, and it is well known how he eluded his British adversaries when they thought that he had been safely netted.'[14] As is well known, Nana Saheb Peshwa, the successor of the last Peshwa Baji Rao II had taken up arms against the British and had succeeded in establishing his position at Kanpur. Nana Saheb was one of the three adopted sons of Baji Rao II. Two others were Sadashiv Pant alias Dada Saheb, and Gagadhar Rao alias Bala Saheb. At the time of the demise of Baji Rao II, Nana Saheb and Bala Saheb were alive but Dada Saheb had died earlier leaving a son Pandurang Rao, better known as Rao Saheb.

British Bundelkhand[15] and Bundelkhand Agency[16] areas were also not quiet. Nawab Ali Bahadur II of Banda was the son of Nawab Zulfiqar Ali of Banda and grandson of Ali Bahadur He succeeded his father on his death in 1849. The former Nawab enjoyed many privileges but Nawab Ali Bahadur II on his succession was deprived of almost all his privileges and was reduced in position and rank. On the outbreak of insurgency it was the people who took the lead in the revolt and the troops followed them. Nawab Alibahadur II established his independent authority and received a *firman* from the Mughal Emperor. He solicited Nana Saheb's support in men and matters. Raja Mardan Singh of Banpur, had sent his emissary to Ali Bahadur and sought his assistance in driving away the British. The Nawab also received agents of Raja Bakhatbali of Shahgarh. Ali Bahadur mooted the possibility of making Kalinjar, the headquarters of the revolutionaries. Meanwhile, the rebel force from Dinapur had arrived at Banda under the leadership of Kunwar Singh of Jagdishpur and after some days proceeded to Kalpi. By the end of October 1857 Nana Saheb, Kunwar Singh and Tatya Tope had gathered at Kalpi.[17]

Over November and December of 1857, Kalpi was going to play an important role in saving Lucknow from falling into taking Kanpur from the hands of the British. The combined troops of Kunwar Singh and tatya Tope marched to deliver an atttack on Kanpur, but they failed to recover it. After his deafeat on 6th December 1857, Tatya Tope fell back to Kalpi. Meanwhile Tatya had to attack Charkhari to extract tribute from Raja Ratan Singh of

Charkhari to meet his dwindling resources. At this time in early February 1858, Nana Saheb still in the northern territories was attempting to take control of the north Doab area that Campbell had 'cleared' in his December campaign.

It was at this time that Firoz Shah and Adil Mohammad Khan, after leaving Rahatgarh wandering in Bundelkhand, ultimately came to Jhansi in the fourth week of February 1858 and took refuge under Rani Laxmibai of Jhansi, who made arrangements for them and also kept some attendants in their service. The Rani also gave employment to the followers of Firoz Shah.[18]

The Bareilly Proclamation

During his wanderings in Bundelkhand, a proclamation was issued on the name of Firoz Shah on 18th February 1858 from Bareilly. It was produced and circulated by one Wazir Khan, previously a subordinate assistant surgeon at Agra[19], who had met Shahzada Firoz Shah at Farrukhabad and had become his ardent follower. In this proclamation, a brief review of the activities of Firoz Shah in 1857 was given.

The proclamation was addressed to both Hindus and Muslims and tried to point or the doings of the British against the Indians. It said that the British want to spread Christianity and destroy Hinduism and Islam from India. This has created enmity between the Indians and the English. Causes of the rebellion were mentioned point wise in the proclamation- The British are destroying the descendants of the former Rulers. Religious books are being destroyed. They will not allow to hold a single *biswa* of land in the hands of Indians. They are intermarrying with the natives by force. Indians are not taught artillery and arms are not left in the hands of the Indians. Jobs are not given to the Indians unless food is eaten with them. Hindus and Muslims to pursue are not allowed to pursue their religious activities and construction of Mosques and temples is not allowed. Laws are made according to the Christianity and Indian systems of marriage are discouraged. Indian systems of medicine are not allowed and Hindus and

Muslims are not allowed to proselytes. English physicians attend Indian women in child birth.

Indians were exhorted to exert to save their religions and murder all the Europeans. Firoz Shah then describes as to how he, after alighting in Bombay, traveled to the north and persuaded the people to stand against the British and proceeded with his followers to Gwalior and Agra. Though lost the battle with the British, they fought bravely. 'I have again collected 1,50,000 soldiers and with their help this country will be cleared off the Englishmen.'

The Proclamation also exhorted all sections of the society to assist him in this religious war against the British and should keep in their mind that the followers of Mirza Birjis Qadr and of Khan Bahadur Khan should join him only with the consent of their chiefs. Analysing the delay in achieving his object, the proclamation says that it was caused because the army of insurgents mercilessly murdered women and children in violation of the orders of their *Sardars*, and indulged so much to plunder that they turned victory into defeat. They likewise oppressed the people. He emphasized that all the people were equal and all should defend our faith. He relied on the blessing of God for the victory.

It appears that through this proclamation, Firoz Shah tried to establish himself as a distinctive leader in Awadh and Ruhelkhand. Its contents tried to exploit the fears of the Hindus and Muslims regarding the policies of the British administration in India. Emphasis was given to the religious concept of the struggle against the British and the Hindus and Muslims were called upon to unite against the British. No other rebel leader condemned the massacres so openly and in such unreserved terms.

Following is the full text of Bareilly Proclamation[20]:

Be it known to all Hindoos and Mussulmans of Hindoostan, that power and dominion are one of the greatest blessings of Providence and that this blessing cannot long be enjoyed by a deceitful tyrant.

For some years past these wicked Christian Kafirs commenced tyranising over India, intending to cause the spread of Christianity by violence, and to do away with the religion of Hindoos and Mussulmans, but it pleased God to turn the minds of the people against them, so much so, that all of a sudden they became intent upon destroying them; and of a truth they are very nearly annihilated, but owing to the loss of power and dignity, they have collected themselves here and there, in wretched plight, and are making useless efforts to regain their power. Please God in a short time they will be so annihilated as not to leave a single trace behind them. Let it be known to all Hindoos and Mussulmans of India, that owing to the circumstances mentioned above, there exists the bitterest enmity between the natives and the English; an if after all that has past (passed), the latter regain their former power in India, it is certain that they will destroy the religion, honor, life, and property of every one. I, therefore, give a short account of the resolutions passed with the joint concurrence of the Judicial Council, the Supreme Court, and the Parliaments in hope that our Indian brethren, becoming aware of their evil intentions, will join together in extirpating them. When the army mutinied for the sake of their religion and killed without mercy these kafirs with their swords, then with regard to the cause of the mutiny, and the loss of life, their Priests and Sages came on the following resolution, viz., that if the former Governors had properly looked to the following points there would have been no rebellion :

1st- "The Government took measures for protecting the heirs and descendants of the former Rulers instead of extirpating them. They ought to have taken them, on the pretence of conveying them to England, on board, a ship, and to have drowned them in the sea."

2nd- "They ought not to have preserved the religious books of any tribe in Hindoostan, but they should have taken them by force and burnt them."

3rd- "They ought to have deprived all natives of the power of holding a single 'Biswah' of land."

4th- "They ought to have intermarried with the daughters of natives of rank, compelling the parents by force, and bribing hem with money, to give them their daughters, so that in a few years they would all have become one."

5th- "They ought not to have taught artillery practice to any natives of India."

6th- "They ought not to have left arms or weapons in the hands of the natives."

7th- "They ought not to have given service to anyone, unless he had eaten food with them."

8th- "They ought not to have permitted the Hindoos to relate their religious tales, or granted permission to Mussulmans to preach sermons."

9th- "They ought not to have permitted the erection of Mosques and Temples."

10th- "Decisions in the Civil Courts ought to have been passed according to the precepts of the Christian Religion."

11th- "The marriage ceremonies should have been made over to the English Clergy, instead of allowing the old customs of 'Nikah' and 'Bhowree."

12th- "Hindoos and Mussulman systems of medicine ought not to have been allowed to be practiced."

13th- "(Wanting in the copy furnished to me)."

14th- "They ought not to have allowed the Hindoo and Mussulman Faqueers, unless specially permitted by the Clergymen, to make Proselytes."

15th- "They ought not to have allowed Midwives, but insisted that English medical men should attend women in child birth."

These points were not at all regarded by the English Government, but the superstitions of the perfidious natives were on the contrary respected and encouraged. The consequence is that these very people rebelled : that if the foregoing measures are adopted there will be no fear of any disturbance for a thousand years to come.

Oh men of Hindoostan! see now these Christians. How great is their enmity against you? You have been told of the future schemes of the English as related above. Now you must wash your hands, and try your best to save your religion and lives by murdering all Europeans, make your resolution firm and by the blessing of God you will succeed.

I, the writer of this Proclamation, give you a short account of facts as follows. Hear it attentively and act up to it. Before the rebellion broke out I had gone to Mecca, and on my return, when I arrived at Bombay, having been informed of the wretched condition of these ill-disposed Christians I thanked God; and as I am by nature a believer in Islam, and a lover of justice, and hater of oppression, when I left Bombay on my way back to this part of India, I persuaded the people on the road, as far as Gwalior, to make a Jahad, and to kill all Christians, and to this effect I took pledges from a great number of native chieftains and warriors. A small force accompanied me from Gwalior, and I had intended to fight, as soon as I had matured my plans; but the religious fervor of my troops became so great, that they paid no attention to discipline. They consequently unadvisedly advanced on Agra and commenced fighting with the ill-starred infidels and that place and notwithstanding that they were inferior in numbers to the enemy, they fought well and bravely, and though they were apparently defeated, yet in reality; having killed about a thousand of the Kafirs, they obtained a victory, my property was lost and my relatives and friends were dispersed.

From that day to this, my time as been employed in preparing to fight again, and for three or four months I have been very successful in inducing several princes and other natives of rank, and warrior of every part of the country, to join with me in extirpating the wicked kafirs, and by the grace of God I have been able to collect 150,000 tried soldiers and recruits, and they have taken solemn oaths not to desert the cause; and therefore in a very short time we shall be able to clear the country from the presence of Kafirs. Everywhere ammunitions stored, and money is collected. The only thing which remains to be done for me to commence operations.

The object in view is purely of a religious nature, therefore it is made known to all Hindoos and Mussulmans, that whoever is so fortunate as to possess the grace of God, he will join us in this religious war. After the receipt of this Proclamation it is expected that all will join the "Jahad".

The week and old can join by their prayers for our success; the wealthy, and old should assist us with their wealth, whilst those who strong and in good health should exert themselves in the field of battle.

On joining the "Jahad" everyone must remember the following points:-

1st- Those who are servants of the Raees of Lucknow, 0ur young kinsman, Mirza Burjees Qudur Bahadoor (Birjis Qadar Bahadur), and those who are servants of the Nawab Khan Bahadoo Khan of Bareilly, will not join in this war, without obtaining first the consent of those chiefs; for those chiefs are ready to expel the Kafirs. Deserting those chiefs is in fact, therefore, adding strength to the infidels.

2nd- All should join in this religious war, not for the sake of this world's goods, but in hopes of reaping the fruits of eternity.

After attaining ascendancy and power, by the blessing of God, they will also get high situations in this world.

3rd- The delay that has occurred hitherto in expelling the English has been caused by the Will and Order of Providence, for the army mercilessly murdered women and children in violation of the orders of their Sirdars and gave themselves up so much to plunder that they turned victory into defeat. They likewise oppressed the people, and did not mind the orders of their leaders.

Now having relinquished all these sinful acts and formed your minds for doing good you should join in the "Jahad" and you will obtain complete victory.

4th- The people of all grades should regard themselves as equals, for in religious matters all brothers should equally defend the faith. It is not my object to wage this war for worldly gain, and therefore having placed reliance in the precepts of religion, I gird myself with bravery and enthusiasm, and having wrapped around my head the cerements of the grave (Kuffun), and having armed myself with the sword of "Jahad" I rise repeating the holy

"Bismilah" and relying on the blessing of God, I am sure of obtaining victory.

I do hereby call you again and again to come and join me for the sake of God. I will inform you of the date and is and[21] which I march out of the city. Those who are anxious to join are requested to do so without delay.

Sacrifice your life for your beloved, for death will some day take it from you. Oh Hafiz, do you decide which is the better of the two courses."

Printed at the Bahadoor Press in Bareilly, by the order of the Nawab, the Ruler of Kutair (Katihar), under the superintendence of Moulavie Qutab Shah, by Darogah Shaikh Neeaz Allee, dated the 3rd Rajab 1274 Hizeree, (18th February 1858).

Production of the proclamation and is circulation appears to have been the responsibility of Wazir Khan.[22]

Reference :

1. Extract from Narrative of Occurrences by C.R. Lindsay, Officiating Magistrate, and Collector of Farrukhabad, dated 20th December, 1857. Mutiny Narratives, NWP. Agra, Farrukhabad District, p. 30. S.A.A. Rizvi and Bhargava, *Freedom Struggle in Uttar Pradesh*, 1956-61, Vol. V, p. 927-28. Here after mentioned as F.S.U.P. Khudaganj lies near the left bank of the Kali Nadi, 14 24 kms. south-east of Fatehgarh in Farrukhabad district.
2. Extract from letter no. 21 of 1858 from G.P. Money, Magistrate and Collecor of Shahjahanpur, to R. Alexander, Commissioner of Rohilkhand, dated 9th September 1858. F.S.U.P. V, p. 427.
3. 69 kilometers north-east of Sagar in M.P.
4. Consultation 254 dated 30-12-1859 political supplementary, letter dated 11th January 1859 from the Raja of Banpur to Firoz Shah.
5. 40 kilometers east of Sagar on the bank of Bina river in M. P. district, M.P. The fort of Rahatgarh was quite large and strong .
6 42 kilometers east of Sagar in M.P. on the convergence of Gadheri and Sonar rivers.
7 Shyam Narain Sinha, *The Revolt of 1857 in Bundelkhand*, 1982, p. 49
8 Letter from Major-General Sir Hugh Rose, Commanding Central India Field Force, To the Adjutant-General of the Army, Head-quarters, Bombay,-Camp Saugor, 7th February 1858, G.W. Forrest (ed.), *The Indian Mutiny 1857-58*, Selections from the Letters Dispatches and Other State Papers Preserved in the Military Department of the Government of India,, Vol IV, Calcutta, 1912, reprint Delhi, 2003, pp. 2-8.

9 15 kms. north-east of Ganjbasoda in present Vidisha district of M.P.

10 20 kms. north-west of Sagar (M.P.) on Sagar-Khurai road.

11 53 kms. north-west of Sagar.

12 Published in the New-York Daily Tribune, No. 5104 of August 29, 1857. See Marx Engels, *The First Indian War of Independence 1847-59*, Progress Publishers Moscow, sixth printing 1988, p.54.

13 R.C. Majumdar, *The Sepoy Mutiny and the Revolt of 1857*, p. 155.

14 Sen, op. cit., p. 229.

15 British Bundelkhand was a tract of country in the United Provinces, which included the Districts of Jalaun, Jhansi, Hamirpur and Banda and a part of Allahabad which lied south of the Jamuna and Ganges rivers. It consisted of an area of about 11,600 square miles, lying south-west of the Jamuna from its junction with the Chambal. *Imperial Gazetteer of India*, Vol. IX, New edition, p. 68.

16 It consisted of a collection of Native States in the Central India Agency, under a Political Agent with an area of about 9,852 square miles. There were 9 states, 13 estates in Bundelkhand Agency. Orchha, Datia, Samthar, Panna, Charkhari, Ajaigarh, Bijawar, Baoni, Chhatarpur, Sarila, Dhurwai, Bijna, Tori-Fatehpur, Banka-Pahari, Jigni, Lugasi, Bihat, Beri, Alipura, Gaurihar, Garrauli and Naigawan Rebai. *Imperial Gazetteer of India*, Vol. IX New edition, pp. 74-76.

17 Shyam Narayan Sinha, *Op. Cit.*, pp. 99-102

18 Intelligence from Ganeshilal at Datia 22nd Feb. 1858, F.S.U.P., Vol. III, p. 277.. Also see deposition of Lalu Bakhshi on 6th April 1858. F.S.U.P., Vol. III, p. 53.

19 F.S.U.P., Vol. V, p. 381, Agra correspondent's letter.

20 Foreign Secret Consultations No. 121-122 dt. 30th April, 1858. Also The Dacca News, 8th May 1858, pp. 233-34. National Library, Calcutta. Quoted in F.S.U.P., Vol. V. pp. 376-380

21 Obviously a printing error for the phrase 'the date on which I march out...'

22 F.S.U.P., Vol. V, p. 381, Agra Correspondent's letter dated 26th April 1858 Another translation is given in Abstract N.W.P. Narrative Foreign, 1858 given in F.S.U.P. Vol. II, pp. 459-463.

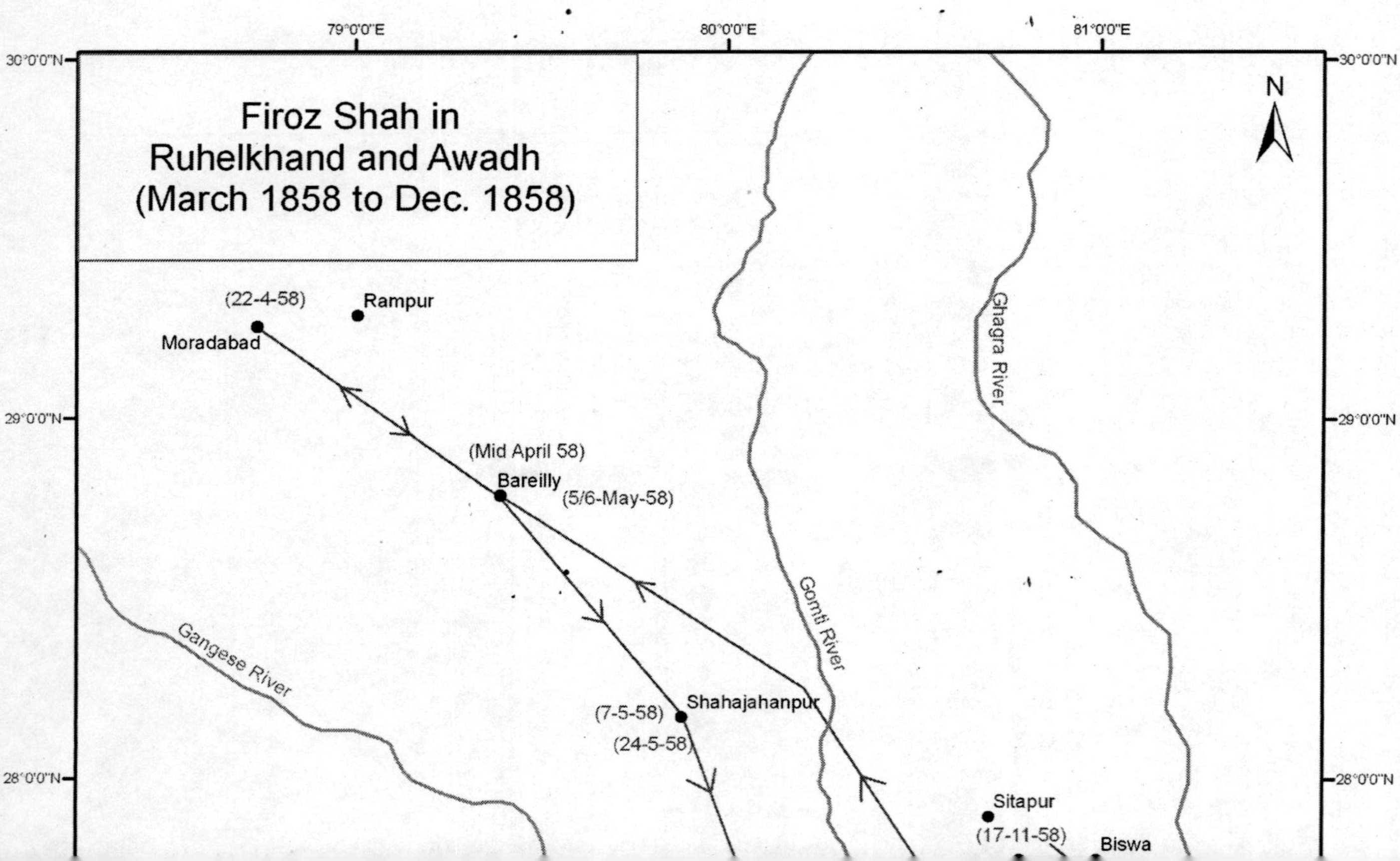

Firoz Shah in
Ruhelkhand and Awadh
(March 1858 to Dec. 1858)
79°0'0"E
80°0'0"E
81°0'0"E
30°0'0"N
29°0'0"N
28°0'0"N
N
(22-4-58)
Rampur
Moradabad
(Mid April 58)
Bareilly
(5/6-May-58)
Gangese River
Gomti River
Ghagra River
(7-5-58)
Shahajahanpur
(24-5-58)
Sitapur
(17-11-58)
Biswa

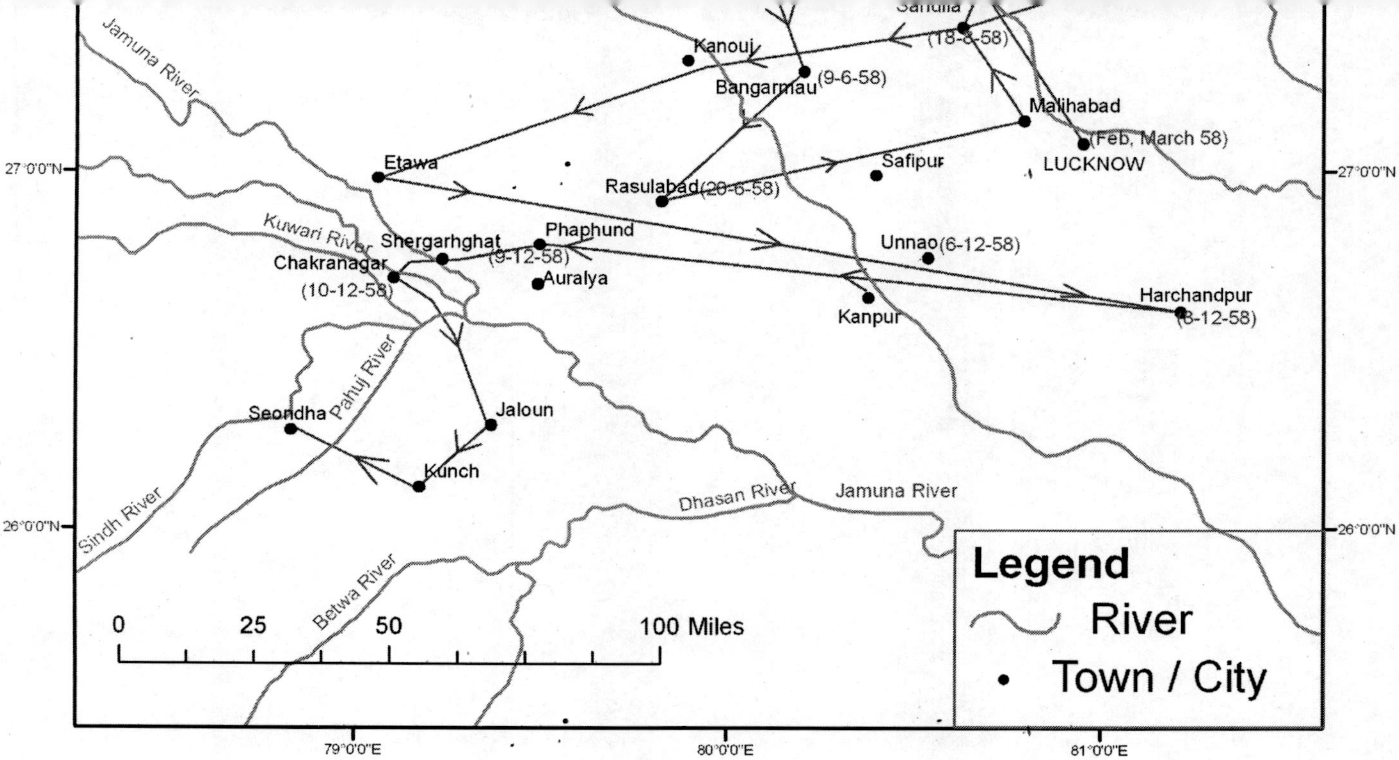
Jamuna River
Kanouj
(18-8-58)
Bangarmau
(9-6-58)
Malihabad
(Feb, March 58)
LUCKNOW
Etawa
Safipur
Rasulabad
(20-6-58)
Kuwari River
Shergarhghat
Phaphund
(9-12-58)
Unnao
(6-12-58)
Chakranagar
(10-12-58)
Auralya
Harchandpur
(8-12-58)
Kanpur
Pahuj River
Seondha
Jaloun
Kunch
Dhasan River
Jamuna River
Sindh River
Betwa River
0
25
50
100 Miles
Legend
River
Town / City
27°0'0"N
26°0'0"N
79°0'0"E
80°0'0"E
81°0'0"E

Map 3

Chapter - 5
Activities In Ruhelkhand

Firoz Shah In Lucknow

By far Firoz Shah had earned a reputation due to his earlier exploits and activities in Malwa, Dholpur, Farrukhabad and Rahatgarh. When he was at Farrukhabad earlier, he must have observed the developments all around and might have learnt about the disturbed condition of Lucknow, where Begam Hazrat Mahal had taken up arms against the British. It seems that after his Jhansi visit, Firoz Shah again went to Farrukhabad and from there, according to Wazir Khan, he joined the insurgents at Lucknow and remained there till it was re-occupied by the British.[1] Looking to the movements of Firoz Shah it is probable that he went to Lucknow during the last days of February 1858 and remained there till the Residency was re-occupied by the British on 18/19 March 1858. Since events in Awadh, including the siege of Lucknow are very important, we may cast an eye over the situation at Awadh which led to the revolt of Begum Hazrat mahal.

Awadh In Revolt

In 1856 the East India Company annexed the state of Awadh and placed it under a chief commissioner - Sir Henry Lawrence. Wajid Ali Shah, the then Nawab, was imprisoned, and then exiled by the Company to Calcutta. 'After the kingdom was annexed, the nobility of Awadh could no longer aspire to the highest offices of the government, which became the close preserve of the rule race. 60,000 of the king's troops were at once thrown out of employment and only a small portion of them could be absorbed in the armed police force.[2] Further, immediately after the take-over, the British ordered a wholesale disarming and demolition of the *talukdars*' forts, which were the symbols of *talukdar's* power and prestige. It was a great jolt to a class which had been enjoying prestige during the Nawabs of Awadh. With their power and prestige, they had a place amongst the people amongst whom they lived. In fact the annexation of Awadh by the British caused not only a political upheaval but also an emotional, social and economic upheaval.

The annexation of Awadh and the policy prescriptions that followed had a snowballing effect. The act of annexation itself alienated the people of Awadh by removing their king. What followed was seen as various orders that rendered topsy-turvy the traditional world of Awadh. What at the time of the annexation was a mere emotional grievance against a foreign power, became linked with real bread and butter grievances as the *talukdars* and peasants were hit by the Summary Settlement.[3]

The expected uprising did not occur till the night of 30th May. It was only after all the major stations between Delhi and Lucknow had risen and the word was around that the rule of the Company Bahadur had collapsed that the regiments in Lucknow mutinied on the night of 30th May 1857. With the collapse of British administration in the districts of Awadh, the British held their sway only in Lucknow, around the Residency. Lucknow now became the scene of action and by the end of June 1857 insurgents from the surrounding districts had started moving towards Lucknow. The defeat of Sir Henry Lawrence's force at Chinhat (Lucknow) on 30th June 1857 caused widespread panic amongst the British and very soon the British were besieged in the Lucknow Residency. The strength of the besieging army of the insurgents was not accurately known, but it was a huge one. The insurgent leaders with huge armies were gradually concentrating in and near the city. They were joined by the *Talukedars* and their followers. Their number had increased in Lucknow after the evacuation of the British from the city on November 1857. Now on the British and the insurgents were struggling for Lucknow because, both sides new that full control of Lucknow is the key to their future success.

It appears that at the end of February 1858, Firoz Shah joined the siege of Lucknow, where other insurgent leaders viz. Begum Hazrat Mahal, Kunwar Singh of Jagdishpur, Khan Bahadur Khan of Bareilly and Maulvi Ahmadullah Shah of Faizabad had gathered against the British. As will be seen later Firoz Shah's association with Maulvi Ahmadullah Shah and Khan Bahadur Khan of Barielly continued in future also.

Khan Bahadur Khan and Maulvi Ahmadulla Shah

Khan Bahadur Khan was the grand son of Hafiz Rahmat Khan, the well known ruler of Ruhelkhand lying in the upper Ganges alluvial plain and has an area of about 25,000 sqm. It was bounded by the Ganges River on the south and by Uttarakhand and Nepal in the north and by Awadh in the east. Before the commencement of the great uprising, Khan Bahadur Khan assumed the office of Viceroy under the Emperor of Delhi and governed the Hindu and Muslim population of Ruhelkhand with statesmanlike wisdom so that all efforts of the enemy to create discord between the two communities were frustrated.[4] He defended Ruhelkhand with great skill, defeating four columns of British troops which had converged upon Bareilly. Khan Bahadur Khan, even at the age of seventy, possessed great military sagacity and knew the British military might and had a plan to meet them and beat them. He was an old man with a long white beard, but not at all bent with age. Unlike the King of Delhi, Begum of Oudh and the Rani of Jhansi, Khan Bahadur Khan was a retired judge of the Company's service, and a descent from the ancient rulers of Ruhelkhand.

Maulvi Ahmadullah Shah hailed from Faizabad. He travelled from place to place, accompanied by some armed men, and had his disciples all over India. He openly declared holy war against the British and made seditious speeches. The police disarmed him and his followers and was placed in in military custody. He was a prisoner when the Mutiny broke out. The insurgents freed him and rallied around him. Very soon he became popular with the insurgents and when the Lucknow Residency was besieged by the insurgents, he joined them.

The insurgents themselves were busy improving their organisation. Shortage of ammunition was being overcome. Percussion caps and all kinds of ammunition were being produced in Lucknow. Artisans were brought in form Delhi especially for this purpose. The services of a Christian who had been taken prisoner were commandeered. Supplies of ammunition from the districts were also maintained. A huge quantity of lead was found in the Dilkhusa and then converted into bullets. Similarly, 3,000 nine pound and 2,000 eighteen pound shot were recovered from wells where the British had left them when they evacuated the Residency. A workshop was set up in Faizabad for the purpose of repairing heavy guns.[5]

The arrangements made by the British for the relief of Lucknow were on a scale hitherto unprecedented in India. In this campaign of Awadh, the number of Europeans alone exceeded that of all the troops sent into Afghanistan. The main army, led by Sir Colin Campbell personally consisted of three divisions of infantry, one of cavalry, and one of artillery and engineers. The first division of infantry, under Outram, held Alambagh. It consisted of five European and one native regiment. The second and third, the cavalry division under Sir Hope Grant and the mass of the artillery, formed Campbell's active force, with which he advanced on the road from Kanpur. In all, the Campbell's force amounted to 30,000 men, to whom must be added the 10,000 Nepalese Gurkhas advancing under Jang Bahadur from Gorakhpur, making the total of the invading army 40,000. Apart from this, contingents were also advancing from different sides towards Lucknow. The force under the insurgents consisted of the remnants of most of the mutinous Bengal regiments and of native levies from the country itself. This force could not have been more than 35,000 or 40,000. This force was disorganized, disheartened, badly appointed and totally unfit to take the field. The new levies were variously stated at from 100,000 to 150,000 men but they were badly equipped.[6]

The British force concentrated before the southern side of Lucknow on March 2 and within a fortnight the British forces prevailed upon them, compelling the insurgents to flee from Lucknow. On the 18th March the insurgents crossed the Ramganga in great force, with four guns; they retired, however, to Baugaon.[7] At that time Nana Saheb Peshwa was at Aliganj.[8] The British had gained a clear victory over the biggest congregation of insurgents at Lucknow. They now controlled the city of Lucknow, the heart of Awadh. But it did not mean that entire Awadh region came under their control. The fall of Lucknow did not ease the situation for the British and, as put up by F. Engels, "altogether, the taking of Lucknow has no more put down the Indian insurrection than the taking of Delhi. This summer's campaign may produce such events the British will have, next winter, to go substantially over the same ground again, and perhaps even to re-conquer the Punjab. But in the best of cases, a long and harassing guerrilla warfare is before them—not an enviable thing for Europeans under an Indian sun."[9] And true to these words, the British faced intense resistance all around.

The insurgents knew that they have suffered a heavy loss. After the defeat at Lucknow it was extremely difficult for them to concentrate their forces. They knew that without a sizeable force they can not now face the British power. Chances to concentrate the force again were quite remote and they had to consider the future strategy suiting to their limitations. Khan Bahadur Khan pointedly expressed this assessment when he formulated the strategy that the insurgents should follow:

Do not attempt to meet the regular columns of the infidels, because they are superior to you in discipline and *bundobust*, and have big guns; but wath their movements, guard all the *ghauts* on the rivers, intercept their communications, stop their supplied, cut up their *daks* and posts, and keep constantly hanging about their camps; give them no rest.[10] Khan Bahadur Khan's advice was taken and the insurgents started harassing the British in every possible manner.

With Muhamadi Government

Defeated at Lucknow the insurgents including Firoz Shah headed towards Ruhelkhand, which had by now become the hot bed of revolutionary activities under its ruler Khan Bahadur Khan. Ahmadullah Shah too retreated to Muhamadi in Lakhimpur-Kheri District. After occupying Muhamadi, he raised mud walls around it and declared himself as an independent King. General Bakht Khan became his Wazir. Sarfaraz Ali Jaunpuri became his *Qazi-ul-uzzat* and Nana Saheb Peshwa was made Diwan. The members of the council were Maulvi Liaqat Ali Ilahabadi, Dr. Wazir Khan Akbarabadi and Maulvi Faiz Ahmad Badauni. Sahzada Firoz Shah joined it under compulsion as he himself was desirous of Kingship. The coin struck at this occasion read : *Sikandar Haft Kishwar Khadim-i-Mehrab Shah/ Hami-i-Din-i-Muhammad Ahmadullah Badshah.*[11] It means 'The Slave of Mehrab Shah struck his coins in the seven countries/ A supporter of the faith of Muhammad is King Ahmadullah.' The coronation is said to have taken place on 15th March 1858. According to Saiyid Zaheer Husain Jafri no such coins seem to have survived. The measure was probably announced to boost the sinking morale of the fighting forces. At Muhammadi the Maulvi received many insurgent leaders, like Azimullah Khan, Shahzada Firoz Shah, Khan Bahadur Khan of Bareilly and one Ismail Khan under the banner of Ahmadullah Shah. Besides these generals some sixteen thousand sepoys also gathered there.[12]

Nana Saheb in Ruhelkhand

Meanwhile, on the 15th of March the Nana was at Shahjahanpur and some important of the insurgents were with him. They also entered the district, attacked Kumpil[13], and driven off the *thana* people. On 16th instant Nana was five *koss* to the eastward of Bareilly. The houses of the people living there had been taken forcible possession of, for the accommodation of himself and his followers; and Khan Bahadur Khan was taking houses at Bareilly for his use.[14] Reports on 27th March were there that the Nana Saheb had an interview with Khan Bahadur Khan whose protection he asked. Khan Bahadur Khan gave him the command of his army which he was to lead to Kutchla Ghat to fight the British two days hence.[15]

Colin Campbell's plan

The affairs at Ruhelkhand were worrying the Commander-in-Chief of the British army in India, Sir Colin Campbell. After solving the crisis of Lucknow he proceeded to Ruhelkhand. He was a veteran soldier and had served in the West Indies and fought in China and was a soldier of mature ability and established reputation when he landed in India in 1846. He was present at Chilianwala and Gujarat and commanded the Peshawar division. On 11th July 1857 he was made the Commander-in-Chief of the Indian Army. For the past eight months he was painstakingly trying to regain the position of the British.

As regards Ruhelkhand, it was to be entered from different points. Brigadier General Walpole was to clear the left bank of the Ganges. The Commander-in-Chief was to proceed personally from Fatehgarh and join Walpole on the frontier of Ruhelkhand. Major-General penny was to march from Meerut and join the Commander-in-Chief at Miranpur Katra between Shahjanpur and Bareilly. A fourth column under Brigadier-General Jones was to penetrate into Ruhelkhand from their base at Roorkee. All the columns were to converge on Bareilly and there deal a decisive blow at the main rebel army, while Major-General Seaton was to watch the movements of the insurgents along the Ganges from his headquarters at Fatehgarh. The scheme was implemented according to the schedule but not without some loss.[16] These forces were advancing to take position against the insurgent concentrations.

Firoz Shah with Nana Saheb in Bareilly

After leaving Lucknow in the second week of March 1858, Firoz Shah, as mentioned earlier, headed towards Ruhelkhand and reached Bareilly in the second week of April 1858, with wounded cavalry. The intervening period of a month he took to cover a distance of about 125 miles, explains the difficulties and problems faced by him in traversing his way through that country, having British contingents around. With a tattered following devoid of provisions and ammunitions, Firoz Shah must have traveled surreptitiously till he reached Bareilly. When Firoz Shah arrived at Bareilly, Nana Saheb Peshwa was also there with his followers in the Government College and intended to attack Rampur. He had ordered entrenchments near the lunatic prison. Some Sikhs who had come to Bareilly were required to give up their arms. Some consented, others refused. Another Shahzada named Khurshid Tilak had also reached Bareilly.[17]

It can safely be assumed that Shahzada Firoz Shah had some close associates at Bareilly, because when Firoz Shah was in Jhansi his proclamation of 18th February 1858 was issued from Bareilly by one Wazir Khan. This base of his acquaintances there, was to prove helpful to him. Further, presumably it was the first time that Firoz Shah met Nana Saheb Peshwa at Bareilly, but it can be assumed that earlier also they were in touch with each other. Nana Saheb must be aware of the Bareilly Proclamation issued by Firoz Shah from Jhansi a month ago. Besides, Nana Saheb had been sending letters to insurgent leaders of North India since the beginning of the insurgency and it is quite probable that there must have been correspondence between Firoz Shah and Nana Saheb. But here Firoz Shah had to keep a low profile, as he did not have much force with him.

Without an effective fighting force, Firoz Shah could not place himself in an important position as was reported by a spy, who wrote that "Shahzada Firuz Shah is stated to be in no way influential— he has 200 Punjaubee Musulman horse and about 200 others with him"[18] but nevertheless gradually he built up a sufficient following[19] to play a significant part in the resistance to the British reoccupation. The main leader of insurgency in Ruhelkhand was Khan Bahadur Khan and his capacity and commitment rallied around him a large following consisting of mutinous sepoy regiments, *talukdars* and resurrected army of Ruhelkhand. He could get the support of insurgent leaders like Maulvi Ahmadullah Shah of Faizabad, Begam Hazrat Mahal of Awadh. They all were attempting to hold Awadh and Ruhelkhand against the British forces under Campbell.

Very soon, Nana Saheb undertook to manage Bareilly city and liberated many prisoners. He kept Daroga Moolchand as a hostage. Thousands were coming from Lucknow to Bareilly and thence proceeding to Rampur. Nana Saheb got 10,000 rupees from Khan Bahadur Khan for the expenses of an expedition against Fatehgrah.[20] Meanwhile, Firoz Shah put a demand for provisions before the Nawab of Rampur, and the Nawab after refusing his demand, informed Commissioner Bareilly about his step on 21st April 1858. The Bareilly Commissioner very much approved of his action and also wrote that if the news of Firoz Shah's march with an army towards Sambhal was true, and if the five hundred men dispatched against him, were, inadequate for the purpose, then an additional force will be sent to meet the requirements.[21]

It is also to be noted that certain influential Wahabi *maulvis* were included among the followers of Firoz Shah, especially during his activities in Ruhelkhand. For example Kutub Shah Wahabi, a teacher at Bareilly College did accompany Firoz Shah force on its march to Moradabad as deputy.[22]

Raid on Moradabad

Firoz Shah starting from Bareilly reached Moradabad and beat the Rampur force.[23] Before his arrival 1600 men, residents of Moradabad, had fixed their seals to a *Muhzur* in testimony of their readiness to co-operate with him. Abdul Ali Khan fled to Rampur. His party plundered the houses of Government well-wishers.[24] This attack of Firoz Shah on the 22nd April caused frustration to the British. He at once, on the departure of the Nawab's mutinous army and the retreat of the few who remained faithful, made for the treasury and *kutcheries*, sacked the contents of the treasury, and burnt those of the *kutcheries*, so that the record of the Nawab's administration was annihilated.[25]

On 25th April 1858 British column marched towards Moradabad. On its arrival there, Kasim Ali, the younger brother of the Nawab of Rampur came out to meet General Jones. The British troops encamped on the race course; immediately after arrival, the Magistrate and Collector Bareilly rode round the city with Brigadier Coke and posted guards at the entrance to prevent the escape of certain of the rebel leaders reported to be there. After the Guards had been posted, he entered in the town with Brigadier Coke and his Regiment of Punjab Rifles and 2 guns. After a long search he succeeded in arresting Majiduddin Khan (Majjo Khan), Asad Ali Khan, Abid Ali Khan, Sajid Ali Khan, Neaz Ali Khan, Kabir Ali Khan and other leaders of the rebellion. Majiduddin Khan was shot in the evening and his body afterwards exposed at the *Kotwali* to assure he people of the fact of his death.[26]

On the 30th April, the Commissioner, in company with the Nawab of Rampur arrived at Moradabad and found that every building in the cantonments fit for sheltering European troops had been destroyed by order of the Nana Saheb, who, however, did not himself wait for the arrival of the British. But the bridge of boats across the Ramganga river was not destroyed, and some of the buildings in the jail, and the wall round it, were still standing. Colonel Hale and a wing of the 82nd were left there with some guns, to make the best of their position in the jail, which partly dominated the city.[27]

Next day the town of Moradabad was illuminated on account of the restoration of Government authority and on 2nd May, District of Moradabad was made over to the Nawab of Rampur and the British Column marched on to Bareilly.

Battle of Bareilly

The insurgent force in Bareilly was estimated at 1,00,000 strong, and was provided with 70 or 72 guns of sizes. They were under the leadership of Firoz Shah, Khan Bahadur Khan, the Nawab of Ruhelkhand and Nana Saheb Peshwa. They were determined to show fight to the Commander-in-chief 's force. Firoz Shah lately marched with a Brigade to Rampur, compelled the loyal Nawab to fly to Nainital and took possession of is territory in the name of the Prophet. The British garrison in Shahjahanpur was besieged by 8000 rebels with 12 guns and the Commander-in-chief was said to be returning from his Ruhelkhand expedition to Farrukhabad for want of provisions.[28]

Ruhelkhand was to be entered from different points. Brigadier-General Walpole was to clear the left bank of the Ganges. The Commander-in-chief would personally proceed from Fatehgarh and join Walpole on the frontier of Ruhelkhand. Major-General Penny was to march from Meerut and join the Commander-in-Chief at Miranpur Katra between Shahjahanpur and Bareilly. A fourth column under Brigadier-General Jones was to penetrate into Ruhelkhand from their base at Roorkee. All the columns were to converge on Bareilly and there deal a decisive blow at the main rebel army. The column under Brigadier Jones halted at Moradabad. He resumed his march on the 3rd May and on the 5th reached Mirganj, within fourteen miles of Bareilly. At Mirganj was posted Shahzada Firoz Shah who retreated without offering any resistance.[29]

On the 2nd of May the British contingent left Shahjahanpur en route for Bareilly, and on the next day reached Fatehganj. Every village was totally deserted, but no plundering was allowed. The British sent the proclamations everywhere for the people to remain in their villages, but it had no effect. Two days later, the British party reached Faridpur, which was also found deserted. The *bazars* were full of reports of the great strength of the army of Khan Bahadur Khan and Firoz shah. The usual estimate was thirty thousand infantry, twenty-five thousand cavalry, and about three hundred guns, among which was said to be a famous black battery that had beaten the European artillery at ball-practice a few months before the army had mutinied at Meerut. The left wing of the 93rd was thrown out, with a squadron of the Lancers and Tombs' battery, as the advance piquet. As darkness set in the British could see the fires of the outposts of the insurgents, their patrol advancing quite close to the British sentries during the night, but making no attack.[30]

A detailed description of the battle of Bareilly has been given by William Forbes-Mitchell in his memoirs, who took part in the battle of Bareilly.[31] Here are the excerpts-

"About 2 A.M. on the 5th of May, according to Sir Colin's usual plan, three days' rations were served out, and the whole force was under arms and slowly advanced before daylight. by sunrise we could see the enemy drawn up on the plain some five miles from Bareilly, in front of what had been the native lines; but as we advanced, they retired. By noon we had crossed the *nullah* in front of the old cantonments, and, except by sending round-shot among us at long distances, which did not do much harm, the enemy did not dispute our advance. We were halted in the middle of a bare, sandy plain, and we of the rank and file then got to understand why the enemy were apparently in some confusion. We could hear the guns of Brigadier Jones hammering at them on the other side [..................] The Sikhs and our light company advanced ikn skirmishing order, when some seven to eight hundred matchlock-men opened fire on them, and all at once a most furious charge was made by a body of about three hundred and sixty Rohilla Ghazis, who rushed out, shouting *"Bismillah! Allah! Allah! Deen! Deen!"* [............] The Ghazis charged in blind fury, with their round shields on their left arms, their bodies bent low, waving their *tulwars* over their heads, throwing themselves under the bayonets, and cutting at the men's legs." Colonel Cameron of the 42nd was pulled from his horse by a Ghazi but was saved by Colour-Sergeant Gardener. General Walpole was also pulled off his horse, but was rescued. The struggle was short but every one of the Ghazis was killed. "None attempted to escape; they had evidently come on to kill or be killed, and a hundred and thirty-three lay in one circle."

Describing his confrontation with Firoz Shah, Mitchell writes "I was detached with about a dozen men of No. 7 company to find the ammunition-guard, and bring our ammunition in rear of the line. Just as I reached the ammunition-camels, a large force of the rebel cavalry, led by Feroze Shah in person, swept round the flank and among the baggage, cutting down camels, camel-drivers, and camp-followers in all directions. My detachment united with the ammunition-guard and defended ourselves, shooting down a number of the enemy's *sowars*." Mr. Russell of *The Times* was also present in this encounter and after being wounded, was rescued by Mitchell. After this charge of the insurgents, the British forces were advanced; but the thunder of Jones' attack on the other side of the city evidently disconcerted the insurgents and they made off to the right of the British line. The British force suffered more from the sun than from the insurgents.

On the 6th of May the troops were under arms, and advanced on the city of Bareilly. But little opposition was offered, except from one large house on the out-skirts of the town, in which a body of about fifty Rohilla Ghazis had barricaded themselves, and a company was sent to storm the house, after several shells had been pitched into it. But the house was taken by the British and the whole of the Ghazis were slain. It was reported that Khan Bahadur Khan and the Nana Saheb had fled in the direction of the Nepal *Tarai*, while Firoz Shah, with a force of cavalry and guns, had gone to attack Shahjanpur.

Brigadier Jones after a skirmish and taking guns at the entrance of the city took three-fourth of the new town of Bareilly without opposition, losing one man killed and three wounded. It was also reported that Firoz Shah was killed in the battle and Nana Saheb got off towards Awadh and Khan Bahadur Khan was entrenched with one thousand men determined to fight. [32] Death of

Firoz Shah was reported in other sources[33] also but as will be seen, he was not killed and was alive to continue his struggle.

A correspondent of *The Englishman* says; "It appears the battle of Bareilly was a farce; for three hours the troops were kept under a burning sun, looking in the direction of the town. A few Ghazis came out and were killed. The Artillery fired into a tope of trees, and then instead of proceeding onward, the Commander-in-Chief pitched tents. This was to wait, as we noticed before, for the heavy guns and baggage."[34]

Shahjahanpur Attacked

After the force under Sir Colin Campbell had left Shahjahanpur a strong band of insurgents from Muhamadi in Awadh made an attack on the few troops that had been assigned for the protection of the station. They surprised and cut off the piquet of De Kantzow's Horse and destroyed many of them. The insurgents were reported to have plundered the city of Shahjahanpur and to have massacred many of the inhabitants and to be in possession of the fort which was an old dilapidated building on the outskirts of the city. The insurgent patrols were on the river and communication was difficult and dangerous.[35]

Brigadier General Jones, with a strong Column left Bareilly on the 8th May, to relieve the garrison at Shahjahanpur, where the right wing of 82nd Regiment had been besieged since he Commander-in-Chief's advance on Bareilly. On the 11th May, Brigadier-General Jone's Column relieved the garrison of Shahjahanpur, and took one gun. The insurgent force was principally Cavalry and was well mounted but British casualties were small.[36]

A local Urdu chronicle *Tarikh-i-Shahjahanpur* gives some details of the events. According to it when the British forces advanced towards Shahjahanpur, Ahmadullah Shah vacated the city but returned back after 2-3 days and assaulted the city. The British forces, which were here went to the old jail and raising mud walls there entrenched themselves. Ahmadullah Shah put to the fire the

Jali Kothi taking it to be the house of the anti-rebels. The attack of Ahmadullah Shah lasted from 3rd to 9th May, 1858. Sir Collin Campbell got its news at the nick of time and sent an army under the command of Brigadier Jones. They made a vain attempt to check the rebels at Nayaghat. Turning the rebels from the fort *Pul Khanaut* and other entrenched positions, they moved through the east of the city on its fringes and joined Col. Hubal. Since Ahmadullah Shah was occupying a strong entrenchment, he could not be pressed and unsystematic warfare was going on. The forces of Firoz Shah and the Begum of Awadh arrived for the help of Ahmadullah Shah, who delivered a very severe attack upon the mud walls on 15th May, 1858 but Jones maintained his place.[37]

The force at Shahjahnpur under General Jones was attacked by the insurgents on Saturday. Khan Bahadur Khan, Mahmood Khan of Najibabad, Firoz Shah and others were said to be there. Brigadier Coke was at Pilibheet on the 16th. Mr. Ricketts sent in several insurgents found hiding in the villages near the time of march. He made over a number of carpenters, black-smiths, *bildars* etc. to the Executive Engineer. Small bands of the insurgents were moving about the district. Banne Mian, Nizam Ali Khan and the Nawab of Fatehgarh were reported to be at Mohanpur and were said to be going to a dinner party at Shergarh in the evening. The *Tahsildar* of Shahi tried to catch these fellows. Some 200 of the insurgents assembled near Bisulpur but were dispersed by the *Tahsildar* Bilas Singh with the assistance of Habibullah *zamindar*.[38]

Battle of Shahjahanpur

Brigadier General J. Jones, Commanding Shahjahanpur Field Force had an encounter with the insurgents. The insurgents opened their guns in quick succession, and for a few minutes their fire was heavy; but the effect produced by 24-pounders of the British force was soon seen and the insurgents had to withdraw their bullock cart guns at once but they continued the fire with the guns put on their horses. As the British force advanced, these horse-guns were also withdrawn and the British force entered the fort of Shahjahanpur easily. The Cavalry Regiment of the British was charged by a large body of insurgents under cover of a tope of trees; about thirty of them were able to get into the rear of the British Regiment but were cut to pieces and the insurgent leader was also killed. The town and fort were found to be evacuated and they were immediately occupied. The insurgents had commenced their retreat from Muhamadi about noon on the 24th, their families and valuables had been carried far into te jungles that skirted the north-eastern portion of Awadh. The British Cavalry was employed during the 26th in clearing the country in the direction of the retreat of the insurgents and found large quantity of gun-powder in a nearby fort, some guns and large number of gun-carriages. Several villages were burnt, and after completely scouring the country, the British force returned to Shahjahanpur on the morning of 29th.[39]

On the 24th May 1858 Campbell had a second engagement with the insurgents at Sahjahanpur. He drove them back on Muhamadi which place was evacuated by the insurgents. The Begum of Awadh, Shahzada Firoz Shah and Khan Bahadur Khan all affected their escape. Maulvi Liaqat Ali attacked and plundered the small town of Bilgram, about eighty miles to the north-west of Lucknow.[40] The Commander-in-Chief arrived Fatehgarh on the morning of 25th May from Shahjahanpur, where he left Brigadier-General Jones with orders to attack the insurgents and destroy Muhamadi.[41] The Muhamadi set back greatly reduced the strength of the insurgents and facing adversity all around they now decided to try their luck in the eastern districts of Awadh, viz. Lakhimpur, Sitapur, Lucknow and Unnao.

Fortunately, on the western side of the Awadh province, Narpat Singh had restored and replenished his fort at Roohia and was joined by Maulvi Ahmadullah Shah and Firoz Shah. Now they had the whole country within a few miles of the Kanpur road in their possession. The Chief Commissioner expressed his deep regret that Narpat Singh was not destroyed by General

Walpole. Failure at Roohia, and the fruitless marches of General Grant to the south 'had done incalculable harm to the British throughout the Oudh'.[42]

Towards north of Lucknow large number of sepoys and rebel chiefs had gathered. They were supposed to join Rana Beni Madho of Shankarpur in a co-ordinated attack on Lucknow on 2nd June. It may be mentioned that Rana Beni Madho of Shankarpur was the most valiant of the Baiswara Rajputs. In April 1858 he had interfered with settlement operations in South-east Awadh and chastised all *zamindars* who had come to terms with the British. Lord Clyde asked him to surrender his person, but he refused and left Shankarpur.[43] He collected a large force and entered Awadh to join other insurgent leaders. The insurgents took up a position at Nawabganj with 9,000 infantry and cavalry and thirteen guns, but their attempt was[44] foiled by General Hope Grant cutting off Rana Beni Madho and the defeat of the insurgents at Nawabganj on 12th June.

This defeat further weakened the position of the insurgents in western Awadh. The loss of the defeat of Firoz Shah at Shahjahanpur on 24th May was yet to be replenished. Maulvi Ahmadulla Shah was still exerting to take the deteriorating situation in his hand but he met his tragic death at Pawain.

Maulvi Ahmadullah's death

On 5th June 1858 Maluvi Ahmadullah Shah, an associate of Firoz Shah, appeared before Powain, a small fort on the Awadh-Rohilkhand border, a few miles from Shahjahanpur. But the Raja closed the gates of his fort against the Maulavi. He changed the gates with his elephant but was shot dead by the garrison. The severed head was then sent to the magistrate of Shahjahanpur and it was exposed at the *Kotwali* of the town. The body was burnt and the ashes thrown into the river.. The Raja got Rs. 50,000 the price of the Maulavi's head.[45] According to Sir Thomas Seaton, the Maulavi was "a man of great abilities, of undaunted courage, of stern determination, and by far the best soldier among the rebels."[46] Malleson describes him as "a man of great abilities, of undaunted courage, and of stern determination, and by far the best soldier among the rebels."[47] He adds, "If a patriot is a man who plots and fights for the independence, wrongfully destroyed, of his native country, then most certainly the Maulavi was a true patriot. He had not stained his sword by assassination, he had connived at no murders; he had fought manfully, honourably, and stubbornly in the field against the strangers who had seized his country, and his memory is entitled to the respect of the brave and the true-hearted of all nations."[48]

Holmes also pays a high tribute to him and describes him as "probably the most capable, as he was certainly the most determined of the men who fought against us in the Indian Mutiny."[49] According to S.N. Sen, he had no military training, but he had the natural instincts of a born leader. He never missed a weak point in the enemy line and always strove to strike at it.[50]

Ahmadullah Shah was a firm minded patriot, possessing in ample measure the qualities of a writer, orator and organizer. Though with no military training, he never missed vulnerable point in the enemy line and always strove to strike at it.[51] Even his British opponents who fought against him could not help praising Maulvi's balance of mind, courage and daring and outstanding efficiency. F.H. Fisher has observed that Maulvi Ahmadulla was one of the three best strategists of the 1857 revolutionaries. The other two were Tatya Tope and Babu Kunwar Singh.[52] The main field of action of Maulvi Ahmad Ullah during the 1857 revolt was Awadh although he also demonstrated his valour at Shahjahanpur and in Rohilkhand. He was the true representative of the discontented masses of Awadh.

While the insurgents struggled hard against the powerful British forces in Ruhelkhand and suffered the loss of their valiant leader Ahmadullah Shah, Bundelkand witnessed two more losses in the same month of June 1858 in the shape of death of Rani of Jhansi and defeat of Tatya Tope at Jaura-Alipur.

Reference :

1. Foreign Department, Political Proceedings, Deposition of Wazeer Khan, 30-12-1859, No. 311, letter no. 54, dt. 9-3-1859.
2. Sen, op. cit., p. 173
3. R. Mukherjee, *Awadh in Revolt* 1857-58, p. 63
4. Couper to Edmonstone, 1 Dec. 1857: '. . . [Chief Commissioner] had authorized the sum of Rs. 50,000 to be expended in an attempt to raise the Hindoo population of Bareilly against the Mahommedan rebels. . . the attempt was quite unsuccessful and has been abandoned. . .': Foreign Department Secret Cons., 27 Aug. 1858, Cons. No. 25
5. R. Mukherjee, *Op. Cit.*, p. 89.
6. Marx and Engels, *The First Indian War of Independence 1857-59*, Moscow, fourth printing, 1975, pp. 123-125
7. Spelt as *Bangaon* on page 126 of Further Papers (No.8), 1858, Inclosure 43 in No. 9. May have been spelt for *Baugaon (Bhogaon)* in *Mainpuri* District, if *Bangaon* in District *Shahjahanpur* is not meant here.
8. Narrative of events, dated March 1858. F.M.U.P. Vol. V, pp. 428-29
9. Marx and Engels, *Op. Cit.* p. 133.
10. Quoted in Russell, *My Indian Mutiny Diary*, p. 73.
11. Hamid Afaq Qureshi, 'East India Company Aur Baghi Ulema' in *1857: Urdu Sources (Translations)*, ed. by Ansari and Qureshi, 2008, p. 158.
12. Saiyid Zaheer Husain Jafri 'The Profile of a Saintly Rebel : Maulvi Ahmaduallah Shah' in *Facets of the Great Revolt, 1857* (ed.) Shireen Moosvi, 2008, p. 45
13. 45 kms. north-west of Farrukhabad in Uttar Pradesh.
14. Narrative of Events, dated March 18, 1858. Further Papers (No. 8 in continuation of No. 6) relative to The Insurrection in the East Indies, 1858, Inclosure 1 in No. 9, p. 116. F.S.U.P., Vol. V, p. 428.
15. Telegraphic Message from G.F. Edmonstone, Allahabad, to E.A. Reade, Agra, dated 28th March 1858., Original Telegrams sent to Mr. E.A. Reade, 1858. Secretariat Records Room, Lucknow, F.S. U.P., Vol. V, pp. 429-30
16. Sen, op. cit., p. 355.
17. Bulletin dated 13th April 1858, Originals of Daily Bulletins issued by A.E. Reade during March-July 1858. Secretariat Records Room, Lucknow. F.S.U.P., Vol. V, pp. 434-35.
18. Report of 16th April in Bulletin 25 April 1858, Originals of Daily Bulletins issued by Mr. E.A. Reade during March-July 1858, Secretariat Records Room, Lucknow F.S.U.P. Vol. V, p. 438
19. Narrative Kanpur District week ending 27th June "F.S. has 8000 (half cavalry) and 12 guns" F.S.U.P., Vol. IV, p. 764
20. Bulletin dated 16th April 1858. Originals of Daily Bulletins issued by A.E. Reade during March-July 1858. Secretariat Records Room, Lucknow, F.S.U.P. V, p. 435.

21. Translation of a Vernacular Letter from Commissioner, Bareilly, to the Nawab of Rampur, dated Naini Tal, the 23rd April 1858. Mss. 'Rampur Darbar and 1857' prepared under the authority of the Ex-Nawab of Rampur. Rampur Collectorate Records Room. F.S.U.P., Vol. V, pp. 407-08.
22. Office Memorandum from the Assistant Secretary to the Govt. of the North-Western Provinces, dated Fort William, 27th May 1859. Trial of Kutub Shah. Foreign Political Proceedings, 27th May 1859, Cons. No. 81, pp. 163-64. F.S.U.P., pp. 583-584.
23. Telegraphic message from Commissioner, Meerut, to E.A. Reade, Agra, dated 24th April 1858,Original Telegrams sent to Mr. E.A. Reade, 1858. Secretariat Records, F.S.U.P., Vol. V, p. 408.
24. Extract from Letter no 88 from R.H. Dunlop, Officiating Magistrate of Moradabad, to R. Alexander, Commissioner of Rohilkhand, dated 18th Novebmer 1858. Mutiny Narratives, N.W.P. Agra, Moradabad District, p. 3. F.S.U.P. , Vol. V, p. 408
25. Extract from letter no. 350 from Commissioner of Rohilkhand Division, to Secretary to Government, North-Western Provinces, dated the 6th December 1858. Mss. "Rampur Darbar and 1857" prepared under the authority of the Ex-Nawab of Rampur. Rampur Collectorate Records Room . F.S.U.P., Vol. V, p. 409
26. Enclosure (narrative of events) to a letter no. 1 from he Magistrate and Collector Bareilly, to R. Alexander, Commissioner of Ruhelkhand Division, at Bareilly, dated 13th May 1858. F.S.U.P. Vol. V, p. 480. Also see F.S.U.P., Vol. V, pp. 410 and 442.
27. William Forbes-Mitchell, *Reminiscences of the Great Mutiny*, reprint 1989, p. 252
28. The Hindu Patriot, 20th May 1858, p. 155. National Library, Calcutta. F.S.U.P., Vol. V, p. 446
29. Foreign Department, Secret Consultations, G.P. Money to R. Alexander, 17 June 1858, no. 138, 27 Aug., 1858.
30. William Forbes-Mitchell, op. cit., p. 252-53
31. Ibid, pp. 253-262. Also see Ball, Vol. II, pp. 328.
32. Telegraphic message from Commissioner. Meerut to E.A. Reade, Agra, dated 10th May 1858. Original Telegrams sent to Mr. E. A. Reade, 1858. Secretariat Records Room, Lucknow. F.S.U.P., Vol. V, p. 467
33. Bulletin dated Agra, 11th May 1858 F.S.U.P. Vol. V, p. 469 and Extract from 'The Friend of India', dated May 20, 1858. F.S.U.P., Vol. V., p. 448.
34. The Friend of India, June 3, 1858, p. 511. National Library, Calcutta. News dated Thursday, May 27, 1858. F.S.U.P., Vol. V, p. 449.
35. Telegraphic Message from G.F. Edmonstone, Allahabad, to E.A. Reade, Agra, dated 7th May 1858. F.S.U.P., Vol. V, pp. 442-43.
36. Further Papers (No. 8, in continuation of No. 6) relative to The Insurrection in the East Indies, 1858, Inclosure 1 in No. 16, p. 157. F.S.U.P., V, p. 510-511.

37. Maulvi Muhammad Sabih-ud-din Khalil, *Tarikh-e-Shahjahnpur*, Lucknow, 1936, English translation by Ishrat Husain Ansari and Hamid Afaq Qureshi in "*1857: Urdu Sources*", Lucknow, 2008, p. 91.
38. Narrative of Events for 16th and 17th May 1858 submitted by Collecor of Bareilly to the Commissioner of Rohilkhand Division at Bareilly, dated Bareilly Collectorship, 18th May 1858. Department-XXIV, file No. 25; Bareilly Commissioner's Office Mutiny Records. State Archives of Uttar Pradesh, Allahabad. F.S.U.P., V, p. 494-95.
39. Message from Brigadier-General J. Jones, C.B. Commanding Shahjahanpur Field Fore, to the Deputy Adjutant-General of the Army, dated Camp Shahajanpur, 1st June 1858, Government Gazette, North-Western Provinces, Allahabad, Tuesday, July 6, 1858, pp. 295-96- F.S.U.P., V, pp. 524-525
40. The Friend of India, 3rd June, 1858, p. 512. National Library, Calcutta. F.S.U.P., V, p. 523.
41. Telegraphic Message from the Commander-in-Chief to the Governor General of India, dated Fategarh, May 25, 1858. Further Papers (No. 8, in continuation of No. 6) relative to *The insurrection in the East Indies*, 1858, Enclosure 3 in No. 19, p. 157. F.S.U.P., V, p. 524.
42. Letter no. 461 of 1858 from T. D.Forsyth, Secretary to the Chief Commissioner, Oudh (Awadh), to G.F. Edmonstone, Secretary to the Governor General, dated Lucknow, 12th June 1858. Quoted in F.S.U.P., Vol. II, p. 434.
43. S.N.Sen, op. cit., p. 362.
44. Forsyth to Edmonstone, 5th June 1858; and also Forsyth to Edmonstone 19th June 1858: Foreign Department Secret Cons. 30th July 1858, Cons. Nos. 63 and 82 respectively.
45. G.P. Money to R. Alexander, 17 June 1858, Foreign Secret Consultations, no. 138, 27 Aug., 1858. as quoted in S.N. Sen pp. 355-57. A first hand account of the death of Maulvi Ahmadaullah Shah at Pawayan is given by Maulana Fazle Haq Khairabadi, who was an eye witness on the occasion. Quoted by Iqtidar Alam Khan in his article in *Facets of the Great Revolt* edited by Shireen Moosvi, p. 45.
46. G.B. Malleson, *History of the Indian Mutiny,*. Vol II, p. 541.
47. Ibid.
48. Ibid, p. 544
49. T. Rice Holmes, *A History of Indian Mutiny*, p. 506
50. Sen, op. cit., p. 356.
51. A.S. Misra, *Nana Saheb Peshwa*, 1961, p. 403
52. F.H. Fisher, *Azamgarh Gazetteer*, 1883, p. 140

Chapter - 6

Awadh Exploits

The defeat in the battle of Shahjahanpur on 24th May 1858, greatly reduced the strength of the insurgent leaders including Firoz Shah and they were facing adversity all around. They now decided to try their luck in the eastern districts of Awadh.

By early June 1858 the situation in Awadh further worsened for the British. Purwa had to be entirely given up by them and was immediately re-occupied by the insurgents. Mehndi Hussain remained in occupation of Ayodhya and Faizabad, and to the west of Lucknow, Narpat Singh was back in his fort at Ruiya.[1] This he restored and replenished, and 'joining the Maulvi Ahmadulla Shah and Firoz Shah they have the whole country to within a few miles of the Cawnpore road in their possession'. The last British post to the west was at Malihabad.[2]

Firoz Shah's close associate Maulvi Ahmadulla Shah was killed on 5th June 1858 at the battle of Powain. As we know, his other associates Begum Hazrat Mahal, Nana Saheb Peshwa and Khan Bahadur Khan were wandering as fugitives in Nepal territories.

Death of the Rani of Jhansi and defeat of Tatya Tope

Events had moved rapidly at Gwalior in June 1858. On the 1st June the insurgents under the leadership of Rao Saheb occupied Gwalior without any resistance. The British force under Sir Hugh Rose invaded Gwalior and the Rani of Jhansi died fighting on

17th June 1858. Loss of the fort of Jhansi coupled with the death of the Rani cast a severe blow to the insurgents in Bundelkhand. She was greatly revered by her people and her heroic death left an indelible mark in the minds of generations to come. 'If the reverence of her own people is any compensation for vilification by her enemies the Rani of Jhansi stands more than vindicated. Thousands of unsophisticated villagers still sing of the valour and virtues of the women who held her own against her Bundela enemies to fall under a British bullet.'

Her associates Tatya Tope and Rao Saheb had to take a flight but they were hotly pursued by General Napier and were routed after an artillery action followed and cavalry charge on the 28th June 1858 at Jaura-Alipur.[3] Both of the insurgent leaders now crossed the Chambal river and fled to Rajputana to resume their activities. They had lost their guns and had but a small following. With their limited resources, they decided to take recourse to guerilla fight against the British.

These two incidences within 11 days were great blows to the struggle against the British and the insurgent leaders Firoz Shah, Nana Saheb, Khan Bahadur Khan, Begum Hazrat Mahal, Mardan Singh and Bakhatbali not only lost two of their best warriers, but also felt a great psychological set back. Death of Rani of Jhansi meant loss of Jhansi which was an important stronghold of the insurgents and defeat of Tatya Tope meant that days of open warfare with the British were over.

With an army of over five thousand soldiers in his attempt to spread the resistance, Tatya was going mobile. More familiar with the terrain and the area, Tatya's army had the ability to be far more agile than the English were. He would march into areas and rekindle local insurrections, which would force the English to mobilise their troops. His warfare was more than 'guerilla'. In some cases, Tatya marched with a full-fledged rmy, complete with all logistical elements that a regular army would have.[4] Tatya Tope now planned to enter Malwa and Rajputana, where he hoped to get support from the local chiefs against the British. He had already sent secret emissaries to several of the capitals in Rajputana. We will see that after six months Shahzada Firoz Shah, after his unsuccessful attempts in Awadh, entered Rajputana to join Tatya Tope.

Very soon Firoz Shah was to hear about the Tatya Tope's defeat at Jaura Alipur in June 1858, following which Tatya Tope abandoned open warfare and took up guerilla warfare and decided to leave for Rajputana and Malwa. It was followed by the surrender of Bakhatbali of Shahgarh and Mardan Singh of Banpur in the first week of July 1858. Deprived of this tangible support of important insurgent leaders in a very short period, Firoz Shah had to go alone in Awadh. In fact now he was the only principle leader left in Awadh to continue the struggle against the British power.

Firoz Shah at Bangarmau

On 9th of June 1858 Firoz Shah was reported staying at Bangarmau 48 miles west of Lucknow in Tahsil Safipur, District Unnao. He had a strength of about 4000 horsemen and *Tilangas*. Other insurgents had deserted, but his horsemen committed acts of plunder as far as Asiwan[5], which was 2 miles west of Mianganj and 32 miles west of Lucknow. It was rumoured that they will reach up to Mohan which was 16 miles west of Lucknow. Firoz Shah summoned all the *Zemindars* of Bangarmau[6] and Safipur and encouraged them to revolt in order to support his claim for royalty. He said to them that he had exempted them from payment of Government revenue for 3 years; and could condone even the dues of the current year; but they must help him. As a result of this, the *Zemindars* of *Ilaqa* Bangarmau went over to his side and he gathered a following. Firoz Shah appointed Allahdad Khan *Risaldar* as the *Tahsildar* of *Ilaqa* Bangarmau. Firoz Shah made Safipur his *Thana*, and devised plans for setting up Narpat Singh, son of Jassa Singh at Fatehpur Chaurasi.[7]

As regards the influence of Firoz Shah over that area, the entire *Ilaqa* had gone against the government owing to Narpat Singh. Now, because of Firoz Shah, they had become still more rebellious and sided with Firoz Shah and Narpat Singh. Of the

Zamindars, the Mewatis of Sitalganj and Bangarmau ravaged the whole *Ilaqa* and blockaded the road to Lucknow, to the extent, that even the wayfarer could not pass.[8]

Gathering forces

Firoz Shah collected his force to threaten Unnao from the west, and the *Thannah* of Rasulabad[9] was occupied by the insurgents. General Grant withdrew a portion of his force from Nawabganj[10] on the 21st June 1858 leaving a sufficient body to hold that part of the country. Captain Reid, Deputy Commissioner, was placed in charge of Nawabganj and the surrounding country as far as the Ghagra river, which was now clear of insurgents.

The insurgents were showing fresh signs of activity in the neighbourhood, but across the Awadh border, because their object was to attack Pawayan[11], if not Shahjahanpur itself. There was to be a great gathering of the insurgent forces at Sikandarabad and two of their regiments had already come on from Garhi Roya (Ruia)[12] and Har Prasad, the *Chukladar* of Khairabad[13], was soon expected with other chiefs and their forces. Khan Ali Khan was appointed to the chief command by the Begum and Khan Bahadur Khan, and a brother of Maulvi Ahmadullah and several other men of note were with him under his authority. He was to come first to Muhamadi which was his depot for commissariat stores, but it was decided that the chief camp would be formed at Sikandarabad and a division would be at Gokurnanath (probably *Gola Gokarn Nath* in *Kheri* District). The number of the insurgents was estimated as being certainly not less than 30,000 and probably 40,000 with 30 guns of sorts but all the rebels were not armed. Probably the effective strength might be about one third of the total and the remainder were camp followers. Azul Haq, a resident of Muhamadi was appointed Tahsildar of Perora (?).[14] Meanwhile Khan Bahadur Khan, an important and formidable ally of Firoz Shah was busy with his contingent elsewhere against the British forces.

In the middle of July Firozshah and other insurgents were to approach Powayan, but as the river Gomti had risen, there was not much possibility of their coming in that direction. It was earlier reported by Bengal Harkaru that the insurgents were at logger-heads about the division of the Maulvis treasure and Begum Hazrat Mahal sent up Khan Ali Khan with a force to bring the treasure to her, but Khan Bahadur, Ismail Khan and Firoz Shah, declined to give it up.[15] But after some time the Bengal Hurkaru amended its earlier report and said that the decapitated Maulavi's property was not, as previously reported, contended for and distributed amongst the rebels, but had been safely send by Khan Ali Khan and Khan Bahadur Khan to the Begum. The train of carts, elephants and camels conveying it, was as large as one of the British commissariat trains.[16]

On the 16th July 1858 Firoz Shah and Lakkar Shah attacked Mohan *Thanna* and on the 18th the insurgents cut off the hands of the *Thanadar*. They then moved on the *Thanna* of Malha, N.W. of Bunnee, which was evacuated by the Police at their approach, but subsequently reoccupied by the British after a skirmish in which 7 or 8 of the insurgents were killed.[17]

Firoz Shah and Mir Mansab Ali

It seems that Firozshah was also assigned some administrative responsibilities by Birjis Qadar and he discharged his duties meticulously. It has to be remembered that though he was the youngest amongst the insurgent leaders, every where he was given equal importance, rather better treatment as he belonged to the Mughal dynasty. The way he dealt with one Mir Mansab Ali shows his administrative capability and perseverance. Mir Mansab Ali was given the *sanad* of the *Chakledari* of the villages of the *Mahal* of Rasulabad and Safipur by Birjis Qadar, son of Begum Hazrat Mahal. We find six letters written to Mir Mansab Ali by Firoz Shah about some revenue arrangements. In a letter Firoz Shah wrote to him that because he (Firoz Shah) had an identity of interest with Birjis Qadar, Mansab Ali should consider himself permanently appointed to his office from Firoz Shah's side as well and should exert himself faithfully and assiduously in the discharge of his duties.[18]

In another letter Firoz Shah wrote to Mansab Ali, "As my government have granted the *Sanad* of free-hold, exclusive of proprietary rights, to Sheikh Ali Hasan *Risaldar* of *Mouza* Phikai, you are, therefore, ordered to put him in possession of the above-named *Mauza*." [19] He again wrote to Mansab Ali on 22nd July 1858, "I have been waiting for the fulfillment of your promise up to this time. The army is making importunate demands. Without the money promised by you, nothing can be done. You have not sent any money as yet. It is, therefore, ordered that you should soon send in the money promised, so that I may be relieved of the persistent demands of the army. If you cannot do this, send an unequivocal reply and dispatch the persons committed, to me. When, in spite of my presence here there is no much delay in sending the promised amount, what reliance can be placed on your promises when I am away. It is, therefore, proper that clear reply be at once sent to me."[20]

On 24th July Firoz Shah wrote to Mansab Ali that the letter of Dalpat Singh regarding the inability of realizing the money to be levied from Safipur and about other matters was perused. Mansab Ali was ordered to arrange soon for the amount because the soldiers at Safipur were in trouble. An order was given to Wilayat Ahmad for the dismissal of the *Tahsildar* of Harayya[21] and in case of non-compliance necessary action was to be taken.[22]

On 26th July Firoz Shah wrote- 'Perused your letter. Be sure Ganga Singh and others shall not go to Safipur. You should make all haste in the collection of money. Now that Wilayat Ahmad is present here for giving account of the government money levied, his house etc. should not be confiscated till these accounts are settled and cleared. Puran Chand should also be taken captive. If he resists, steps will be taken, in case you send the information. It should be announced by beat of drums, in the *Ilaqa* that all those from whom Wilayat Ahmad had taken money either for force or in the form of government revenue should report the matter in my presence and those who will not do so will be punished, if this is discovered.'[23]

On 7th August he wrote- 'Your letter has come to my notice. As you did not come in spite of repeated orders the work of the government was considerably delayed. This is why a new arrangement has been made. I have already written to you what I intended and therefore there is no use repeating it. You should now reach Rasulabad and make a new settlement of the *Ilaqa* till further orders. You should act according to this new settlement. Later, necessary orders will be sent to you.'[24]

Towards Malihabad and Sandila

For many days past the raids of Lukkarshah, Hushmut Ali and Firoz Shah had caused considerable annoyance in the British quarters. Their success at Mohan and Malha, emboldened them to press close upon Malihabad. The movement of European troops under Colonel Maxwell from Muriaon cantonments towards Kakori on the road to Malihabad induced Lakkurshah to withdraw in the direction of Sundeela, and on the 29th July the insurgents having abandoned Ruheemabad, half-way between Malihabad and Sundeela, Kavanagh thought this opportunity favorable for establishing a *Thanah* there. This was no sooner done, than the *thanah* was surrounded by the insurgents from Sundeela. On 30th July, Kavanagh at once proceeded from Malihabad with 400 infantry and 90 sowars and after a sharp skirmish drove the insurgents out with a loss of 15 or 20 killed, and followed them up on the road to Sundeela. Nurput Singh, on hearing of the movement of Colonel Maxwell's force, at once withdrew into his fort of Rohya, and recalled his gun and men from Bilgram. He had now 1700 men and 9 guns inside his fort. The tidings of the approach of a British force spread alarm amongst the rebels at Palee, Bilgram and other places to the west. Meanwhile Beni Madho, after making a demonstration of going towards the South-Eastern frontier, returned to his own fort at Shankarpur and his troops have ceased from all active proceedings against British outposts during the week.[25]

Firoz Shah and the other Delhi Princes were at Nourangabad 14 miles south of Muhamadi with 1500 men and 5 guns. Hushmut

Ali who was sent by Mr. Kavanagh, acting under orders of the Chief Commissioner to Meerganj 18 miles south of Sandila, occupied that place with his followers and held the surrounding country quiet.[26]

There was rumour that on the Muhamadi side at Biror and Naurangabad, 7 or 8 *Kos* east of Muhamadi, there were seven or eight thousand rebel *Tilangas*, horsemen and new recruits and six or seven guns under Firoz Shah, Khan Bahadur, Ismail Khan, Wilayat Shah and Bunney Mian. Persons were sent by the British for investigation and to find out the true news about Fazlul Haq who had marched with his followers towards Shahabad and about Mazhar Ali Khan, brother of Jan Ali Khan who was known as the General of the army in *Mauza* Sheora.[27]

The supplies of the city of Lucknow were checked by the insurgents at Sandila, which was sixteen miles west of Malihabad where insurgent force consisting of fifteen hundred infantry, two hundred cavalry, and five guns was stationed. The British contingent planned to attack Malihabad. The time seemed favourable for attacking them, for the spirited progress of Sir Hope Grant towards Fyzabad and Sultanpoor had somewhat disheartened the rebels throughout the province. British troops on the Kanpur road were also threatening Shahzada Firoz Shah.

Battle of Sandila

T.H. Kavanagh[28], one of the participants of the battle of Sandila,[29] gives a detailed account of the battle. The account says that on the afternoon of the 10th of August, Captain Dawson advanced with a small force to Rahimabad,[30] where he was joined by two small Talukdars and some of the natives of Sandila and Malihabad, and Chowdhry Hushmat Ali, a man with considerable influence. In the evening, his cavalry contingent reached within five miles of Sandila, and a watchman was sent by him to warn the insurgent leaders that they would be attacked in the morning. It was expected that the message would cause them to make early arrangements for retreat.

Midway to Sandila the British contingent halted for breakfast where they learnt that in consequence of the message to the Chiefs, the insurgents had been reinforced during the night, and now had six hundred cavalry under Shahzada Firoz Shah, three thousand regular and irregular infantry under Namdar Khan and Ghulab Singh, and five guns.

The British officer found large bodies of insurgent cavalry and infantry standing under extensive woods screening the town in our front. Captain Dawson arranged to attack them to the south, and made over the gallant troop of cavalry to Kavanagh, and with them Kavanagh covered his advance from the insurgent cavalry and assembled in columns of troops with the intention of sweeping down upon Kavanagh's handful of horsemen. Kavanagh put on a bold front, and sent them further back.

The six hundred cavalry led by Firoz Shah drew closer, and their steady advance was so menacing that, as Kavanagh puts it, "I was forced to decide at once between attacking them or going into the town. The first would have disheartened our infantry, who were already engaged at great odds, and I, therefore, invited the Sikhs to say whether they would follow me. With one accord they lifted their swords, and called to me to go on." Shahzada Firoz Shah drew nearer, but, as Kavanagh turned to engage him, he halted on the edge of a large grove of trees, apparently uncertain what to do. In another minute Kavanagh's contingent suddenly turned from the straight line, and were engaged hand to hand with the left flank, which broke at once, and threw the whole body into such confusion, that they turned about and went away, pursued by the Sikhs.

Followed by a dozen Sikhs, Kavanagh started after the Shahzada Firoz Shah, who was conspicuous from riding a grey horse and being dressed in white. Within no time Firoz Shah distanced the contingent of Kavanagh. A shot disabled Kavanagh's horse and threw him to the ground. The insurgents went post haste, eight miles off, to the fort of Birrwa.

The insurgents were led by Firoz Shah in person and with him were Lukkarshah and others. The police force returned after having established Hushmut Ally with his own seven hundred retainers. The loss of Firoz Shah was estimated at one hundred killed and wounded while the British losses were 13 killed & 17 wounded. The Sultanpur Bitish Column on the 11th was at Thulner 11 miles from Sultanpur and was expected to reach Sultanpur next day. [31]

A 19th August, 1858 news reported that the Begum of Awadh with her troops stands far beyond the Ghagra. She had in her camp Khan Bahadur Khan and his men, as well as a number of other chiefs. A portion of the Awadh insurgents had crossed into the Azamgarh District.[32]

Meanwhile the Governor General directed in his Ruhelkhand proclamation that only rebel leaders should be capitally punished. The local authorities construed a 'leader' to mean every man who held any office under Khan Bahadur Khan. They were now warned of their mistake.[33]

Azamgarh Proclamation

It was about this time that Firoz Shah issued a Proclamation on 25th August 1858 from Azamgarh[34] on the name of Bahadur Shah II. By now the British had already tried and found Bahadur Shah guilty and while they were making plans to exile him from India, Shahzada Firoz Shah attempted to rally the Indians by issuing this Azamgarh Proclamation on the name of Bahadur Shah, in which he highlighted various grievances of different classes of Indian society. The *zamindars* were told that the British assess lands very highly and this had been the cause of their ruin. They have to pay for stamp paper and Court fees which are ruinous. The merchants were reminded that the British have appropriated to themselves the monopoly of all lucrative trade such as indigo, opium, cloth etc. and left the less remunerative merchandise to them. The officials were reminded that in the Civil and Military Departments the natives are given less lucrative situations and paid far less than the Europeans. The artisans were reminded that the Europeans imported every sort of article from Europe and have left but a small trade in their hands. Scholars of both the creeds of Hindus and Muslims were reminded that the British were opposed to their religion.

This proclamation was published by Delhi Gazette, 1857 and was reproduced by The Friend of India, published from Serampur, in its issue of October 7, 1858, under the heading, "The Delhi millennium" with the following comments:-

"The Delhi Gazette publishes a most valuable contribution to the history of the rebellion. It is the first manifesto in the European sense which has been published in India, the first list of grievances, the first step to stir up the people by promises unconnected with religion. It is in the form of a proclamation issued by the King of Delhi on 25th August, 1858, to the people of Hindoostan. The grievances of each class are specified, and a remedy promised if they will but fight boldly for the old regime. It is scarcely conceivable that such a document can be wholly without foundation, that intriguers plotting for a throne should promise reforms they knew were not desired, the removal of grievances they knew were never felt. And yet if these were indeed the changes for which the people sighed, how fatally have Anglo-Indians mistaken their temper and their wants, after attending to the plot which the princes have been framing for years, and the prophesies current among both Hindoos and Mussalmans of the approaching extirpation of the British, the King addresses to *zemindars*:- (as above) ....The declaration that the land tax is oppressive and ought to be lowered was only to be expected. Leaders who appeal to the populace, from Jack Cade to Mr. Cobden, have always promised cheap bread and lowered rents. The promise, too that every zemindar should be absolute on his domain was natural from one who knew what we did not know, that the feudal aristocracy was still strong. But if we have priced ourselves on one popular innovation, it has been on the demolition of privilege. That the *Ryot* and *Zemindar* could stand in the same court was in one belief the one thing which made our rule savoury to the mass. It is quoted here (in the Proclamation) as one of the heaviest oppressions."[35]

According to Rudrangshu Mukherjee the Azamgarh Proclamation seems to suggest that undoing all that the British had done was their stated aim. At least some sections of the Indian population were anxious to expel the British from India and were counting days for that fateful event. This is clear from the paragraph in the proclamation where we are told that all religious works of both Hindus and Muslims, astrologers and miracle-workers are agreed that the English will no longer have any footing in India. As this section of the population consisted of the religious men who were respected and honoured in the countryside, it is obvious that many of the peasants believed in the prediction and were ready to bring about what they thought was god's wish.[36]

He adds that earlier on 18th February 1858 Firoz Shah had issued Bareilly proclamation and Begum Hazrat Mahal had also issued a proclamation exhorting the people to join hands against the British. Every proclamation mentioned Hindus and Muslims and their religions. Though many of the leaders who issued proclamations were Muslims, no divisive issues between Hindus and Muslims were invoked. The rebellion was seen as a war in which both Hindus and Muslims had equally to lose or gain. The emphasis was always on pre-British Hindu-Muslim coexistence within the Mughal imperial framework. Bahadur Shah's proclamation emphasized the standard of Mohammad and the standard of Mahavir.[37]

It is remarkable that the proclamation shows concern about the decline of Indian artisans and handicrafts under the impact of British rule while intellectuals like Ram Mohan Rai forgot to realise this fact. In the Azamgarh proclamation the artisans have been promised that under the *badshahi* government they will "exclusively be employed in the services of the kings, rajahs and the rich".

Though the proclamation deals about the problems of the merchant class, during the insurgency the mercantile classes, urban traders, bankers and moneylenders stood by the British and resultantly the rebels looked upon them as pro-British and these bankers and moneylenders were attacked almost in all places and the leaders of insurgency exacted money from them to cope up with their expenses.

The proclamation makes a terse statement on the grievances of the *zamindars*. There is no doubt that the traditional landholding classes, the *zamindars*, were the hardest hit by the British innovations in the sphere of land and revenue. The rendering of the right to engage for the government revenue (*malguzari*), alienable and salable, led to a vast transfer of land rights: and to the displacement of much of traditional elite, the *zamindar*, by the urban trading and mercantile classes and moneylenders, who were becoming more and more interested in the collection of land-revenue as a profit-making enterprise.[38]

Full text of the Azamgarh Proclamation is as follows[39]:

It is well known to all, that in this age the people of Hindoostan, both Hindoos and Mohammedans, are being ruined under the tyranny and oppression of the infidel and treacherous English. It is therefore the bounden duty of all the wealthy people of India, especially of those who have any sort of connection with any of the Mohammedan royal families, and are considered the pastors and masters of their people, to stake their lives and property for the well being of the public. With the view of effecting this general good, several princes belonging to the royal family of Delhi, have dispersed themselves in the different parts of India, Iran, Turan, and Afghanistan, and have been long since taking measures to compass their favourite end; and it is to accomplish this charitable oject that one of the aforesaid princes has, at the head of an army of Afghanistan, &c., made his appearance in India; and I, who am the grandson of Abul Muzuffer Serajuddin Bahadur Shah Ghazee, King of India, having in the course of circuit come here to extirpate the infidels residing in the eastern part of the country, and to liberate and protect the poor helpless people now groaning under their iron rule, have, by the aid of the Majahdeens, or religious fanatics, erected the standard of Mohammed, and persuaded the orthodox Hindoos who had been subject to my ancestors, and have been and are still accessories in the destruction of the English, to raise the standard of Mahavir.

Several of the Hindoo and Mussalman chiefs, who have long since quitted their homes for the preservation of their religion, and have been trying their best to root out the English in India, have presented themselves to me, and taken part in the reigning Indian crusade, and it is more than probable that I shall very shortly receive succours from the West. Therefore, for the information of the public, the present Ishtahar, consisting of several sections, is put in circulation, and it is the imperative duty of all to take it into their careful consideration, and abide by it. Parties anxious to participate in the common cause, but having no means to provide for themselves, shall receive their daily subsistence from me; and be it known to all, that the ancient works, both of the Hindoos and the Mohammedans, the writings of the miracle-workers, and the calculations of the astrologers, pundits, and ramals, all agree in asserting that the English will no longer have any footing in India or elsewhere. Therefore it is incumbent on all the give up the hope of the continuation of the British sway, side with me, and deserve the consideration of the Badshahi, or imperial Government, by their individual exertion in promoting the common good, and thus attain their respective ends; otherwise if this golden opportunity you are to meet with the ball of fortune; but if you do not avail yourself of the opportunity that offers itself, you will have to bite your finger through grief.

No person, at the misrepresentation of the well-wishers of the British Government, ought to conclude from the present slight inconveniences usually attendant on revolutions, that similar inconveniences and troubles should continue when the Bahshahi Government is established on a firm basis; and parties badly dealt with by any sepoy or plunderer, should come up and represent their grievances to me, and receive redress at my hands; and for whatever property they may lose in the reigning disorder, they will be recompensed from the public treasury when the Badshahi Government is well fixed.

Section I- Regarding Zemindars:- It is evident, that the British Government in making zemindary settlements have imposed exorbitant Jumas, and have disgraced and ruined several zemindars, by putting up their estates to public auction for arrears of rent, in so much as, that on the institution of a suit by a common Ryot, a maid servant or a slave, the respectable zemindars are summoned into court, arrested, put in goal and disgraced. In litigations regarding zemindaries, the immense value of stamps, and other unnecessary expenses of the civil courts, which are pregnant with all sorts of crooked dealings, and the practice of allowing a case to hand on for years, are all calculated to impoverish the litigants. Besides this, the coffers of the zemindars are annually taxed with subscription for schools, hospitals, roads etc. Such extortions will have no manner of existence in the Badshahi Government; but, on the contrary, the Jumas will be light, the dignity and honour of the zemindars safe, and every zemindar will have absolute rule in his own zemindary. The zemindary disputes will be summarily. The zemindary disputes will be summarily decided according to the Shurrah and the Shasters, without any expense; and the zemindars who will assist in the present war with their men and money, shall be excused for ever from paying half the revenue. Zemindars aiding only with money, shall be excepted in perpetuity from paying one-fourth of the revenue; and should any zemindar who has been unjustly deprived of his lands during the English Government, personally join the war, he will be restored to his Zemindary, and excused from paying one-fourth of the revenue.

Section II- Regarding Merchants:- It is plain that the infidel and treacherous British Government have monopolized the trade of all the fine and valuable merchandise, such as indigo, cloth, and other articles of shipping, leaving only the trade of trifles to the people, and even in this they are not without their share of the profits, which they secure by means of customs and stamp fees, &c. in money suits, so that the people have merely a trade in name. Besides this, the profits of the traders are taxed, with postages, tolls, and subscriptions for schools, &c., Notwithstanding all these concessions, the merchants are liable to imprisonment and disgrace at the instance or complaint of a worthless man. When the Badshahi Government is established, all these aforesaid fraudulent practices shall be dispensed with, and the trade of every article, without exception, both by land and water, shall be open to the native merchants of India, who will have the benefit of the Government steam-vessels and steam-carriages for the conveyance of their merchandise gratis; and merchants having no capital of their own shall be assisted from the public treasury. It is therefore the duty of every merchant to take part in the war, and aid the Badshahi Government with his men and money, either secretly or openly, as may be consistent with his position or interest, and forswear his allegiance to the British Government.

Section III- Regarding Public Servants:- It is not a secret thing, tht under the British Government, natives employed in the civil and military services, have little respect, low pay, and no manner of influence; and all the posts of dignity and emolument in both the departments, are exclusively bestowed on Englishmen for natives in the military service, after having devoted the greater part of their lives, attain to the post of soobadar (the very height of their hopes) with a salary of 60r. or 70r. per mensem; and those in the civil service obtain the post of Subder Ala, with a salary of 500 r. a-month, but no influence, jagheer, or present. But under the Badshahi Government like the posts of colonel, general, and commander-in-chief, which the English enjoy at present, the corresponding posts of Pansadi, Punj-Hazari, Haft hazari, and Sippah-salari, will be given to the native in the military service; and, like the post of collector, magistrate, judge, sudder judge, secretary and governor, which the European civil servants now hold, the corresponding posts of Wuzeer, Quazi, Safir, Suba Nizam (Nazim) and Dewan, &c. with salaries of Lacs of Rupees, will be given to the natives of the civil service, together with jagheers, khilluts, inams, and influence. Natives, whether Hindoos or Mohammedans, who fall fighting against the English, are sure to go to heaven; and those killed figting for the English, will, doubtless, go to hell. Therefore, all the natives in the British service ought to be above to their religion and interest, and abjuring their loyalty to the English, side with the Badshahi Government, and obtain salaries of 200 or300 rupees per month for the present, and be entitled to high posts in future. If they, for any reason, cannot at present declare openly against the English, they can heartily wish ill tot their cause, and remain passive spectators of passing events, without taking any active share therein. But at the same time they should indirectly assist the Badshahi Government, and try their best to drive the English out of the country.

All the sepoys and sowars who have, for the sake of their religion, joined in the destruction of the English, and are at present on any consideration, in a state of concealment, either at home or elsewhere, should present themselves to me without the least delay or hesitation.

Foot soldiers will be paid at the rate of three annas, and sowars at eight or twelve annas per diem for the present, and afterwards they will be paid double of what they get in the British service. Soldiers not in the English service, and taking part in the war against the English, will receive their daily subsistence money according to the rates specified below for the present; and in future the foot soldiers will be paid at the rate of eight or ten rupees, and sowars at the rate of twenty or thirty rupees, per month; and on the permanent establishment of the Badshahi Government, will stand entitled to the highest posts in the state, to jagheers and presents:-

matchlockmen ... ... 2 annas a day.

Riflemen ... ... 2 and half annas a day.

swordsmen ... ... 1 and half annas a day.

Horsemen, with large horses ... 8 annas a day.

Horsemen, with small horses ... 6 annas a day.

Section IV- Regarding Artisans:- It is evident that the Europeans, by the introduction of English articles into India, have thrown the weavers, the cotton dressers, the carpenters, the blacksmiths, and the shoemakers, &c., out of employ, and have engrossed their occupations, so that every description of native artisan has been reduced to beggary. But under the Badshahi Government the native artisans will exclusively be employed in the services of the kings, the rajas, and the rich; and this will no doubt ensure their prosperity. Therefore these artisans ought to renounce the English services, and assist the Majahdeens, or religious fanatics, engaged in the war, and thus be entitled both to secular and eternal happiness.

Section V- Regarding Pundits, Fakirs and other learned persons:- The pundits and fakirs being the guardians of the Hindoo and Mohammedan religions respectively, and the Europeans being the enemies of both the religions, and as at present a war is raging against the English on account of religion, the pundits and fakirs are bound to present themselves to me, and take this share in the holy war, otherwise they will stand condemned according to the tenor of the Shurrah and the Shasters; but if they come, they will, when the Badshahi Government is well established, receive rent-free lands.

"Lastly, be it known to all, that whoever, out of the above named classes, shall after the circulation of this Ishtahar, still cling to the British Government, all his estates shall be confiscated, and his property plundered, and he himself, with his whole family, shall be imprisoned, and ultimately put to death.

Gomti to Ganga

A news of 26th August 1858 reported that the insurgents had been burning and plundering villages to the north of the district Kheri. The main body under Khan Ali Khan had moved from Hyderabad (Tahsil Mohammadi, District Kheri) nearer to the Gomti river with the view, apparently, of crossing it. Another body of them was preparing a bridge of boats over the Gomti river at Sirsa Ghat, about 8 miles north-east of Pawayan.[40]

On 2nd November 1858, Colin Campbell, now Lord Clyde of Clydesdale, left Allahabad for Oudh. His plan was to encircle the rebel troops and gradually push them towards the Nepal frontier and there crush them in toto or leave them to die of privation and disease in the fever-infested forests of the Terai. Rana Jang Bahadur, the Prime Minister of Nepal had openly ranged himself on the side of the British. Lord Clyde's plan was simple. One column was to enter Oudh from his old headquarters, Fatehgarh, another from Shahjahanpur, a third from Azamgarh and he himself would advance from Soraon near Allahabad. The campaign had, however, gone according to Lord Clyde's plans. Beni Madho, Devi Baksh, Muhammad Hasan, Mehndi Hasan, Amar Singh, Khan Bahadur Khan, Begum Hazrat Mahal, Mannu Khan, Nana Saheb, Bala Saheb, Jwala Prasad, with other prominent rebel leaders were driven out of their home districts and hemmed in a narrow region on the border of Nepal. It now remained to push them north into the inhospitable land of Nepal.[41]

But Firoz Shah refused to walk into the trap. With two thousand followers Firoz Shah doubled back and crossed the Ganges and appeared near Etawa. Brigadiers Troup and Barker failed to intercept him. Firoz Shah later joined Rao Saheb and Tatya Tope.[42] Narpat Singh of Rohia and Firoz Shah, etc. joined with their troops and guns at Minaoli. On November 9 of 1858 the British army sallied forth to crush the insurgents. After a short combat the insurgents unable to resist the British army dispersed and took to flight. They fled to the jungle and left the *garhi.* A large number of the insurgents were killed although only 7 or 8 were wounded on the Government side.[43]

Queen's Proclamation

Meanwhile, in England, it had been found necessary, as usual to find a scapegoat for the disasters which had fallen upon India. With a singular agreement of opinion the scapegoat was declared to be the Company. Consequently it was decreed to transfer the administration of India from the Company to the Crown. An Act carrying out this transfer was signed by the Queen on the 2nd of August 1858.

On the 1st November Queen's Proclamation was issued to pacify the Indian subjects declaring the principles under which the British Government intended to administer India. To the native princes of India the Queen announced that all treaties in force with them would be accepted and scrupulously maintain; that she would respect their rights, their dignity, and their honour as her own; that she would sanction to encroachments on the rights of any one of them; that the same obligations of duty which bound her to her other subjects would bind her also to them. To her Indian subjects she promised not only complete toleration in matters of religion, but admission to office, without question of religion, to all such persons, as might be qualified for the same by their education, ability, and integrity. The Queen declared, further, that she would direct that, in administering the law, due attention should be paid to the ancient rights, usages, and customs of India; that clemency should be extended to all offenders (in the matter of the Mutiny) save to those who had been or should be convicted of having taken part in the murder of British subjects; that full consideration should be given to men who had thrown off their allegiance, or who had been moved to action by a too credulous acceptance of the false reports circulated by designing men; that to all others who would submit before the 1st of January 1859 unconditional pardon should be granted.[44]

Soon after it, the Begam Hazrat Mahal of Awadh issued a Proclamation in the name of her son Birjis Qadr and urged the people concerned not to place their faith in the offer of pardon. She strongly criticized the promises made in the Queen's Proclamation and condemned every single act of annexation in north and central India. Her reply to Queen's Proclamation was a mirror of the feelings of the Indian people.

Firoz Shah at Khairabad: Biswan[45] set back

A British spy Munnalal Pandey sent information to Captain A. Orr on 18th November 1858 that "on November 17, it was learnt through Ram Din *Jamadar of Harkaras* and Bhogia *Harkara* that Har

Prasad, rebel, *Chakledar* of Khairabad, Lakkar Shah *Badmash* and Firoz Shah, rebel, are all staying at Khairabad with a body of eight or nine thousand men and eight guns and the picket is stationed on the river-bridge, two miles to the south. The rebels are encamped in a garden south of Khairabad at the place where previously there was the camp of Har Prasad, but they intend going to the side of Bari. There is no army of the rebels at Machhrehta. A camel-rider of Har Prasad, rebel, named above, had come with a letter for Agha and other Moghals".[46]

In November 1858, Brigadier Barker advanced northwards from Sandeela, clearing the country right and left, and at the end of the month secured Khyrabad and Biswan; leaving, however, a gap on the Lucknow side, though nearing Brig. Troup on the other flank. To co-operate with him, Brigadier Troup, after capturing Mitauli, also moved northwards in advance of his left; driving the enemy before him to Aligunj[47], near the Ghagra, across which most of them were forced after a sharp action on the 17th. Then he turned to his right, marched along the right bank of the Ghagra, and reaching Biswah on the 2nd December, affected his junction with Barker. At this time Eveleigh, in the middle line, had been directed to operate on the north-west of Lucknow, to fill up the gap between Lucknow and the site of Barker's operations. In doing this he took the fort of Umaria, on the 2nd December. So that now all that western district had been subdued, and all its rebel troops, with one exception, driven across the Ghagra by Barker's forward and Troup's flank movement. That exception was that Prince Firoz Shah, when being hemmed in on the Ghagra near Biswah, dodged and escaped through British troops with some 1500 men.[48]

Raja Loni Singh of Mitauli was captured and charged of leading the rebellion and to have maltreated Captain Orr and other European gentlemen and ladies and betrayed them to the Rebel Government.

Firoz Shah Crosses the Ganges

After the defeat at Biswa on the 1st December 1858, Firoz Shah fled with his followers to Mahmudabad, with the intention of crossing the Ghagra and joining the Begum. But he received an intimation from the Begum's Camp, that he would not be permitted to cross, because her funds were at too low an ebb, to allow her to swell her force. Now Firoz Shah found himself in a dilemma, as Brigadier Barker's force was coming from behind, and a column was advancing from Lucknow in front. Finding his escape by the Ghagra suddenly cut off, Firoz Shah formed hastily the bold determination to make direct for the Ganges and across to Central India. Leaving Biswa on the morning of the 4th with 900 followers, mounted and equipped, he dashed across the Gomti river and the Mullaon District [?], till he reached the Ganges on the morning of the 5th at Nanamow *ghat*. The passage of the river at this point he found impracticable, but proceeding a few miles higher up, he, by the aid of elephants procured boats from the opposite bank, and crossed with his party from Akum *ghat* near the old city of Kanauj by the morning of the 6th.[49]

Crossing the Ganges river was a great feet for Firoz Shah and his army. Inability of Begum Hazrat Mahal to give him shelter and support him, while the British force was quite close to him, Firoz Shah had no other way out than crossing the Ganges. Had he not done that, he would have been caught by the British. With this the scene of struggle shifted from Awadh to Bundelkhand and Rajputana, where Tatya Tope and Firoz Shah with Rao Saheb became a formidable force against the British.

In his flight he was supported by Mohsin Ali Khan of Mau Shamsabad, one or two leading Risaldars of Irregular Cavalry and the two Maulvies, Gulab Shah and Lakkar Shah together with about 1500 Cavalry; 500 Foot, 4 or 5 guns of various sizes, several elephants and a number of followers, many women and much baggage. On quitting the field of battle they passed north of Sandila and evaded the detachment there and had reached the Ganges.[50]

Firoz Shah intended to join Tatya Tope by entering Bundelkhand with his force consisting of 900 horsemen of whom 400 were well mounted and armed, the rest were badly equipped; 300 foot, camp followers etc. including 100 women; 6 elephants, 1 small gun called a *Goorda*. The leaders of this body were – Firoz Shah, Lukkur Shah, Gulab Shah *alias* Peerjee, Mohsin Aly Khan of Mow Shumshabad (Furrukhabad) who posed himself as an European, Fazlul Huq Moulvi, formerly *Sherishtehdar* in the Delhi Commissioner's Office, Hari Singh of the 12th Irregular Cavalry, Jareeb or Yakub Khan of 12th Irregular Cavalry, Summund Khan of Jhujjur. Saligram 11th Cavalry, Diler Singh of Pareechitgurh were last seen at sunrise on the 6th instant at Akum Ghat, by the *Kotwal* of Sundeela. The insurgents were making for Kalpi *en route* to Ranthambore 20 *Koss* distant from Kotah in the Jaipur territory. They hoped to join Tatya Tope who, they believed, ruled at Agra.[51]

Firoz Shah, Walidad Khan and others with some thousand men were at Arroul on the 6th and they were going via Etawah. All communication was cut off with Kanpur. Road below Miran Ki Sarai[52] was in the hands of the insurgents. They had only one gun having lost one in the Ganges. Force was partly Cavalry with four elephants and numerous women. Government Troops were sent from Fatehgarh to prevent the rebels coming up the Grand Trunk Road. Five Companies Police Infantry were going from here to Etawah.[53]

The news of Firoz Shah crossing the Ganges was flashed telegraphically from different locations. A telegram from Allahabad announced that Firoz Shah broke through all British posts and crossed the Ganges at Bithoor.[54] He had 1500 *Sawars* and intends to traverse Bundelkhand and join Tatya Tope. He was last heard of at Huttiah, whither he had been pursued by the Magistrate of Kanpur with some troops.[55] Another telegraphic message from Miran Ka Sarai informed that Firoz Shah with large force crossed Sundeela road on 3rd instant having been defeated by English force. There seems to be no doubt of Firoz Shah's having been with the force which crossed the Ganges on the 5th and 6th instant. There was a rumour that Tatya Tope is either this side of the river Jamuna or at all events on the right bank to render assistance to Firoz Shah.[56]

Battle of Harchandpur

Though Firoz Shah with his force had crossed the Ganges to cross the Jamuna river for Bundelkhand, he had to change his plan as the British contingents were heading for a decisive fight with the insurgents. While Firoz Shah was on the verge of crossing the Ganges, Nana Saheb Peshwa crossed at some *ghat* near Meeran ki sarai at about 4 P.M. of the 5th December with a considerable force. A. Hume, Magistrate of Etawah marched from Etawah with Lt. Forbes to Phaphund with every available man. He chose Phaphund[57] because it commanded all the favourite routes of the insurgent forces in crossing the Doab from Awadh into Bundelkhand, via Oraiya and Shergarh ghat, Dalelnagar and Bijalpur *ghat* and lastly Ajitmal and Joheka *ghat* on the *Jamuna* river. Hume and Forbes arrived at Phaphund before daylight of the 7th December and sent their *sawars* at once to Sehar, Rasulabad and Mangalpur,[58] who returning in the course of the day reported that no insurgents were seen, though strong rumours of their having crossed the Ganges were everywhere afloat. About 5 P.M. letters reached from Beylah and Sehar that both places were attacked by the insurgents and that the former had been taken and plundered. The insurgents numbered at least 3000 and many reports said them to be 5 to 7 thousand.

At day break on 8th December, Hume marched from Phaphund for Harchandpur[59] with 200 infantry, 4 guns and 46 artillery, infantry under Maconochie and 207 cavalry under Doyle, the total 453 men under command of Lt. Forbes. The British force reached Kundhon bridge over the canal 14 miles from Phaphund. Soon after crossing the bridge insurgent horsemen were seen. They had 1600 well mounted and armed *sawars*, 400 badly mounted men on tattoos, armed for the most part with rifles, muskets and carbines, about 125 Regular Infantry, 200 women and children, some 4 or 5 thousand unarmed or badly armed camp followers servants etc., two small guns, 8 elephants, a few camels and a host of tattoos, baggage cattle etc. The leaders were Firoz Shah, Lakkar Shah, Gulab Shah, Masum Ali Khan, Fazlul Haq, Diler Singh of Parichatgarh, Jussa Singh, Murad Ali Khan alias the Nazim and Alidad Khan. The main leader was Firoz Shah but the General in the field of the whole force was Alidad Khan, a Mewati Pahalwan. The main body of the insurgents consisted of Cavalry. In the British side, Doyle was with the Etawah Cavalry. There was a village between the centres of both the parties. The insurgents were hugely outflanking the British force and Lieutemant Forbes gave the word to advance and went off to the right with Doyle and the Etawah Cavalry. Doyle was cut to pieces in an encounter. After a fierce battle which lasted for about three and half hours, the insurgents disappeared. The British lost heavily. Besides Doyle, 21 killed and 19 wounded, while the insurgents lost their two leaders Murad Ali Khan alias the Nazim and a Mahomedan Risaldar along with 55 to 58 killed.[60]

After Harchandpur, the insurgents retired towards Phaphund and were on their way to Shergarh *ghat*.[61] Obviously they intended to cross the Jamuna river. On the 9th December Hume with a column sent by Brigadier Percy Herbert proceeded to Phaphund only to find that the insurgents had left that place on getting news of Herbert's column. Meanwhile, the Kanpur column had reached Oraiya and shut the insurgents out from the Shergarh *ghat*.[62]

Hither they were closely pursued by Brigadier Percy Herbert from Kanpur with detachments of Cavalry and regiments, but the main body of the insurgents had crossed at Jaleeka near the Bureh fort into the Doab, between the Jamuna and Chambal. A few men only were left and these were cut up to the number of 40 to 50 by a detachment under Lt. Angelo who also captured a small gun. Many of the insurgents, their horses and baggage were also lost in the quicksand of the river Jamuna at that spot. This spot prevented the British detachment to cross the river in pursuit. The insurgents subsequently moved across the Chambal at Chakranagar[63] and down the Pahooj river pursued by Br. Macduff, and on the 11th December were at Lohar in the Jalaun District. Br. Gen. Napier had however started with a force from Gwalior to intercept them and on that day was moving parallel to them at a short distance. From Agra, too, a force was sent to Etawah but it reached only after the insurgents had passed.[64]

The insurgents under Firoz Shah continued their march by the left bank of the Jhooi river. They passed through Sohar on 11th December 1858 making for Sikandra.[65] Another news was that the insurgents with Firoz Shah had started for Koonch.[66] They were watched by Captain Mc Mohan with his party. General Napier was to leave Gwalior for Datia the day before, to intercept them.[67] Now Firoz Shah was to proceed towards Bundelkhand.

At the beginning of the year 1859, Sir Colin Campbell was able to report to the Governor General, that there was "no longer even a vestige of rebellion in Oude." Begum of Awadh, Khan Bahadur Khan, Nana Saheb Peshwa, Bala Saheb, Jwala Prasad and Rana Beni Madho of Shankarpur with other prominent insurgent leaders were driven out of their home districts and hemmed in a narrow region on the border of Nepal. It now remained to push them north into the inhospitable land of Jang Bahadur.

Among the chief leaders who surrendered themselves to the British was Lal Madho Singh of Amethi. Many more either surrendered before the British or perished fighting.[68] Firoz Shah and Tatya Tope were not with Begum Hazrat Mahal. While Hazrat Mahal group was surrounded by the British force and was cornered between Indian Nepal border, Shahzada Firoz Shah had a vast area to roam in Bundelkhand and Rajputana.

With two thousand followers Firoz Shah doubled back and crossed the Ganges and appeared near Etawa. Brigadiers Troup and Barker failed to intercept him. Firoz Shah later joined Rao Saheb and Tatya Tope. He shared their adventures but not their fate.[69]

On the morning of the 7th January 1859, the Nawab of Farukkabad crossed the Rapti river with his followers and surrendered to Major Barrow. Another insurgent chief Mehndi

Husain also surrendered the same day. While Mehndi Hasan was granted a pension, the Nawab of Farrukhabad was tried and condemned to death, for he was held responsible for the murder of some Europeans, but his life was spared according to Major Barrow's promise at the time of surrender. He was packed off to Arabia and there left to shift for himself.[70]

Reference :

1. Eighty kilometers south-west of Lucknow.
2. Foreign Department Secret Consultations, 30 July 1858, Cons. No. 70. Forsyth to Edmonstone, 12 June 1858:
3. Thirty two kms. west of Gwalior
4. Parag Tope, Tatya Tope's Operation Red Lotus, 2010, p. 238.
5. Tahsil Hasanganj, Distt. Unnao, U.P.
6. Fifty kilometers north-west of Unnao, U.P.
7. Letter written on Wednesday, June 9, 1858 addressed to the Office of Captain Adolphus Orr, Intelligence Department, Akhbar No. 55, submitted from Mallawan. Lucknow Chief Court Mutiny Basta. F.S.U.P., Vol. II, pp. 399-401.

   Fatehpur Chaurasi lies 10 kilometers south of the road from Unnao to Bangarmau on the north bank of the river Kalyani.
8. Letter written on Wednesday, June 9, 1858 addressed to the Office of Captain Adolphus Orr, Intelligence Department, Akhbar No. 55, submitted from Mallawan. Lucknow Chief Court Mutiny *Basta*. F.S.U.P., Vol. II, p. 402
9. Twenty kilometers north of Unnao, UP.
10. Twenty kilometers north-east of Unnao.
11. Forty eight kilometers north-east of Shahjahanpur, UP.
12. Ruia, Tah. Bilgram, Distt. Hardoi. It lies at a distance of 60 kilometers south-west of Hardoi.
13. Eight kilometers from Sitapur, UP.
14. The Bengal Hurkaru and India Gazette, August 3, 1858, p. 116. National Library, Calcutta. F.S.U.P., V, p. 553-554.
15. The Bengal Harkaru and India Gazette, July 23, 1858, p. 80; (Reproduced from Delhi Gazette July 14). National Libary, Calcutta. F.S.U.P., Vol. V, p. 553
16. The Bengal Hurkaru and India Gazette, August 3, 1858, p. 116. National Library, Calcutta. F.S.U.P., V, p. 554.
17. Letter No. 753 of 1858 from T.D. Forsyth, Secretary to the Chief Commissioner, Oudh (Awadh), to G.F. Edmonstone, Secretary to the Government of India with the Governor General, dated Lucknow, 24th July 1858.Quoted in F.S.U.P., Vol. II, p. 456.
18. Letter from Firoz Shah addressed to Mir Mansab Ali, *Chaudhri* and *Chakledar* of Rasulabad, dated 16th July 1858. Unnao District Court Mutiny *Basta*. F.S.U.P., Vol. II, p. 468

19. Letter from Firoz Shah addressed to Mir Mansab Ali, Chaudhri and Chakledar, dated 6th Zilhijja 1274 A.H. (18th July 1858). Unnao District Court Mutiny *Basta.* F.S.U.P. Vol. II, p. 473
20. Firoz Shah's Letter to Mir Mansab Ali, Chaudhary and Chakledar, dated 10th Zilhijja 1274 A.H. (22nd of July 1858). Unnao District Court Mutiny *Basta.* F.S.U.P., II, p. 473.
21. Probably in Kalyanmal Pargana and Tahsil Sandila Distt. Hardoi.
22. Firoz Shah's letter addressed to Mir Mansab Ali, Chaudhri and Chakledar of Rasulabad, dated 12th Zilhijja 1274 A.H. (24th July 1858). Unnao District Court Mutiny *Basta.* F.S.U.P. Vol. II, pp. 473-474.
23. Firoz Shah's Letter addressed to Mir Mansab Ali, Chaudhri and Chakledar of Rasulabad, dated 14th Zilhijja 1274 A.H. (26th July 1858). Unnao District Court Mutiny *Basta,* F.S.U.P., Vol. II, p. 474.
24. Firoz Shah's letter to Mir Mansab Ali, Chaudhri, dated 26th Zilhijja 1274 A.H. (7th August 1858). Unnao District Court Mutiny *Basta,* F.S.U.P., Vol. II, p. 474.
25. Letter no. 786 from T.D. Forsyth, Secretary to Chief Commissioner, Oudh, to G.F. Edmonstone, Secretary to Governnent of India with Governor General, Allahabad, dt. Lucknow, 31st July 1858. F.S.U.P., II, p. 484-485.
26. Letter no. 1088 of 1858 from T.D. Forsyth, Secretary to the Chief Commissioner Oudh), to G.F. Edmonstone, Secretary to the Government of India with Governor General dated Lucknow, 18th September 1858. Foreign Political Consultations, 8th Oct. 1858 no. 196. F.S.U.P., Vol. II, p. 503.
27. News letter from Baldeo Bax, Mohalla Rangmahal, Shahjahanpur, dt. Oct. 17, 1858, Lucknow Chief Court Mutiny Basta. F.S.U.P., Vol II, p. 518.
28. T.H. Kavanagh: *How I won the Victoria Cross* (London 1860), pp. 172-176.
29. About fifty kilometers north-west of Lucknow. It is an important Tahsil of Hardoi District of UP.
30. In District Sitapur, U.P.
31. Telegraphic Message from G.F. Edmonstone, Allahabad, dated 15th Aug. 1858, to E.A. Reade, Agra. Original Telegrams sent to Mr. E.A. Reade, 1858; Secretariat Records Room, Lucknow. F.S.U.P., Vol. II, pp. 487-488.
32. The Hindu Patriot, August 19, 1858, p. 259. National Library, Calcutta. F.S.U.P., Vol. V, p. 560-61.
33. The Hindu Patriot, August 19, 1858, p. 259. National Library, Calcutta. F.S.U.P., Vol. V, p. 561.
34. Azamgarh is a town near the Gogra with Balia to the east, Jaunpur and Ghazipur to the south, and Faizabad and Gorakhpur in the north
35. F.S.U.P., Vol. I, p. 455.
36. R. Mukherjee, 'The Azamgarh Proclamation and some questions on the revolt of 1857 in the North Western Provinces', in *Essays in Honour of S.C. Sarkar* ,New Delhi, 1976. p. 479.
37. R. Mukherjee, *Awadh in Revolt*, 2008, p. 153
38. R. Mukherjee, in *Essays in Honour of S.C. Sarkar* ,New Delhi, 1976, pp. 482-483

39. Ball, Vol. II, pp. 630-632, quoted in F.S.U.P., Vol. I, pp. 453-458. This proclamation or manifesto was published in the Delhi Gazette on 29 September 1857.
40. *The Bengal Hurkaru and India Gazette*, dt. August 26th, 1858. F.S.U.P., Vol. V, p. 555.
41. Sen, pp. 362-63. In the light of this, William Forbes-Mitchell's statement that Khan Bahadur Khan was captured by the Bareilly police-levy early in July, 1858 and was hanged in front of the Kotwali in Bareilly a few days after his capture is misleading. See William Forbes-Mitchell, Reminiscences of the Great mutiny 1857-59, Reprint 2005, p. 263.
42. Sen, op. cit., pp. 362-63
43. News letter from Chhedilal, resident of Shahabad, staying then at the house of Dulhe Rai, Mukhtar of the Rani of Jatpura Mohalla Unchapura, Shahjahanpur, to Captain Adolphus Orr, Supdt. Intelligence Department, dated, November 12, 1858. Lucknow Chief Court Mutiny Basta. F.S.U. P., Vol. II, p. 543.
44. Ibid, p. 403-404
45. 32 kilometers east of Sitapur, UP.
46. News-letter from Munna Lal Pandey to Captain Adolphus Orr, Superintendent Intelligence Department, dated 18th November 1858, 9 o'clock in the night, dispatched from Sandila. F.S.U.P., II, p. 557.
47. Tahsil Aonla, District Bareilly, UP. It stands on the road from Bareilly to Aonla.
48. Letter no. 145 from Lord Clyde, the Commander in Chief in India to Rajah Lall Madho of Amethi, dt. Army Headquarters, Camp Partabgarh, the 3rd November, 1858. Innes: "*The Sepoy Revolt*" (London 1897), pp. 260-71), F.S.U.P., Vol. II, p. 536.
49. Foreign Political Consultations, 30th September 1859, Nos. 204/6. & K.W.; Letter No. 1633 from T.D. Forsyth, Secretary to the Chief Commissioner, Oudh (Awadh), to G.F. Edmonstone, Secretary to the Government of India with the Governor General, Allahabad, dated Lucknow, 11th December 1858. F.S.U.P..Vol. II, pp. 564-565.
50. Foreign Deparment, North-Western Provinces, Nrrative (Abstract Proceedings) 1858. Narrative of Events for Etawah for the week ending 11th December 1858. Secretariat Records Room, Lucknow. F.S.U.P., Vol. V, pp. 807-809
51. News-letter sent for information of the Magistrate and Collector of Hamirpur by the Secretary to the Chief Commissioner, Oudh (Awadh), dated Lucknow, 8th December 1858. F.S.U.P., Vol. II, p.563.
52. In district Kannauj, UP. Fifty two kilometers south-east of Fatehgarh.
53. Telegraphic Message from Goodall, Mainpuri, to E.A. Reade, Agra, dated 7th December 1858. Original Telegrams sent to Mr. E.A. Reade, 1858. Secretariat Records Room, Lucknow. F.S.U.P.,Vol. V, pp. 806-807.
54. North west of Kanpur on the right bank of river Ganga.
55. "The Friend of India", Dec. 6, 1858, p. 18— "Weekly Epitome of News Dec. 9", National Library Calcutta. F.S.U.P. Vol. III, p. 664

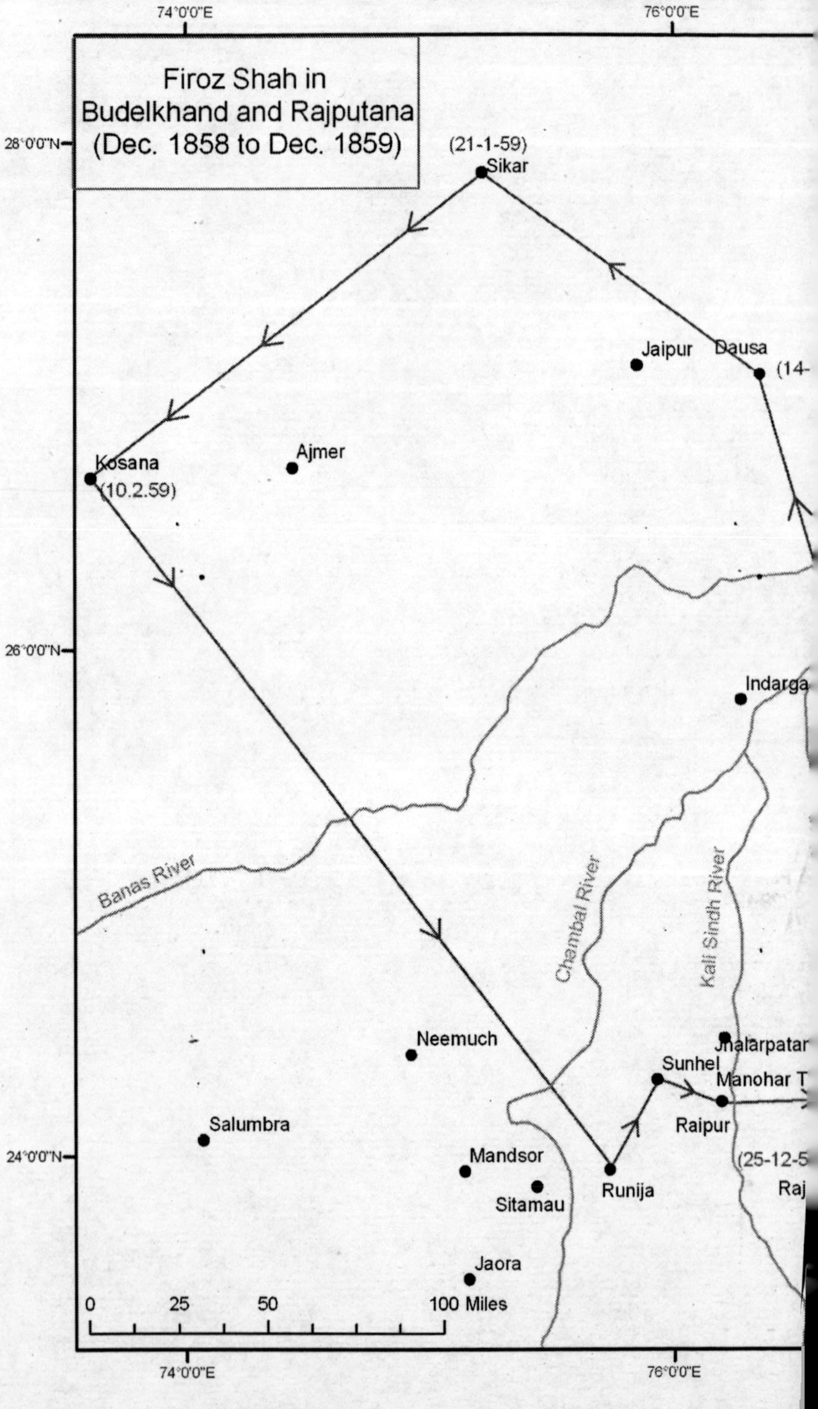
74°0'0"E
76°0'0"E
Firoz Shah in
Budelkhand and Rajputana
(Dec. 1858 to Dec. 1859)
28°0'0"N
26°0'0"N
24°0'0"N
(21-1-59)
Sikar
Jaipur
Dausa
(14-
Kosana
(10.2.59)
Ajmer
Indarga
Banas River
Chambal River
Kali Sindh River
Neemuch
Jhalarpatar
Sunhel
Manohar T
Raipur
(25-12-5
Salumbra
Mandsor
Sitamau
Runija
Raj
Jaora
0
25
50
100 Miles

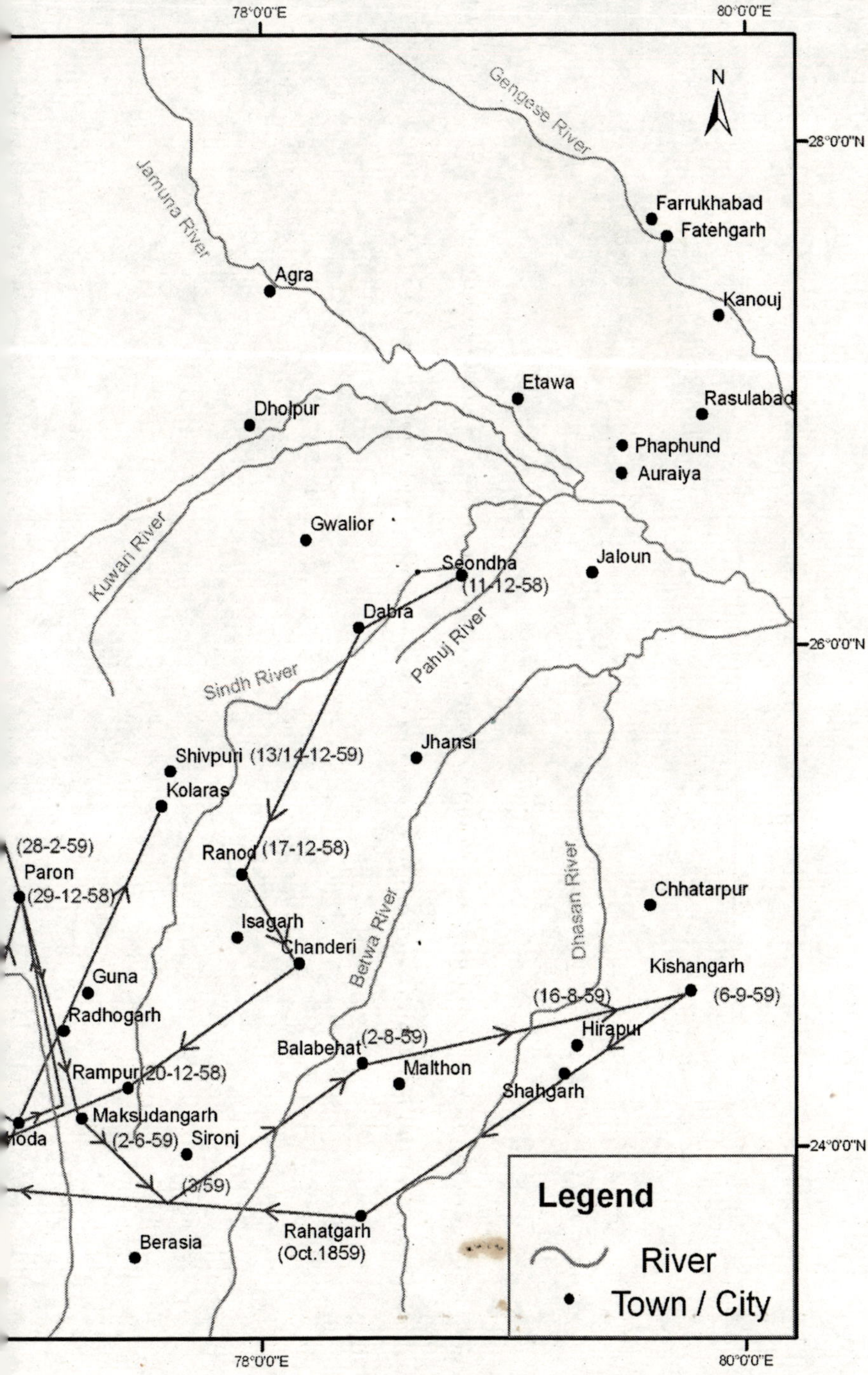

78°0'0"E
80°0'0"E
28°0'0"N
26°0'0"N
24°0'0"N
N
Gengese River
Jamuna River
Farrukhabad
Fatehgarh
Agra
Kanouj
Etawa
Rasulabad
Dholpur
Phaphund
Auraiya
Kuwari River
Gwalior
Seondha
(11-12-58)
Jaloun
Dabra
Pahuj River
Sindh River
Jhansi
Shivpuri (13/14-12-59)
Kolaras
(28-2-59)
Ranod (17-12-58)
Paron
(29-12-58)
Dhasan River
Chhatarpur
Isagarh
Chanderi
Betwa River
Kishangarh
Guna
(16-8-59)
(6-9-59)
Radhogarh
Hirapur
Balabehat (2-8-59)
Malthon
Rampur (20-12-58)
Shahgarh
Maksudangarh
(2-6-59)
Sironj
(3/59)
Rahatgarh
(Oct.1859)
Berasia
Legend
River
Town / City

56. Telegraphic Message from C.R. Lindsay, dated Miran Ki Serai, the 8th December 1858 to E.A. Reade, 1858. Secretariat Record Room, Lucknow. F.S.U.P., III, p. 664.
57. Twenty kilometers north-west of Auraiya, in Auraiya district, UP.
58. Twenty kilometers east of Auraiya.
59. Fifteen kilometer north of Raibareli, UP.
60. Letter No. 107 from A. Hume, Magisrate, Etawah, to the Secretary to Government, N.W.P., dated Camp Sahson, December 12, 1858, Etawah Collectorate Mutiny *Basta*, File no. 11-XVI-8. F.S.U.P., V, pp. 817-824 For another brief description of the battle see Foreign Department, North-Western Provinces, Narrative (Abstract Proceedings) 1858. Narrative of Events for Etawah for the week ending 11th December 1858. Secretariat Records Room, Lucknow.
61. Telegraphic message from E.A. Reade, Agra, dated 11th December 1858, Copies of Telegrams sent by Mr. E.A. Reade from 11th May 1858 to 12th January 1859. Secretariat Records Room, Lucknow. F.S.U.P., V, p. 829
62. Letter No. 107 from A. Hume, Magistrate, Etawah, to the Secretary to Government, N.W.P., dated Camp Sahson, December 12, 1858. F.S.U.P., V, pp. 825-826
63. Twenty three kilometer from the district headquarter Etawa on the right bank of river Jamuna.
64. Foreign Department, North-Western Provinces, Narrative (Abstract Proceedings) 1858. Narrative of Events for Etawah for the week ending 11th December 1858. Secretariat Records Room, Lucknow.
65. Service Message from G.F. Edmonstone, dated Allahabad, 16th December. Original Telegramis sent to E.A. Reade, 1858. Secretariat Records Room, Lucknow. F.S.U.P. Vol. III, p. 665.
Sikandara is about 35 kilometer south-east of Auraiya in UP.
66. Konch is 25 kilometer south-west of Jalaun in UP.
67. Ibid, p. no. 46. Quoted in Purwar, H.M. and Singh, D.K. (ed): *Kuchh Telegram, Kuchh Dastavez: Janpad Jalaun*, 2007, p. 35.
68. F.S.U.P. Vol. II, pp. 625-28
69. S.N. Sen, op. cit., p. 363
70. Ibid, pp. 364-365

Chapter - 7
Traversing Bundelkhand And Rajputana

Firoz Shah enters Bundelkhand

By the beginning of December 1858, the force of Firoz Shah had dwindled down to some 700 cavalry, without guns, and nearly without resources. After leaving Doab the insurgents under Firoz Shah moved on 10th December 1858 to Taongari on the Sind river proceeding towards Bundelkhand. On hearing this, Capt. Mac Mohan's detachment was near Aron[1]– 12 miles from Taongari and Gen. Robert Napier left Gwalior to intercept Firoz Shah and his party and halted at Antri. The insurgents, keeping on the left bank of Parvati, were making for Seondha[2] in the Sind river in Datia district.[3]

On 10th December 1858 Brigadier Herbert was at Oraiya. He proposed crossing Jamuna and Chambal after the insurgents who consisted of about fourteen hundred men chiefly Cavalry. Some were with carbines but no guns. The report at Mainpuri was that the insurgents had with them forty elephants, but it was seemed doubtful.[4]

On the 11th December, the insurgents crossed the Sind river close to Seondha. They halted at Naraila for 12 hours and then started again. On the 12th they crossed the Sindh river at village Sabey (Datia area) and halted at Burgoor, close to Pichhor.[5] The next day on the 13th, they burnt the staying bungalow at Dabra[6] and put up in a village called Baglan which was plundered next day. They stayed in the jungles near Magroti. This whole party consistsed of about 4000 *sawars*. They gave out that they were going to Tatya Tope. They had two *Jinjals* which they carried on elephants and had no guns, no footmen or ammunition. It was reported that Firoz Shah was with them. On the 15th, this party plundered the villages of Amah in the vicinity of Akuola.[7]

Battle of Ranod

Continuing his pursuit through Narwar, Napier pressed forward and reached Ranod on the morning of the 17th December. The same morning Firoz Shah, who had marched on a line almost parallel to him, left the jungle to attack Ranod.[8] He knew not that Napier had arrived there and Napier did not know where Firoz was, until he saw a mass of men extended in a front of nearly a mile advancing. There was man to man fighting. Four hundred and fifty of the insurgents were killed at Ranod and the pursuit continued for nearly eight miles.[9] Among the killed were several persons of distinction, including Maulvi Fazlul Haq and Risaldar Zahur Ali of the 12th. Six elephants and numbers of horses and arms were lost to the British. The insurgents were completely scattered.[10]

Firoz Shah fled towards Chanderi, but forces under Brigadier Ainslie from Jhansi and Colonel Liddell from Lalitpur, moving respectively in the direction of Ranod and Chanderi, obliged him to turn, and he made for the jungles of Aroni, passing south of Isagarh.[11] Near Rampur, between Guna and Sironj, the insurgents accidentally came upon Lieutenant Stack's detachment of 40 men of the 1st Bombay Lancers on the 20th December.[12] Three Lancers were killed and a portion of his camels and carriage taken.[13] Lt. Stack and the horses managed to escape.

British Apprehension

The movement and speed of Firoz Shah was such that the British feared that he may cross Narmada river any time to go to the south.

They had witnessed the crossing of Narmada river by Tatya Tope on 31st October 1858 despite all their precautions. After that Tatya Tope, traversing long distances through Nimar, Gujarat and Malwa had now reached the Bhil country of Banswara in Rajputana. When Firoz Shah was taken on by Lieutenant Stack's detachment near Sironj, Tatya Tope was heading towards Pratapgarh.

George Plowden, Commissioner of Nagpur wrote to the Government of India that on the 21st of December, when the Field Columns had been recalled a second time, it again became necessary, consequent upon the probability of a force under Firoz Shah crossing the Narmada to the East of Hoshangabad, to direct the Kamptee Column under Lt. Col. Blogg to diverge to Pandurna in the Chhindwara district, and the Sitabuldi column, under Captain Shakespear, to retrace its steps to Chhindwara. It was not until the end of January that the two Columns finally returned to their respective cantonments.[14]

Captain Rice takes on

On the 22nd of December, a party of Firoz Shah had an encounter with a detachment of the 25th Bombay Native Infantry from Guna, under the command of Captain Rice. On arriving at Aroni, Rice heard that some two thousand insurgents, mainly cavalry, were encamped in a dense jungle near a village about eleven miles away. Leaving forty-two men to guard his camp, he started with the column. Slowly they pushed forward the guns through the trees which grew more dense as they advanced. After pushing through rocky wooded glens for four hours, they caught a glimpse of the insurgent camp in a deep ravine. Rice swiftly made his way down the ravine and charged through the camp. The insurgents fled into the jungle, leaving behind them a hundred horse, several camels and a large amount of arms.

Firoz Shah having been driven across the Parbati river by Brigadier General Sir Robert Napier, was at Puprail near Mohna Thanah on the 25th December.[15] General Napier returned to Guna on 29th December from near Shivpuri. Firoz Shah and his followers had by now joined Man Singh near Parone[16] via Shivpuri.[17] There after Firoz Shah fled to Rajgarh and then made his way north to Indargarh, where he met Tatya Tope and Rao Saheb (nephew of Nana Saheb).[18]

Tatya Tope and Rao Saheb

Let us now see the activities of Tatya Tope before Indergarh. After his defeat at Jora Alipur on 21st June 1858, Tatya Tope had adopted guerilla tactics. He was accompanied by Rao Saheb who took a prominent part in the uprising and was with Tatya Tope in all his exploits and wanderings. When Nana Saheb Peshwa's whereabouts were not known, after Lucknow set back, Rao Saheb was considered his representative and commanded respect from his associates. In his deposition, after his capture, he gave details of his activities.[19]

When Tatya Tope was in Bundelkhand in October 1858, being surrounded on all sides by the British columns, he went towards Narmada river and had crossed it on 31st October, advanced towards west and made a dash towards Baroda. Tatya tope was defeated by Brg. Parks near Chota Udaipur on 1st December 1858. There after Tatya Tope and Rao Saheb took shelter in the forests of Banswara. On 25th December, as he neared Partabgarh[20], he encountered a column under Maj. Rocke.[21] On 31st December 1858 Colonel Somerset defeated the army of Tatya Tope near Chapra Bursaud (Chhipa Barod). After his defeat Tatya fled to Nahargarh[22] in Kota territory, where he halted and was joined by Mansingh. Leaving Mansingh on the banks of the Chambal, he again went north and affected a junction with Firoz Shah at Indargarh[23], on the west bank of that river.[24]

Firoz Shah with Tatya Tope and Rao Saheb

Reinforcement offered by Firoz Shah did not alter Tatya's position much. Throughout his pursuit, his followers had kept on deserting him in such a large number that by now his army, combined with the troops hardly numbered 2000. The British had tightened its net on Indargarh and there was no way to escape. They were almost checkmated by Napier on the north and north-east, Brig. Showers was on the north-west, Brig. Somerset was at Barod[25] on the east and Brig. Smith was on the south-east, Maj-Gen. Michel was on the south while Brig. Honner, commanding the Nasirabad Brigade, was on the south-v .st and west.[26]

On 4th January Man Singh was at Parone, while Tatya and Rao Shaeb had marched to Didwana[27] en-route for Kharuara. Tatya and Rao Saheb, with a force said to be large, but chiefly cavalry, had marched on 3rd January towards Madhopur beyond Tonk. Man Singh was at Parone and Firoz Shah on the road to Madhopur. Brg. Smith marched on the 5th January to Nahargarh and General Napier to Shahabad. In the meantime, Mansingh of Narwar was planning to submit to the British and on 7th January, he wrote to Sir R. Hamilton expressing his readiness to come in.[28] This was an important step which went against the interests of the insurgents, ultimately leading to the capture of Tatya Tope in future.

Set back at Dausa

Brig. Showers reached Hindoun on the 8th January 1859. He was in communication with Captain Eden of Jaipur, Captain Mevin of Bharatpur and Dr. Mathias of Karauli. General Napier was at Sheopur, Brig. Smith at Kylowara, Brig. Honner of Rajputana Field Force was said to be advancing on Tonk. As regards the insurgents, the news about them was conflicting. There appeared to be three separate parties of them: 1. Rahim Ali 2. Firoz Shah and 3. Tantya Tope with the Rao Sahib. All these three parties were advancing towards Tonk and Jaipur.[29]

The united forces of Firoz Shah and Tatya Tope were at Dausa between Jaipur and Bharatpur, about thirty miles from Jaipur. On the 13th January, the insurgents left Dausa, but there was no positive information of the direction they had taken. On the same date i.e. on the 13th itself, Brig. Showers' force moved from Chaksu[30] to Tangah and Detachment of the Nasirabad force almost without cavalry under Colonel Holmes was moving from the same place towards Lalsout.[31] Brigadier Showers, Smiths and Parkes' forces were some 30 miles in the rear. The insurgents appeared moving either towards Alwar or Bharatpur, to the north and north-west unencumbered with guns or baggage. The A.G.G. Rajputana Br. Gen. G.P. Lawrence suggested to his higher ups that a light force of cavalry and Horse Artillery be sent from Delhi towards Alwar, to intercept the insurgents, in case, if after being driven back from Rajputana, they should make for Shekhawati,[32] where the British were totally unprovided with troops. The British, therefore, did not want the insurgents to go that side.[33]

Showers threw forward a strong advanced guard to Ripliwara, 18 miles distant, to intercept stragglers and followed with the main body during the night. The insurgents had passed the village only a few hours before, and Brigadier Showers took up the pursuit, and, following close on their heels, came up with them at Dausa at 3 A.M. on the 14th January 1859. Dausa was situated on the western slope of a rocky hill, bounded to the west by fields with high banks, among which the insurgents took up their position. The approach to it was difficult, as there were only two roads leading out of the town in this direction. having no guide on whom he could rely, Brigadier Showers proceeded with his column for some distance down one of those roads, in hope of finding an opening to lead him to the insurgent camp. Failing in this, and day beginning to break, he determined to begin the attack, with the cavalry, leaving the artillery to follow, with the infantry as escort. He pushed up on the high ground, the Agra Mounted Police on the left, the squadron of Alexander's Horse on the right, and then, advancing at a charging pace across the intervening fields, came upon the insurgents preparing to march. The insurgents were taken by surprise. Being unable to escape from the enclosures, many were killed. The attack was made on the centre of the position of the insurgents and separated their force into three parties; one went off to the right, another to the left, while a considerable body was driven to the front and vigorously followed up by Alexander's Horse and Agra Mounted Police under Lt. H. Chapman and H.T. Oldfield. The guns were brought up to within 1200 yards of the insurgents who had fled with Firoz Shah to the right, although at that long range not much damage could be inflicted. The party under Tatya Tope disappeared to the left early in the action.[34] Three hundred insurgents were killed in the encounter. But a greater surprise and a greater disaster awaited them.

Sikar Disaster

Colonel Holmes marching with a field detachment from Nasirabad for the protection of Tonk and Jaipur, heard at Tonk that the insurgents were marching towards Jaipur, and he went after them. He surprised the insurgents on the 21st January 1859 before dawn at Sikar, about sixty four miles north-west of Jaipur. 'The confusion heard in their camp was very great, their horsemen galloped off in every direction without attempting to make a stand, and numbers without even saddling their horses.' The insurgents were routed and were chased for some hours but missed the roads which the Tatya Tope, Rao Saheb and Firoz Shah took. The defeat of the insurgents by Holmes had a most important political result. After their flight Firoz Shah, with the 12th Irregulars, left Tatya. The next day Tatya and the Rao Sahib were joined by three *thakurs* related to Mansingh.[35]

In small bands they hoped to elude the British and find shelter in remote jungles but together they will be tracked. Tatya is said to have told his followers to find their way as best as they could, because now he is unable to continue his fight against the might of the British. He left the company of Rao Saheb with three attendants, three horses and a pony and decided to go in the Paron Jungles under the protection of his ally Mansingh. The state of mind of Tatya Tope at this juncture can well be imagined. After the defeat of Jaura Alipur he did or could no longer stay at a place to take respite. The British columns were pursuing him every where and from every direction. Ultimately he lost his heart and decided to abandon his struggle. It was a jolt to not only Firoz Shah and Rao Saheb but for the entire struggle against the British. Minus Tatya Tope, the strength and determination of Firoz Shah and Rao Saheb became feeble and they knew that now on they too will have to abandon their struggle.

Tatya Tope captured

In April 1859 Man Singh betrayed Tatya Tope and connived his capture with the British Officer Captain Meade. Tatya was captured on 8th April and was court marshaled on 15th April on the charge of "having been in rebellion, and having waged war against the British Government between January 1857 and December 1858 especially at Jhansi and Gwalior. He was found guilty and was sentenced to death.[36] In his deposition he gave details of his campaigns.[37] He was hanged on 18th April 1859 at Shivpuri. Tatya's elimination from the scene was a great blow for the insurgents. He had inherited the tradition of the original guerilla tactics of the Marathas and he gave a superb demonstration of his talents in the unequal fight which he carried on for two years against very heavy odds. With lightening swiftness he would move from place to place stoking the fires of rebellion, outmaneuvering and routing his opponents, avoiding pitched battles, escaping after defeat and eluding his adversaries in pursuit. He kept large British forces engaged in chasing him across Central India into Rajputana, backwards and forwards. Defeat could not depress his ardor nor fear of ruin and destruction diminish his loyalty to the cause.[38] Tatya Tope, in the words of Malleson, 'was a marvelous guerilla warrior. In pursuit of him, Brigadier Parke had marched, consecutively, 240 miles in nine days; Brigadier Somerset, 230 in nine days, and, again, seventy miles in forth-eight hours; Colonel Holmes, through a sandy desert, fifty four miles in little cover twenty-four hours; Brigadier Honner, 145 miles in four days. Yet he slipped through them all-through enemies watching every issue of the jungles in which he lay concealed.'[39]

Commenting on the pursuit of Tatya Tope by British Generals, 'The Friend of India' of 16th December, 1858 reported : "Tantia Topee has fled but a degree faster than he has been pursued......He has raced across India, chiefly through Native States, always through a territory less under European control than any portion of the continent, and everywhere his ubiquitous foe is still present, fully armed, neither guns nor commissariat wanting for the work. Some of the generals have been (for) months in the field. Almost all have been hunting for a period sufficient to try men and beasts, yet we all know, and none better than Tantia that if he keeps in motion for the next years till his followers' beard reach their feet, and their sabre hilts have been worn to a nedle's fineness he will still be hunted down with the same perseverance as at present ..... Tantia Topee may yet find out that he has aced as a training maser for the Indain Armies."[40]

Firoz Shah and Rao Saheb

Firoz Shah and Rao Saheb decided to stay together and they crossed the Chaturbhuj pass and took shelter in the jungles of Sironj.[41] 'But even there they were not left in peace. With their superior resources the British Generals tried to cordon the jungle and search it foot by foot and inch by inch. At last the four columns combined to sweep the forest clean and the rebel camp was reached. But the British officers were doomed to disappointment. Rao Saheb and Firoz Shah had vanished in thin air.'[42]

One of the spies of Holkar Maharaja, Hari Trimbak wrote from Biaora[43] camp on 31-1-59 that a rumour was current there that a force of insurgents was posted inside the Raghogarh fort.[44] Some say that this force had been concealed in a thicket. They went to Shivpuri for a meeting. There Firoz Shah and others had rallied their forces.[45]

Meanwhile Rao Saheb with his followers moved towards the west, then to the south, and reached Kushana, west of Ajmer, about 80 miles east of Jodhpur on the 10th February. General Michel ordered Brig. Somerset to proceed by forced marches and take up a position near to the south of Udaipur side of the Chaturbhuj pass, which was the principal road across the hills. Brig. Showers was ordered to the north, Park to the west, and Honner to the south. On the east lay the great desert. On the 10th February Honner's column left Guna and after a march of 43 miles reached on the following evening at the encampment of the insurgents at Kushana. Eight miles before they arrived at this place, the insurgents began to flee, a body going under Firoz Shah to the south-west, the remainder under Rao Saheb to the south-east. On arriving near Kushana, the British army found that the insurgents were gone off.[46]

Things were gradually becoming problematic for the insurgents due to desertions of some of their sections. Abdul Sutar Khan of Jaora with 10 horsemen broke off near Sadree during the flight and remained back in the jungles. There are about 2200 men with the Rao Saheb mounted on horse and camel, 1800 of which did not agree with the Rao Saheb and wanted to surrender themselves to the British force. So Rao Saheb with 400 trustworthy horsemen (chiefly *Poorbeas*) separated from the rest.[47]

Pir Zahoor Ali Surrenders

On the 19th February two men were arrested near Neemach who claimed to be envoys from the camp of the insurgents. Two letters were found on their person, one in English from Wazir Khan, addressed to the Officer commanding at Neemach and the other in Persian, without any address or date, signed by Syed Zahur Ali on behalf of himself and his brother officers. Wazir Khan began by saying that he was 'neither a rebel nor a mutineer' and was compelled to leave his post at Agra under peculiar circumstances. He claimed to have persuaded the rebels to surrender and to have written to that effect to the Officer commanding the column in the district of Bikaner. But he received no reply. he now requested for a clear explanation of the terms of the Proclamation and concluded with a prayer for amnesty on behalf of Firoz Shah and Rao Saheb. He wrote, "I believe if the Prince Firoz Shah and the Rao are both convinced of safety not a single soul will remain in arms against Government—Should Government not deem Rao worthy of pardon I think the Prince alone will bring away almost all the mutineers to surrender provided he will be pardoned for joining the mutineers." Zahur Ali wrote, "We received a copy of Her Majesty's

Proclamation from Sikar—In that the limit is fixed for submission by 1st January. 1859—but in the margin a further extension of six months is granted—merely for the purpose of explanation on certain points. We have sent our Vakeels Sirmust Khan and Abdul Kareem Khan to you. According to what they say if we can be assured of safety, whenever you may direct we will surrender ourselves." Captain Dennys, Superintendent of Neemach, promptly replied that with regard to every one who may surrender under the terms of the Queen's Proclamation, every promise made therein would be rigidly observed. This applied equally to Rao Saheb, Firoz Shah and the common soldiers.[48]

Three hundred rebel cavalry, under Pir Zahoor Ali, surrendered on the 27th, at Sunhail, and more were said to be coming in and on 3rd March. Pir Zahoor Ali and his party of insurgents surrendered to General Michel, and laid down their arms on the 1st of March General Michel afterwards marched to Sonail.[49]

At Paron and Sironj Jungles

Firoz Shah and Rao Saheb, with their followers took a north-easterly course from Runija and pursued the same via Misroli, Sunhel, Raipur, Asnawad (near Cheepa Barod) where they suddenly doubled south, and pursued their way by the circuitous route of Manohar Thana[50], Chachora[51], Antralia, crossed Parbati river at the Kharar Barar *ghat* and thence through the jungles arrived on the 28th February at Paron[52] which was situated in the heart of the jungle tract lying between Shahabad[53] and Bamori Rampura.[54] They halted at Paron on the 1st March, being under the protection of the rebel Raja of that place Bhanwarji. Rao Saheb probably kept aloof from Firoz Shah and the rest, mistrusting the latter after the late negotiations for surrender, and surrender of Firoz Shah's principal followers Pir Zahoor Ali and Maulvi Wazir Khan.[55] It seemed that after leaving Paron Firoz Shah left for Sironj Jungles. He had with him Imam Ali, Woordie Major and Adil Mohammad Khan with eight or nine thousand men. Emam Ali, Woordie Major of the 5th Irregular Cavalry even wrote to Tatya Tope to come and join him.[56]

Rao Saheb also wanted to settle his terms with the Government. From a telegraphic message from Sir Robert Hamilton of the 14th March we learn that an agent of Rao Saheb had been to Sir Robert Napier with peace proposals. Sir Robert Napier wrote that if Rao Saheb surrenders, his life will be pardoned. He will not be put into irons or imprisoned—nor suffer any indignity, a provision will be made for his maintenance, and he will have to reside in such part of India as the Govt. will fix for him.[57] Rao Saheb, however did not agree to these terms.

Firoz Shah was seen there on the 19th March 1859 though separate from the rest.[58]

Col. DeSalis Takes on

On the 2nd April Colonel DeSalis was at Maksudangarh[59] and Colonel Rich at Lateri[60], when arrangements were made for a movement of the columns to the south to sweep the jungles. They accordingly reached on the 3rd, but the insurgents escaped to the west, crossing the Parbati river, and a body of their cavalry cut through the long column of the baggage which had been sent by the level road skirting the forest. The insurgents killed the bandmaster of the 10th Bombay Infantry and severely wounded two sepoys, taking some rifles and camels. That night Colonel DeSalis camped at Ganjari, 12 miles south of Maksudnagar, and Colonel Rich at Deogarh, about 8 miles to the east of Ganjari but on the other side of the belt of jungle. Colonel DeSalis had reason to believe that the insurgents who had crossed the Parbati would try to return and having few cavalry he could not spare them for pursuit. He knew that other insurgents under Firoz Shah had been left behind, and on the 4th April information of their position was obtained, and Colonel DeSalis arranged with Lieutenant-Colonel Rich to make long marches to the north that night and attack the insurgents simultaneously from different sides. Colonel DeSalis marched at 7 P.M. with a force. The column marched 13 miles beyond Maksudangarh to a point north of the jungle village of Burdah, 10 miles north-north-east of Maksudangarh , sending a detachment to Tinsiah, a village in the heart of the jungle about five miles south of Burdah. He advanced quietly through the thick jungle in the direction where the insurgents were said to be camping. On nearing the camp they at once charged them. Many insurgent infantry were killed, but the cavalry escaped. The insurgents, who were commanded by Firoz Shah numbered some 1500. It was estimated that 300 were killed including *Subadar* Chhatar Singh, a General in the insurgent force, and formerly of the Gwalior contingent. Many of the insurgents flying from Colonel DeSalis went towards Kotra and made for some villages on the edge of the jungle. They were surrounded and attacked and were killed. This was practically the final dispersal of the rebels under Firoz Shah whose following was again broken up by Brigadier Showers, with a force from Guna, near Patan on 15th of April.[61]

Firoz Shah's final defeat

G.W. Forrest gives us the intimate description of the final struggle with Firoz Shah. He says, "General Michel ordered the pursuing columns to take up carefully selected positions adjoining the jungle at Manawar [Manohar] Thana, between fifty and sixty miles almost west of Sironj, Pachore about 35 miles north of Sironj, and Berasia about 35 miles south-south-west of Sironj. Brg. Wheeler moved out from Saugor towards the Betwa river, ready to take up the pursuit should the insurgents break cover. A strong detachment under Major Chetwode formed a cordon between Sironj and Berasia, and thus cut off a portion of the extensive jungle and reduced the field operations considerably. A column under Col. DeSalis, which General Michel had placed at the disposal of Sir Robert Napier, another under Col. Rich, and a detachment of the 92nd Highlanders on their way to Jhansi under Col. Lockhart, thoroughly swept the northern portion of the jungle, but without success. The impenetrable screen of trees and brushwood enabled the insurgents to evade their pursuers. Ultimately, the insurgents were defeated with a heavy loss. The insurgents were commanded by Firoz Shah.

It was his final defeat. He and Rao Saheb disappeared, and no trace of them could for some time be found."[62]

The Vaqil of Rao Saheb told Sir Hamilton that Firoz Shah was anxious to come in but fears. The Vaqil was told that if they do not come in Hamilton shall proceed against them but any who chose their submission by proceeding to Jabalpur shall not be attacked there.[63]

Question of Surrender

Repeated defeats had now disheartened the insurgents and gradually they started thinking of opening negotiations with the British for terms of their surrender.

We get a glimpse of the issue of surrender of Firoz Shah and Rao Saheb from the deposition of Wazir Khan, a close associate of Firoz Shah, who was captured by the British force. He was formerly an Asstt. Surgeon of the Agra dispensary having been educated and received his diploma in Calcutta Medical College, early education at Delhi College. Regarding the question of surrender of Firoz Shah he alluded to the following facts in his deposition.

At the time of discussion for surrender, Wazir Khan was to the closest intimacy with the leaders and indeed was the medium of English papers that found their way into their camp. The most reliable information they received of the movement of the several British columns in the field against them, was from the papers and also regarding that of such of their leaders as got separated from them or were in rebellion in distant parts. At first, none of the leaders was disposed to surrender, as they were not aware of the safety of their lives, but in some of the English papers reading about the amnesty, Wazir Khan opened the subject for surrender to Firoz Shah the only leader who would take his advice. Firoz Shah willingly understood the proposal and discussed the matter with the Rao Saheb. It was agreed that a copy of the amnesty should be procured and its contents well understood. The insurgents had no opportunity of getting one. However when they arrived in the Bikaner territory the question of surrender then mooted.[64]

According to Wazir Khan the question of surrender was first mooted when the rebels were in Bikaner territory, the Raja having sent one of his officers with a notification to the address of Risaldars and others of the Rao's force stating that a proclamation of pardon had been issued by the British Government, and enclosed its copy. On the receipt of the same Firoz Shah and Rao Saheb appointed myself and 3 others to go to the Bikaner Officer not being changed with any guarantee for our safety we continued our fight towards the south hearing the approach of British Force.[65] The persons deputed were Mohamed Wazir Khan, Sarmust Khan, Gaurishankar and Desai Gangadhar Pant and adds that the *risaldar* of Bikaner somehow or other sent the deputation back.[66]

Wazir Khan said in his deposition that in the middle of a forced march from Kankraoli in Mewar, while at Akala, Firoz Shah after getting all his officers to agree to the proposal of surrender, sent Wazir Khan with the Darpan Gaure and Imam Ali, to speak to the Rao Saheb on the subject. Rao Saheb after listening with earnest attention said that he could not be the first to open negotiations in the matter on account of his relations and head of his House, the Nana Saheb not having made any offer of submission, but "if we thought fit to open the correspondence he would have no objection to go as we did, if the terms granted were favourable, since he would then have alternative but to join us in submission." It was then agreed by all the *Sardars* to depute some persons with letters touching the question of surrender to the nearest station.[67]

Negotiation for Rao Saheb

When Firoz Shah was roaming with Rao Saheb in Sironj forests they could not stay long as the British Generals were vigorously combing the forest. Meanwhile overtures had started for surrender under the terms of the Queen's Proclamation; but a reward of 10,000 rupees had already been proclaimed for the arrest of Rao Saheb.[68] G.F. Edmonstone had directed Robert Hamilton that if Rao Saheb was captured he was to be tried by a Court Martial but the sentence passed by the Court was not to be carried into effect without the approval of the Governor-General. He added that if Rao Saheb tendered submission on guarantee of his life, the same might be given.[69] Rao Saheb first sent Mohammad Ishaq as a *Vakil* to the British General at Sironj with a verbal request of presenting himself. According to his own statement, General sent a *parwana* asking him to come to him but he could not go.[70] Baba Saheb Apte, son-in-law of Baji Rao II and Sindhia's *Subedar* in Malwa represented the cases of Rao Saheb, Bala Saheb and Nana Saheb to Sir Robert Hamilton. Sir Robert Hamilton replied that he could do little for Bala Saheb and Nana Saheb, but he could deal with Rao Saheb so long as he remained with the limits of his jurisdiction. He added that the order of the Governor-General with regard to him was that "if Rao Saheb surrenders, his life will be pardoned. He will not be put into irons or imprisoned nor suffer any indignity; a provision will be made for his maintenance. He will have to reside in such part of India as the government will fix for him. These promises are made to him provided he has not with his hand o tongue incited or caused the murder of British subjects."[71] Rao Saheb, however, did not take advantage of this offer. After leaving the forest of Sironj, he moved from place to place in northern India.[72]

Firoz Shah's Terms

It was reported on June 2, 1859 that Firoz Shah was staying in the north of Sironj in a thick forest. His party consisted of about 50 Vilaitees, 200 Telangas and 300 other men. These were very watchful and seldom stayed in one place. It was understood that Firoz Shah was willing to surrender if he could secure his terms, which were: full liberty to reside wherever he liked and a suitable provision for his future maintenance.[73]

"Even dire adversity" says S.N. Sen, " could not make the proud prince forget that he was a descendant of Timur and Babur. He would not relinquish the title of his imperial ancestors, and to a man of Wazir Khan's rank and status he could address only a *Parwana*, not a letter."[74] The *Parwana* ran as follows:

Parwana from the Lord of World and Mankind, the son of the holy preceptor of the Universe and its inmates, Mirza Mahomed Firoz Shah Bahadur to his confidential servant Maulvi Mohammad Wazir Khan, dated 3rd Zikad, 1275 A.H. (4th June 1859).

As your petition has been received and the contents learned, I write certain conditions. Should these be agreed to; and full assurance obtained I have no objection in coming to terms.

What arrangement has been made for my maintenance?

2nd- I should be allowed full liberty, that is, I should be allowed to remain or go wherever I like, without molestation.

3rd- The arms of my followers, about ten or twenty in number, will not be given up. After obtaining an answer to the above conditions give me information.

On a former occasion, I had sent a man to Indore from whom I have not heard to this hour. Enquire about him and communicate to me and result of your enquiries.[75]

Colonel R. , Agent Governor General for Cental India forwarded a copy and translation of the above *Parwana* written to his Agent by Firoz Shah to Cecil Beadon, Secretary to the Govt. of India Foreign Deptt. from Indore Residency on 15th June 1859 and commented that “had Firoz Shah worded his conditions of surrender in more humble and reasonable terms, I should have felt disposed to offer him (on my own responsibility) a provision for it is obvious that some allowance must be made for one so utterly unable to gain his own bread; but to do so now might have a bad effect in encouraging his unreasonable request. I hope the instructions by post will fix an allowance for Firoz Shah.”[76]

Sir R. in his letter of 9th June 1859 requested his Government to tell him whether Firoz Shah may be called in and if so, on what terms.[77] On this, Sir R. was asked to tell Firoz Shah that he will not be brought to trial but that he will be required to reside under surveillance at such place as the Govt. may fix.[78]

To this Cecil Beadon, Secretary to the Govt. of India informed Brigadier-General R.C. that "Firoz Shah, if he gives himself up, will not be allowed to chose his own place of residence but will be kept under surveillance and will have an allowance made to him sufficient for his maintenance."[79] Firoz Shah could not accept the terms of amnesty from the Government and continued his struggle, though with reduced force and meager resources.

In Balabehat Jungles

On the 2nd August 1859, 500 insurgents under Firoz Shah having passed through the Saugor district entered the Balabehat jungles of Chanderi in which a considerable body of insurgents under Rao Hamirsingh, Debisingh and others of the Chanderi district had always found a retreat. The people of Pargana received them well and supplied them with provisions freely. After some fruitless attempts to come up with Firoz Shah, Colonel Nott, Commanding 19th Madras Native Infantry, completely surprised him as Putrai 4 miles N.W. of Narhut,[80] killed 25 of his band and took all their horses, tents and several arms. The remains of the band at once fled from British territories, leaving only local insurgents in Chanderi namely about 150 under Rao Hamirsingh and 100 under Debisingh. About this time the insurgent leader Tilok Singh of Sunauri[81] was taken in the north of Chanderi district.[82]

On 16th August Firoz Shah had a skirmishes with the Thakur of Bijawar[83] in Bundelkhand. Firoz Shah's party consisted of 100 and the Thakur lost his life in this skirmish. On that day he was in the north of Hirapur (Chhatarpur). On the 20th August Firoz Shah suffered defeat from Nutt's force following which he broke into three parties. He had only 100 mutineers and 6 men riding wretched ponies, 80 *sawars* and 50 infantry who had proceeded with him and were on in the 5th September at Daloni[84]. The third fragment of Firoz Shah's force was attacked lately at Patrokola in the Shahgarh territory[85]. His strength may be put down at 100 foot and 40 horse. He plundered villages in the Saugor district. The Government declared a reward of Rs. ten thousand for the apprehension of Firoz Shah.[86] During this period Farzand Ali and Despat Bundela were leading the insurgency in Sagar area but it is unfortunate that there seems to be no contact or cooperation between these three insurgent leaders.

In mid-August of 1859, Bhopal rebel Adil Mohammad Khan of Ambapani, who, for some time acted in concert with Firoz shah, appears to have totally separated from him by now. It may be recalled that Adil Mohammad Khan, with his brother Fazil Mohammad Khan was at Rahatgarh fort with Firoz Shah and other insurgent leaders of Bundelkhand. The Thakurs of Lalitpur did not join Firoz Shah. The British had 150 Europeans infantry, 600 native infantry and 2 guns of Native Artillery at Malthone.[87] Lalitpur was also reinforced. There was also a force from General Napier's Division watching the western *ghats* of the river Betwa.[88] The British were convinced that the appearance of Firoz Shah in the Lalitpur *Pargana* will not cause a general rising in that District of the *Thakurs*.[89]

These days Nawab Adil Mohammad Khan was also creating pressure from the side of Saugor-Dhamoni. In the beginning of September 1859 a party of fifty insurgents had an encounter with the British force at Laxmanjhir on the bank of Dhasan river, wherein three insurgents were killed and three injured. After this defeat this party flew towards the village Silawari on 4th September. Next day the same party consisting of 50 foot and 18 cavalry, reached Dardenia and ultimately they hid themselves in the forests of Majgawan. On 8th September 1859, Firoz Shah was reported to have been seen in the forests of Dhamoni.[90] Firoz Shah wanted to join hands with Despat by reaching Kishangarh. The Thakur of Bamnaura faced the contingent proceeding under the leadership of Firoz Shah on 16th September 1859 in which the Thakur lost his life.[91]

It was reported in early October 1859 that a party of insurgents headed by Firoz Shah rapidly marched from Rahatgarh to Malthone. It succeeded in evading pursuit. Within the trough of Rahatgarh, Beaora and Kolaras, the insurgents were not less than 1000 men, horse and foot.[92]

Messages of the 13th and 14th December 1859 which had been received from the Political Agent at Gwalior, though not very clear, showed that the insurgents under Firoz Shah were in the neighbourhood of the Sind River closely pressed by Napier and were crossing and re-crossing it, with the object apparently of eluding the Major General's force.[93]

After this we don't find any mention of Firoz Shah's activities in India. It seems that looking to his precarious condition and lack of resources and support, Firoz Shah abandoned his activities in India and with some of his followers he decided to leave India and try his hands with the foreign powers like Afghanistan, Turkey, Iraq and Iran. It took him more than two years to reach and settle himself in that far off land.

Reference :

1. Forty five kilometer south of Gwalior. This is different from Araon which is situated south of Guna.
2. Seventy five kilometer north of Datia.
3. Foreign Department Secret Consultations. 108 dt. 26-1-1859, Tel. 14-12-1858, from GI
4. Telegraphic Message from Brigadier Showers, Mainpuri, to E.A. Reade, G. Harvey, Col. Abbot, Major-General Bradford, and Brigadier McCausland, Agra, Meerut, Fatehgarh, dated 11th Dec. 1858. And Telegraphic Message from E.A. Reade, Agra, to W. Muir, dt. 12th December, 1858. Secretariat Records Room, Lucknow. F.S.U.P. Vol. V, pp. 832-833
5. Forty five kilometer south-east of Gwalior. This is not be confused by another Pichhor of Shivpuri district of M.P.
6. Forth kilometer south-east of Gwalior near Pichhor.
7. Foreign Department Political Proceedings, 4-3-1859, SN 377 Intelligence – p. 48 dt. 11-12-58.
8. Forty kilometers south-east of Shivpuri.
9. G.W. Forrest, *A History of The Indian Mutiny*, Vol. III, pp. 612-613. Telegraphic Message from Major Macpherson, Gwalior, to G.F. Edmonstone, E.A. Reade, R. Hamilton and Officer commanding of Lucknow, Allahabad, Agra, Indore, dated 18th December 1858. Secretariat Records Room, Lucknow. F.M.U.P. Vol., V, p. 835
10. *The Revolt in Central India*, p. 227.
11. Thirty kilometer north-west of Chanderi.
12. *The Revolt in Central India*, p. 227
13. Telegraphic Message from Major Macpherson to E.A. Reade, dated Gwalior, the 22nd December 1858. Secretariat Records Room, Lucknow.

14. Letter (No. 24) from George Plowden, Commissioner of Nagpur, to R. Simpson, Under Secretary to the Government of India, Foreign department, Fort William, dated Nagpur, 28th February 1859. F.S.U.P. Vol. III, p. 526
15. Foreign Department, Political Proceeding 4 March 1859 No. 327, from Sir Robert Hamilton, AGG for GOI, 28th Dec. 1858 Indore.
16. Thirty kilometers north of Guna in M.P.
17. Foreign Department, Political Proceeding 4 March 1859 Nos. 480. Telegram from Captain Mayne, Goonah, 29th December to Bombay, Indore, Gwalior and Allahabad.
18. Forrest Mutiny, Vol. III, p. 614. Also Foreign Department, Political Proceeding 4 March 1859 Nos. 481. Telegram from Allahabad dt. 25th Dec. 1858 to from G.J. Edmonstone to different officers.
19. Deposition of Rao Saheb in Appendix 3
20. In Rajasthan. 32 kilometers west of Mandsaur, M.P.
21. Rajnikant Gupta, *Military Traits of Tatya Tope*, 1987, pp. 135-144. A short description of Tatya Tope's activities may also be found in Rao Saheb's deposition in appendix 3.
22. About 100 kilometers east of Kota in Rajasthan.
23. Ninety kilometers north-east of Kota and 25 kilometers south of Sawai Madhopur in Rajasthan.
24. G.W. Forrest, *A History of the Indian Mutiny*, Vol. III, p. 611. Also see Rao Saheb's deposition in Appendix 4, p. 6
25. Seventy kilometers west of Guna.
26. Rajnikant Gupta, *Op. Cit.*, p. 144
27. Sixty five kilometers south-west of Sikar in Rajasthan.
28. Foreign Department, Political Proceeding 4 March 1859 Nos. 500. Telegram circular from Allahabad the 8th January 1859 from G.J. Edmonstone to different officers.
29. Foreign Department, Political Proceeding 4 March 1859 Nos. 502
30. Fifty kilometers south of Jaipur in Rajasthan.
31. Forty kilometers south of Dausa in Rajasthan.
32. In north-east part of Rajasthan comprising of administrative districts of Sikar and Jhunjhnu.
33. Foreign Department, Political Proceeding 4 March 1859 Nos. 475. Copy of letter no. 56 of 1859, dt. 16th January 1859 from Brig. Gen. G P. Lawrence AGG for the States of Rajputana to the Commissioner of Delhi Division. Dt. Camp Ajmer the 16th Jan. 1859.
34. *The Revolt in Central India*, p. 229
35. Forrest Mutiny, Vol. III, pp. 616-17
36. Sen, op. cit., p. 380.

    Parag Tope (on the authority of *Camp and Cantonment: A Journal of Life in India in 1857-59*, Mrs. Leopold Paget, Longman, Green, Longman, Roberts & Green, 1865, Appendix titled: A Short Narrative of the Pursuit of the Rebels in Central India, Major Leopold Grimston Paget, p. 453-4) says that Tatya Tope died fighting dt Chhipa Barod against the British column on 1st

January 1859. *Tatya Tope's Operation Red Lotus*, 2010, p. 289-90. But Parag Tope has not quoted the next sentence of his source, which makes it amply clear that Tatya Tope was not killed on 1st January but continued to live. The lines are "It turned out afterwards that *he lived to give us plenty more trouble,* as I shall presently show, but in point of fact, this was the last stand- if stand it could be called- made by any considerable body of rebels in that par of India".

37. Tatya Tope's deposition is given in Appendix 2.
38. Tarachand, *History of Freedom Movement in India*, Vol. II, pp. 102-03
39. Malleson, op. cit., p. 397.
40. F.S.U.P., Vol. III, pp. 569-570.
41. About one hundred kilometers north of Bhopal and about 75 kilometers south-east of Guna in M.P.
42. Sen, op. cit., p. 376.
    When Rao Saheb was asked during his deposition that if you were not a rebel why were you there with Firoz Shah? To this Rao Saheb's reply was that 'When Tatya Tope left me I thought it was in my power to join the English but I had no friend or acquaintance to introduce me. If I along would join I would be killed'. See appendix 3, page 10-11. It seems that Rao Saheb simply wanted to prove his innocence. Otherwise he was quite intent in his activities with Firoz Shah.
43. Thirty kilometers east of Rajgarh, the district headquarter of the same name in M.P.
44. Twenty five kilometers south of Guna, M.P.
45. Lunia, letter no. 322, pp. 586.
46. Forrest Mutiny, Vol. III, pp. 617-18.
47. Foreign Deptt. Political Consultations, 1859, no. 608. Purport of a *Kyfeeut* from Dajee Sukhwaram on the part of the Gwalior Vakeel attached to the Mewar Agency deputed by Captain Showers offg. Pol. Agent Rajpootana. 26th Feb. 1859.
48. Foreign Department, Political Consultations, No. 618, 15 April, 1859.
49. Ball, Vol. I, p. 583
50. Misroli, Sunhel, Raipur, Asnawad near Cheepa barod and Manohar Thana are in the lower half area of Jhalawad district of Rajasthan.
51. In Guna district of Madhya Pradesh situated at 30 kilometers north of Rajgarh and sixteen kilometers east of Manohar Thana of Rajasthan.
52. North of Guna in Madhya Pradesh, close to the border of Rajasthan.
53. Forty kilometers east of Kishangarh of Rajasthan and fifty kilometers south-west of Shivpuri of Madhya Pradesh.
54. Twenty five kilometers north of Guna in Madhya Pradesh.
55. Foreign Department, Political Proceedings, 1st April 1859, Cons. No. 607, enclosure No. 67 of 1859. Memo. of Intelligence from C.L. Showers, Officiating Political Agent, dated Mewar Agency Camp, the 5th March 1859. National Archives, New Delhi. F.S.U.P. Vol. III, 666-667
56. Deposition of Tatya Tope, F.S.U.P. Vol. III, p. 589

57. Foreign Department, Political Consultations, No. 288, 17 June, 1859
58. Foreign Department Political Consultations. 1-4-1859, no. 358. Telegraphic Message from Seeronge via Goonah, 22nd March to Beorah, Indore, Gwalior and Bengal From Br. Gen. Sir R. Napier to Maj. General Sir R. Hamilton, Major Macpherson, Chief of the Staff.
59. At the southern projection of Guna District of Madhya Pradesh.
60. In Vidisha district of MP. Fifteen kilometer east of Maksudangarh of Rajasthan.
61. *The Revolt in Central India*, pp. 233-35
62. Forrest Mutiny, Vol. III, pp. 620-21.
63. Foreign Department, Political Consultation, 25 March 1859, no. 195-196. From Indore 14th /15th March to Calcutta. From Sir R. Hamilton to Lord Elphinstone
64. Foreign Department Political Proceedings 30-12-1859, No. 311, letter no. 54, dt. 9-3-1959, Wazeer Khan's deposition. His deposition is given in Appendix 1.
65. Foreign Department Political Proceedings 30-12-1859, No. 311, letter no. 54, dt. 9-3-1959, Wazeer Khan's deposition. His deposition is given in Appendix 1.
66. Foreign Department Political Proceedings, 30th Dec. 1859, Part II, Foreign Department Cons. No. 313, pp. 4 to 6. Deposition of Peer Jahoor Ali. His deposition is given in Appendix 1.
67. Foreign Department, Political Proceedings, 30-12-1859, No. 311, letter no. 54, dt. 9-3-1859, Wazir Khan's depositon. See Appendix 1.
    Rao Saheb in his deposition also alludes to the consent of Firoz Shah to surrender before the British. See Appendix 3, page 6.
68. Home Public 'B' Progs. 20 August, 1862, Cons. No. 111.
69. Military Consultations, 2 September, 1859, No. 144.
70. See Rao Saheb's deposition in Appendix 3
71. Foreign Political Consultations, 17 June 1859, No. 288.
72. Rao Saheb, he roamed in north India till he reached Chenani in Jammu territory. But he was betrayed by one Bhim Rao who had been for some time with Tatya Tope. He was arrested and was sentenced to be hanged and was executed in front of his palace at Bithur on August 20, 1862.
73. Memo. of Intelligence from Shahamat Ali, Asstt. to Agent Governor General, Central India, dated 2nd June 1859, Foreign Political Consultations, 17th June 1859, No. 292 A. F.S.U.P. Vol. III, p. 667-668
74. Sen, op. cit., p. 378
75. Foreign Department, Political Consultations, 1st July 1859, No. 172. F.S.U.P. Vol. III, p. 669
76. Foreign Department, Political Consultations, 1st July 1859, o. 171,
77. Foreign Department Political Consultation 17 June 1859, no. 290. Telegram from Sir R. Shakespeare to C.Beadon, Secy to Govt. Calcutta. dt. 9th June 1859

78. Foreign Department Political Consultations. 17th June 1859, no. 291. From Calcutta 10th June from Mr. Beadon, Secy. to Govt., To Indore to Sir R. Shakespeare:
79. Foreign Department, Political Consultations. 1st July 1859, No. 171.
80. Ninety kilometers north of Sagar on Sagar-Jhansi road.
81. In Block Talbehat of Lalitpur District of U.P.
82. Letter no. 568 F of 1860 from F.W. Pinkney, Commissioner, Jhansi Division, to Secretary to Government, N.W.P., Allahabad, dated Jhansi, the 8th June 1860, F.S.U.P. Vol. III, pp. 657-658 .
83. Forty eight kilometers south of Chhatarpur in Madhya Pradesh.
84. Situated at the northern boundary of Damoh District of Madhya Pradesh
85. Northern most part of Sagar District of Madhya Prdesh.
86. Foreign Department, Political Consultations 433-34 dt. 30-12-1859 Memo p. 15 from AGG.
87. Situated about 65 kilometers north of Sagar on Sagar-Jhansi Road.
88. Foreign Department Political Consultations, 9 Sept. 1859 no. 117. From Col. Shakespear, AGG, to Cecil Beadon, Secy to GOI, Foreign Deptt. Fort William, Indore Residency 21st August 1859.
89. Foreign Department Political Consultations, 2 Sept. 1859 no. 115. Camp Tehree. From Col. Sir R. Shakespear, Agent G G for C.I., to Cecil Beadon, Secy. to the GOI in the Foreign Deptt. Fort Williams.
90. Foreign Department, Political Proceedings, 23rd September 1859, No. 206 Dhamoni is situated about 45 kilometers north of Sagar on the Sagar-Jhansi Road.
91. Foreign Department, Political. Consultations 433-4, dt. 30-12-1859.
92. Foreign Department Political Proceedings,. 18-12-1859 - LN.102 dt. 5-10-1859 from AGG to GI.
93. Foreign Department, FC Suppl. 30-12-1859. no. 878

Chapter - 8
In Self-Exile

The great uprising in India subsided till 1860. The great heroes of this rising had either been imprisoned or killed in the battles or surrendered or went or sent in exile. Insurgent leaders of Ruhelkhand and Awadh who were cornered in the Tarai area of Nepal, moved from place to place between Chitwan, Bhutwal and Nayakot and suffered terrible privations. In an encounter with the Nepal force Rana Beni Madho met with his death in November 1859 fighting with the Gorkhas. The deaths of Narpat Singh, Bala Rao, Khuda Baksh and Harprashad were reported in 1860. Nawab Mammu Khan, Khan Bahadur Khan and Brigadier Jwala Prasad with others were delivered to the British authorities. Khan Bahadur Khan was tried, condemned and hanged. Jwala Prasad was also hanged near Sati Chaura Ghat at Kanpur on 3rd May 1860. Begam Hazrat Mahal of Oudh preferred to stay with her son and a small retinue in Nepal itself. Nana Saheb refused the British terms. What happened to him is not known.

Amongst the foremost leaders of the great uprising, Firoz Shah was the only one who was undaunted and continued his struggle till the close of 1859 and when he failed to secure acceptable terms for surrender before the British Government, he, any how, managed to escape from India. He spent several years wandering around Central Asia, Middle East and Iran and ended his life in Mecca. It appears that he tried to inspire these countries to join hands against the British in India. It is yet a secret how he along with his associates managed to leave India for Afghanistan and what route he adopted. It is also not known as to what connections he had there and how they managed to give him shelter in a country like Afghanistan, which had cordial relations with the British. Let us examine the political condition of the countries which were visited by Firoz Shah during his exile from India.

Afghanistan and Bukhara

In 1850 Dost Muhammad, the ruler of Afghanistan, again conquered Balkh and in 1855 the renewal of friendly intercourse between Dost Muhammad and the British Government led to the conclusion of a treaty at Peshawar and the same year Dost Muhammad made himself master of Kandahar. In 1856 Persian forces advanced to Herat and captured it and the same year the British expedition was sent to the Persian Gulf which resulted in its relinquishment to an independent ruler. In January 1857, Dost Muhammad had an interview at Peshawar with Sir John Lawrence, Chief Commissioner of the Punjab, at which he was promised arms and a subsidy for protection against Persia. In consequence of this treaty, a British mission under Major Lumsden proceeded to Kandahar. The Indian uprising followed, but in spite of Afghan excitement the Amir remained faithful to the British alliance.[1] In 1860 Firoz Shah was heard of in Qandahar making his way to Persia.[2] It means that Firoz Shah entered Afghanistan in 1860, when it was being ruled by Dost Muhammad Khan who was having cordial relations with the British Government since a decade and had used this opportunity to extend his domain.

It was certain that Firoz Shah could not muster the support of Dost Muhammad Khan and after some futile months he had to proceed elsewhere. The place he selected was Bukhara which was further west of Afghanistan. This fact is revealed by the fact that a British Minister at Tehran (Iran) noticed that Firoz Shah had proceeded to Bokhara in the beginning of December 1861 and there after his name surfaced in the diplomatic correspondence of the British Government.[3]

The Amir of Bukhara, whom Firoz Shah visited in 1861 and 1863, was fully occupied with the Russian advance and succession wars in the neighbouring state of Khokand.[4] In fact Bukhara had become an object of rivalry between Russia and Great Britain in the middle of the 19th century and envoys were sent by both nations to cultivate the favour of its *amir* Mohammed Rahim.[5]

Iran

It seems that from Bokhara, Firoz shah went to Iran i.e. Persia. It was the time when Persia was facing the encroachments of Russia from the north and had lost some territories in north Persia. The Shah of Persia was desirous of obtaining compensation for the territorial losses to Russia in northern Persia earlier in the century by conquest in the east, Herat being as its primary objective. These aspirations were encouraged by the Russian minister at Teheran. When Persia occupied Herat in 1856, Great Britain strongly objected to it and pressed Persia to sign a treaty of 1857, by which the Shah of Persia undertook to evacuate Herat and to recognize the kingdom of Afghanistan.[6] Persia was balancing its diplomacy between Russia and Great Britain and was not in a mood to spoil its relations with either of the powers. This was the time when Firoz Shah came to Persia.

As late as November 1862, Firoz Shah was residing at Astrabad, a shrine four miles from Tehran in Iran . His object was to obtain money from the Shah of Iran, but as yet he could only succeed in procuring a promise of 300 Tomans, and he endeavoured to get this sum increased. He had contracted debts at Astrabad to the amount of about 700, and unless the Shah gave him a large sum, he was to require to borrow money in Tehran for his current expenses.[7] The British envoy in Persia informed the British Government that Firoz Shah was likely to remain there for 2-3 months. He had about twenty people with him and one of them was said to be Maulvi. The envoy wanted to know whether any sum has been offered for the arrest of Firoz Shah and whether the Government considers it very important that he should be arrested.

The Brit'sh envoy in Persia was informed that no reward was offered for the capture of Firoz Shah.[8]

Firoz Shah\ and the following insurgents were residing a Shahdullazena near Tehran.[9]

1. Mirza Koochek Alias Firoz Bukht s/o Nazom Bukht s/o Noor Bhakht s/o Bahauddin or Mirza Bajoo Saheb s/o Mohammad Bakht Medoo Saheb. He was distantly related to s/oTaimoor family.
2. Imam Ali Khan – a Zamidar from Calcutta, native of Rampoor
3. Alif Khan, native of Queil.
4. Alimoolla, a native of Baroda.
5. Meer Vessee Hussain, relative of Meer Wassim Ali Khan of Baroda.
6. Rehmat Ollah, a one eyed Bagoochi – came with Feroz Shah.
7. Nehha Buksh
8. Meer Kaushar Ali
9. Melloh Khan
10. Mirza Mehdee

While Firoz Shah was at Teheran in 1862 an enquiry was made as to whether a ransom would be paid for his arrest, but the British authorities in India decided he was no longer of sufficient importance to be worth annoying the Persian authorities for.[10]

Mhd. Abbas Ali Khan's narrative

In the middle of February 1863, it was reported that one Mohd. Abbas Ali Khan, a native of Madras, lately traveled with Firoz Shah and his party from Kerman to Meshad and to Astrabad and thus had been living for several months on terms of intimacy with the whole of the insurgent refugees. According to his own statement, this person had no previous connection with these people. Mohammad Abbas Ali Khan wrote a letter to Thomson giving details of the activities of Firozshah. He wrote, "My name is Ghulam Mohammad Abbas Ali Khan s/o Ghulam Mohammad Masga Khan Bahadur of the Mewalwalagarh family, now residing in Madras.

My wife's father who was the Nejahid Daulat, whose son, Abbas Ali Khan is now living in the fortress of the English Government. I left India, with the intention of pilgrimage to Mecca. I came by way of Bushire to Seeraj. Mirza Koochak of Feroz Bakht arrived from Kerman and took up his quarters."[11] He further wrote that the Persian Dabir-ul- Mulk paid 600 Toomans to Vessee Hussain who has assumed the title of `Dabir-ul-Mulk of India' and promised that a further sum would be given. But he requested that Firoz Shah and his party would go away and not trouble the Persian Govt. any long. Firoz Shah replied that he could not travel in the winter season but after two months he would take his departure. Mohammad Abbas Ali Khan further wrote that Firoz Shah dispatched the one eyed Bilochi named Rehmatulla to India by way of Baghdad with letters from Firoz Shah to certain persons in Belochistan and to his friends in India. He sent Akhoond Beloch from Kerman down the Persian Gulf. It was also intended to dispatch Alimulla, who was the person employed to communicate with the Persian Govt., to India on a similar errand. Both these persons were to proceed to Baroda. Alimullah had not yet started. He was living in a *serai* at the New Gate at Tehran. Mohammad Abbas Ali Khan also wrote about an incident related to Firoz Shah's Baroda visit. Abbas Ali wrote that when he was in Meshad with the rebels, they told him that while Firoz Shah and his followers were at Baroda, the Baroda Raja ordered a general illumination on the occasion of Lord Elphinston's visit, and Firoz Shah, the one eyed Baluchi, Rahmatulla, Alimullah and Versee Hussain all determined to assassinate Lord Elphinston. They had left their home and had started with loaded guns on one of the roads where the Governor had to pass, but in the meantime, their friend Maulana Saheb Hislee finding that they were not in their house followed them and dissuaded them from carrying out their intention. This Maulana Saheb was the person who provided them with a house in which they were concealed and from which during their stay at Baroda they did not move except in mid-night.[12]

It is not clear as to when Firoz Shah was in Baroda in his mission. It was quite possible that he might have visited Baroda in the last quarter of 1862, the rumours of which might have prompted the British authorities to apprehend Mahmud Shah alias Pasha on 31st December 1862 at Patan, Gujarat.

In reply to a reference from Persia in January 1863, whether any reward had been offered for Firoz Shah's apprehension, the Government of India stated that it would not be expedient to undertake any such proceedings in a foreign territory.[13]

Pasha of Patan

Meanwhile, in India, a person named Pasha was apprehended on 31st December, 1862 at the city of Patan, Gujarat in the territory of the Gaikwar of Baroda. Pasha had alighted first at Jama Masjid, remained there for two days and then had proceeded to live in a *haveli* in the Motorshah *Mohalla* of that city. People called him Padshah. At Sidhpur a Syed of Radhavpur, aged 80 years had told that he was in his father's service at Delhi about 15 years ago and had nursed Pasha, when he was a child.[14]

Soon after, this fellow was captured by Lance Naik Sheikh Majju of the 6th Regiment, Bombay Native Infantry. He was about 45 years of age. In his statement the so called Pasha said that his name was Mahmud Shah s/o Dara Bakht, the heir apparent of Bahadur Shah, the ex-king of Delhi. He had come to Puttun 8 months ago to make a pilgrimage to the tomb of Makdoom Saheb. He stayed in a *sarai* near the *Masjid*, where he fell sick. He requested for another habitation where he could take medicines. He had no means of paying for a private lodging, he procured him an accommodation in Salerah *Mohalla* where he was apprehended. He remained there and took medicines and got well in 10 or 12 days. He then earned his livelihood by imparting medicines. He said that he had nothing to do with the rebellion at Delhi. He had left Delhi 10 months ago and took two months to reach Patan via Jaipur, Ajmer and Pali. He used to reside at Delhi at Nizamuddin

Dargah. He further told that before the rebellion, he was on the King's household and received Rs.200 p.m. from the British Government for his subsistence. This was stopped at the time of rebellion. His father, who was heir apparent to the late ex-King of Delhi died 15 or 20 years ago. The ex-King annulled his rights of heir ship and appointed Fakhruddin s/o his another wife. The of Rs. 200 p.m. was paid to him by one Mr. Thomas and then Simon Frazer. He was sick in the Dargah of Nizamuddin when rebellion broke out. He had a wife and four sons whom he had left in Nizamuddin Dargah. He had heard a good deal of Peer Patan, and the Peers at the village of Uniara near Patan. He now wanted to return to Delhi. [15] After elaborate enquiry the authorities were satisfied that the man was really what he stated himself to be the son of Dara Bakht. There was nothing against him in connection with the mutiny and he was released.[16]

Firoz Shah's Contacts

Though Firoz Shah was in Persia, he knew the whereabouts of the Indian leaders, particularly Nana Saheb and Bala Saheb, who were staying in Nepal. On 28th February 1863 the British Resident of Nepal informed the Government of India that the Maharaja of Nepal informed him that a Qabul fruit seller had arrived there from Herat and had been apprehended at the house of the families of the Nana Sahib and Bala Rao. He stated that he had received a letter for those persons from Firoz Shah at Herat, which he had destroyed during his journey for fear of its falling into the hands of the British. Firoz Shah had promised him a large reward if he would take the Nana and Bala Rao back with him, disguised as Mahomedans, to Herat.[17]

Another intercepted letter was found to be written by Firoz Shah explaining his plan of journey to India. Firoz Shah wrote that on account of the lateness of the season, he traveled by land instead of sea from the port of Karachi, and arrived on 22nd of Rujjab 1278 A.H. (1862 AD) at Kandhar. As soon as the news of his arrival reached Mohd. Ameen Khan, Ruler of Kandhar, he received him with all honour and treated him with hospitability in his own house.[18]

A letter written from Astrabad on 20th Rajjab, 1279 (1863 AD)[19] by some Imam Ali Khan to His Excellency Ghulam Ali gives some details about the activities of Firoz Shah during his stay in Iran. Code words were used in the letter viz. *Mirzajee* for Firoz Shah, *Ommee* for Imam Ali Khan, *Becheh* for Alif Khan, *Maulvi Saheb* for Aleemullah, *Asp-i-suphed* i.e. white horse for English government, *Jemadar* for Rehmatuual, *Mishkeen-i-asp* i.e. dark horse for Russian government and *Asp-i-Koochub* i.e. little horse for Persian government. The letter said that Meerzaji (Firoz Shah) wrote four letters from Kirman, and delivered them to a Bilochi Akhoond and furnished him with money for the road and sent him to Ghulam Ali and other friends. 'I hope that they have reached you, and that you are fully informed as to the affairs of the rulers of Bilochistan and Lass-bela and Khelat and Mohomed Ameen Khan, Ruler of Kandhar, and his brothers.' Firoz Shah himself went to Tehran and having furnished with money he had dispatched the *Jamadar* (Rehmatullah) and *Maulvi Saheb* (Aleemullah) to go via Baghdad to Hindustan and deliver letters to friends of Raoji and others. 'You will get much information from the Jamadar and Maulvi Saheb in person, which is at present kept close, and as I have (before) brought to your notice in writing letters for the perusal of myself and our friends in different places, keep the meaning carefully conceded, and I too with the assistance of friends will behave with all circumspection.' Firoz Shah was most anxious that Ghulam Ali Khan Risaldar should not cultivate the friendship of the the English government. While the Russian government was of no use, the Persian government was of a very little service, for its power was too small. He considered the British government to be his enemy. Letters were also written by Firoz Shah to the friends in Bilochistan and Kabul and Kandhar and Bokhara. Turkomans were considered fine fellows, and one of their chief had given a written promise for assistance.[20]

Firoz Shah was also in communication with his agents and friends in Afghanistan and India. He had placed his agent at Kandhar, who informed Firoz Shah that he had met with a friendly reception from the s/o Dost Mohammad Khan, who was the Governor of that place. Meanwhile, Imam Ali Khan, one of the follower of Firoz Shah in Tehran wrote to a person named Maulana, residing in Baroda. Persian Government lately offered Firoz Shah the sum of 200 *tomans* and wanted him to go away and not apply for further extension, but as the amount offered would not suffice to pay what Firoz Shah owed in the market, he declined to accept the money on those terms, and took shelter in the Shah's stable where he has been living for the last ten days. This was in April 1863.[21]

Herat

On 12 April 1864, the Assistant Political Agent of Gwadur wrote to the Commissioner of Sindh that Firoz Shah did pass through Kedge in disguise.[22]

It was learnt that in the last week of September 1864 Shahzada Firoz Shah, accompanied by two women and three or four Hindustani followers, arrived at Herat. He had lodgings in an empty house belonging to a Hindu. He then sought an interview with Wazir Wareem Khan, the Governor of Herat. Being disappointed with his reception, he made complaints, which came to the ear of Wazir Wareem Khan and so Wazir Wareem Khan did not allow him another interview. Firoz Shah in despair proceeded to Bokhara via "Mymunah" with the intention ultimately of finding his way into Russia via Mukeya.[23]

Another account says that one Husain Khan had gone to Yaqub Khan in Herat to submit to Sher Ali Khan and, on his return, taken back a refugee Mughal prince Shahzada Firoz Shah, who was wanted by the British for his part in the Indian Mutiny.[24]

Bokhara

When Firoz Shah started from Herat for Bokhara[25] the British *vakeel* at Kabul was instructed to look out for Firoz Shah and report his movements should he proceed thither.[26]

Firoz Shah, having arrived at Bokhara, wished to obtain an interview with the Kosh Begee, who had already heard of his arrival through his spies and sent for him. Firoz Shah expressed his desire for an interview with the ruler of Bokhara. The Kosh Begee from the equivocation of his replies suspected him and sent him to the quarters of the Hindustani and Khorasani merchants to have him recognized. When no one could recognize him, the Kosh Begee gave him a trifle amount for subsistence, made him over to the charge of the in charge of the *sarai* till the king should return, and ordered that he should not be allowed to leave the place. On the arrival of the king twelve days after, Firoz Shah presented his petition for a private interview, but owing to the news received fom Balkh, the King of Bokhara departed shortly after to Koorshee, and Firoz Shah remained under surveillance in the "Serai Gasfundi.".[27]

Beale, without quoting his source of information says that some Arabs who arrived at Hyderabad in 1866, reported that they had seen Firoz Shah in Arabia, and supporting himself by begging among the rich merchants.[28]

Contacts Russians

When Samarkand[29] was taken by the Russians in 1868[30], Firoz Shah returned there and obtained a stipend of five gold *tillahs* (the *tilla* was 5 rupees roughly) per diem from the Russian Governor. He also offered the Governor of Samarkand that, if the Emperor could assist him with an army for the capture of Delhi, he would pay rupees, 1,00,000 per diem at every stage for the expense of the troops, but this application was rejected by the Governor. Firoz Shah at last gave himself up and his allowance was, consequently, reduced to one-half. Afterwards he left Samarkand and proceeded to Shuhur Subz, where he obtained a good stipend, but before the Russian invasion of the latter place he had quitted and proceeded to Khokand, where he drew a subsistence allowance from the Meer.[31]

He seems to be successful in obtaining the support of the Russians against the British in India. He had planned to enter India and with the aid of the Russians wanted to raise the standards of revolt. This fact was revealed in a letter lately intercepted by the British Government. In this letter one Noor Ali Khan (Ilakadar of Mohalla Kukra, District Shahjahanpur) wrote to Maharaja of Charkhari and Diwan Anna Saheb that Firoz Shah was residing in the Western Frontier and wanted to know the number of British troops located in the neighbourhood and also wished that a mutiny may be convened and counsel taken as to whether or not people will join in aiding and helping him. Those who will give help, will have their states saved by Firoz Shah. Nawab Khullun Khan will get all territory he possessed by him. Firoz Shah also intimated that a body of the Russian troops will reach Shahjanahpur from the side of Tibet subduing the country from the British.[32]

Again in Afghanistan

The Shahzada was also an inconvenient guest at Kabul in 1868, whose Amir was easily responsive to British displeasure.[33] Dost Mohammad was succeeded by his son, Sher Ali Khan. Sher Ali Khan passed through many vicissitudes in rivalry with his brothers and nephews, and in 1867 his fortunes were so low that he held only Balkh and Herat. By the autumn of 1868, however, he was again established on the throne of Kabul and his competitors were beaten and dispersed.[34]

In 1868 itself Firoz Shah made his way to Swat and thence to Kabul.[35] In Swat Firoz Shah came into contact with the Wahabis in 1868. He remained sometime with the Wahabi community at Bajkatta,[36] and also used Wahabi messengers to send some letters via his brother (Mirza Izad Bakhash) in Delhi in the hope of persuading some "Rajas of the Deccan" to join him by the river Oxus in preparation for an attack on the British.[37] This conspiracy was brought to light in 1868 by the government enquiry into the Wahabi movement.[38] It shows that how optimist and persistent Firoz Shah was in his efforts to drive the British out of India.

In October 1868 Firoz Shah was ordered to leave Afganistan for Balochistan by way of Kandhar. The Political Superintendent, Frontier Upper Sindh spoke to the Khan of Kalat upon the subject, and expressed the hope that there will be no attempt to afford an asylum to Firoz Shah in Belochistan. The above officer presumed that Firoz Shah probably go to Sibi, and remain concealed there with Afghan connivance. He decided to convey the Khan of Kalat that if Firoz Shah is harboured in Balochistan, the Government of India would not be pleased. He also decided to ascertain about the presence of Firoz Shah at Sibi.[39]

The Government of India wrote to the Govt. of Bombay that Firoz Shah, on no account be allowed an asylum in Khelat or anywhere else on that frontier, and that 'all the influence of our political authorities should be exerted deprive him of the means of carrying on treason and of creating alarm and distrust within oujr own territories.'[40]

In October 1872 the British Ambassador at Constantinople reported Firoz Shah to be residing there.[41] While Firoz Shah was residing at Constantinople, the British Government did not consider it to be expedient to take any measures against him, unless it should appear that, whilst under the protection of the Porte (Sultan of Turkey), he has been engaged in any intrigues, hostile to the British Government in India.[42]

In Mecca and death

The British envoy to Yarkand informed the Government of India in his letter of 11th December 1873 that one Syed Yakoob Khan told him to have met Firoz Shah in Constantinople. Firoz Shah had some problem with his eyes and had a limping gait. Firoz Shah had requested the Syed to intercede for him with the Grand Vizier, who had stopped his allowance.[43]

It was commonly reported in Constantinople that Firoz Shah had left for Mecca with Mirza Mahomed Beg some months ago. The fact that he was still there was only known to the Hindustanis and to such of the Turks as were personally acquainted with him.

The reason assigned for his keeping himself concealed was that some months ago there was a report that two men, said to be Afghans, had been sent from India for the purpose of arresting or killing him. At this time Firoz Shah was a broken down looking man, blind or nearly so of one eye, and lame. He had visited almost every Mahomedan country, but had received no help or encouragement. On one occasion he had been imprisoned in Persia for six months as an impostor. Apparently he was not actively engaged in the Hindustani scheming which went on in Istambul, but he was kept informed of what went on. He received an allowance of 500 *piastres* a month from the Turkish Government. He lived in the house of his father-in-law, a Hindustani, who had been settled there for many years in the quarter, Jami Alli Badshah, Alli Manner.[44]

When Firoz Shah was in Mecca, he was found in the company of other distinguished Wahabi Ulema, for instance, Muhammed Ishaq. Haji Imdadullah etc., who had fled to Arabia after the collapse of the resistance movement.[45]

Firoz Shah was well known at Mecca as a member of the ex-Royal Family of Delhi and connected with the Mutiny. He arrived at Mecca during the month of June 1875 and remained in the city until his death which took place on the morning of the 17th December 1877. He was in a state of poverty and almost dependent on an allowance made to him by the High Sheriff of Mecca, he also at times received assistance from the Indian Sheikhs and people. The only relation he had left at Mecca was a wife to whom the Governor General of Hejaz had made an allowance of Rs. seven per month. It was also stated that Firoz Shah had left another wife and daughter in India.[46]

Pension to Firoz Shah's wife

Following the death of Firoz Shah, his wife Nawab Tooklakha Sultan Zamani Begum requested the Government from Mecca to grant to her a pension for maintenance. This request was declined in December 1878.[47] Probably the Begum pursued the matter with the British Government and in November 1881 sanction was accorded for the payment of Rs. 5/- P.M. to her as compassionate allowance. She was not to be allowed o return to Delhi.[48] This paltry pension continued till the matter was reconsidered in 1882 because the British Consul at Jeddah (Captain Moncrieff) felt that the grant of so small a pension as Rs. 5/- per month might give rise to unwelcome comment amongst the people at Mecca who might be against the British Govt. He suggested a pension of Rs. 30/- or Rs. 50/- per month or even Rs. 100/- per month. Lord Ripon, the Governor General of India, sanctioned on 31st March 1882 the payment of Rs. 100/- per month to the widow. The widow was not to be permitted to return to Delhi.[49] The payment of this pension was made to the Begum from 10th November 1881. The grant of the pension was meant for her only and was not to be treated hereditary.[50] What happened to the Begum after 1882 is not known.

Last days of his associates

Out of the principle associates of Shahzada Firoz Shah in his struggle we know the fate of Rani Laxmi Bai, Tatya Tope, Rao Saheb and Maulvi Ahmadulla Khan of Faizabad and Nawab Tafazzul Husain of Farrukhabad. The remaining principle insurgent leaders viz. Begum Hazrat Mahal of Lucknow, Khan Bahadur Khan of Bareilly and Rana Beni Madhav Singh of Shankarpur after being cornered to *tarai* area, crossed the boundary to Nepal and moved from place to place between Chitwan, Bhutawal and nayakot and suffered terrible privations. The Nepal Government of Jung Bahadur employed their troops for the capture and expulsion of their uninvited guests. It was in such an encounter that Rana Beni Madhav met with his death. Khan Bahadur Khan and Brigadier Jwala Prasad with others were delivered to the British authorities. The malaria of the tarai also claimed Bala Saheb and probably his brother Nana Saheb as well.[51]

Khan Bahadur Khan of Bareilly, was put on trial. In his defense he pleaded that had he been guilty he would not have surrendered. The evidence was strong against him and he was sentenced to be hanged. Begum Hazrat Mahal had taken shelter in Nepal. The British tried to induce her to come back to India by assuring her all honours befitting her rank and promising a suitable pension to her independently of the allowance which was being paid to her husband, the ex-Nawab Wajid Ali Shah, living in Calcutta. But she thought it dishonourable to accept these overtures. She preferred to spend her days in suffering in a foreign land than to accept a pension from the British, and thereby tacitly renounced the rights of her son to the Awadh kingdom.[52]

Firoz Shah's Perception of the Struggle

The question is as to how Firoz Shah visualized his struggle against the British. Unfortunately, we don't have letters of Firoz Shah which could throw light on his mind set regarding the great uprising. We can reach to some conclusion only on the basis of two proclamations issued by Firoz Shah one from Bareilly in Feb. 1858 and another from Azamgarh on 25th August 1858.

The salient feature of these proclamations was their acute anti-British character. He exhorted everybody to participate in some way or other in the struggle against the British. In his Feb. 1858 Proclamation he said that- 'all of us must conjointly exert ourselves for the protection of our lives, property and religion and to root out the English from the country . . .Those that are old should offer their prayers. The rich but old should assist our sacred warriors with money. Those in perfect health as well as young should attend in person.' He also circulated a list of the 'real intentions' of the British.

The preservation of religion also emerged as the dominant cry of the uprising. The struggle was seen as a war of religion. Firoz Shah told the people that 'Within the last few years the British commenced to oppress the people in India, under different pleas and continued to eradicate Hindooism and Mahomedanism and to make all the people embrace Christianity.'

His Azamgarh Proclamation analysed the grievances of different sections of the population – the rich, *zamindars*, merchants, public servants, sepoys, artisans, pundits, fakirs and other learned persons- and appeals to them to join the struggle. Deliberately the most sensitive issues, and those lying closest to the Indian heart were picked to rouse people and show that 'the real purpose of this war is to save religion', and to make 'every Hindoo and Mussulman to render assistance to the utmost'.[53]

In a different version[54] of the same proclamation Firoz Shah saw himself as God's servant and urged others to join him: 'Placing my trust in God; devoting myself solely to God's service; observing the precepts of religion; strengthening my determination . . . my sword taken in my hand, the sword of religious zeal, I arise in the name of God. We shall obtain victory through the grace of God, who promises victory to those who put their trust in him. Therefore again I urge you and urge you one and all, join me prompted solely by the desire of doing God's work.'

The other major theme of Firoz Shah's proclamation was about the British annexations. According to him they did not intend to leave a *biswa* of land with the Indian rulers.

Tribute

This is the poignant story of a valiant warrior who began his historic career at the young age of 22 and in three years he traversed a large territory fighting the British. He was a patriot of the highest order. Without resources or following, he raised a large army and bravely fought the British, suffering heavily for his country. He openly condemned the massacres of English women and children perpetrated at some places by furious sepoys, though he himself was relentless in vengeance against the ruling power. His own hands were never soiled by the blood of innocent victims. He fougt and killed combatants in open warfare.[55] In his proclamation of 17th February 1858, he declared, "The delay in defeating the English has been caused by people killing innocent children and women without any permission whatever from the leaders whose commands were not obeyed. Let us avoid such practices and then proclaim a sacred war.

Tarachand has aptly summarised the life and achievements of this son of the soil. "The royal house of Delhi gave to the cause a representative not unworthy of its noble traditions. Though young in age-for he was in his twenties when the revolt broke out- Prince Firoz Shah was a born leader of men. He raised the standard of independence at Mandsaur and kept the British troops engaged in Central India. Driven out he appeared in Uttar Pradesh and campaigned in Rohilkhand and Oudh. Defeated he joined his forces with those of Tatya Tope in Rajputana and battling against heavy odds and evading his pursuers, he escaped into the jungle of Sironj. The revolt had by now fizzled out and the proclamation of Queen Victoria promising amnesty to those who submitted, had been widely advertised. Although in dire circumstances, he refused to barter self-respect, personal liberty, or the claims of his house for a life in durance vile and humiliating. He had been an intrepid fighter, and his faith in the destiny of his country remained unshaken till the end. He died in exile."[56]

A remarkable thing which is seen in Firoz Shah was his speed and determination. At one time he is seen at a place and at another he is active in a place far off from the earlier scene. He was quick to change the area of operation according to the need of the hour. Distances and lack of resources hardly mattered to him. Earliest example is his dash from Mandsaur to Morar in August 1857. In early October 1857 he is seen at Farrukhabad and immediately after it he is seen fighting at Jeeran on 24th October 1857, a distance of about 330 miles from Farrukhabad. After the battle at Guradia (21-24 Nov. 1857) he fled to Jhalrapatan and from there he shot up to Farrukhabad within a few days at the end of December 1857. In early January 1858 he is in Bareilly and in the last week of that month he is in Rahatgarh to defy Hugh Rose and after the fall of Rahatgarh fort. His last long dash is from Kosana to Runija. He left Kosana on 10th February 1859 and covering a distance of about 350 miles he reaches Runija to proceed to other destinations. In this regard he is ahead of Tatya Tope, with whom he was closely associated for a considerable time.

Edward Thompson says "It was a great relief to many, even to his foes, that the British never captured this brave and skillful man. His horsemanship and his hairbreadth escapes became a legend."[57] P.J.O. Taylor says "his military daring, hair breadth escapes and skillful horsemanship were spoken of with admiration on both sides of the conflict."[58] Wazir Khan, a close associate of Firoz Shah, told in his deposition that Firoz Shah had invariably opposed to plundering during their wonderings, and had on several occasions severely punished his followers for committing excess.[59] As S. N. Sen puts it, "He was still in his twenties; a century earlier a young man of his personality and resourcefulness might have carved out a kingdom, a century later he might have risen to eminence as a popular leader, but he came an age too late and an age too early, and his adventures ended in failure and in a self-imposed exile."[60]

When the vengeance fever subsided, the Europeans began to draw distinctions between the insurgent leaders, and to admit, and even praise, the courage and steadfastness with which certain of them endured prolonged suffering. This change of feeling is very marked in the case of Prince Firoz Shah of Delhi and even Anglo-Indian journals (the Delhi Gazette, for instance) plead his cause, urging his reported intercession on behalf of the European ladies and children massacred at Delhi by the mutinous sepoys of the East India Company. Few persons, how, but would regret to hear that the prince had perished either by jungle fever or the hands of the executioner.[61]

His family

The details of Firoz Shah's family is found in the website of "Royal Arc". According to this Firoz Shah first married in 1853 and had a divorce in 1858. He remarried in 1874 at Mecca with Nawab Tukhlakha Sultan uz-Zamani Begam, (died at Bombay on 26th August 1893) daughter of Mirza Muhammad Alauddin. His second wife was Nawab Malika uz-Zamani alia Khayum Zimani and his third wife was Nawab Rahmat uz-Zamani (born at Bahlolia in 1848 and died there in 1889) whom he married in 1863,. She was the daughter of Meer bin Sayed Muhammad bin Allah Bakhsh Dhund of Bahlolia. Firoz Shah had three daughters by his first wife and one son by his second wife.

His son Mirza Habib ul-Mulk Kalau was *born* at Bahlolia in 1864 by Rahmat uz-Zamani). This son was married at Bahlolia in 1879 with Nawab Khair un-nisa Begum Sahiba (*b.* at Mansehra, Hazara, Punjab, 1868; *d.* at Bahlolia, 1899). Mirza Habib ul-Mulk Kalau died at Bahlolia in1893. One of Firoz Shah's daughters was Malika Begum Sahiba (*d/o* Tukhlakha Sultan Zamani Begum). She *died* young. His second daughter was Ruqiya Begum Sahiba (*d/o* Tukhlakha Sultan Zamani Begum). She also died young. His third daughter was Hajira Sultan Begum Sahiba [Bilqis uz-Zamani Begum Sahiba] who was born in 1854 in India (*d/o* the second wife). *She was married* at Delhi, on 15th September 1871 to Safdar Sultan Mirza (*b.* at Delhi, ca. 1854; *d.* there, 7th July 1874) son of Mirza Gauhar 'Ali, by his wife, Ruqiya Sultan Begum Sahiba, daughter of Shahzada Mirza Muhammad Mu'azzam Shah, Khurrum Bakht Bahadur, of Benares. She died after 1899 leaving behind two sons.[62]

Reference :

1. *Imperial Gazetteer of India,* Vol. V, 1908, p. 39
2. Extracts from Office Notes from the Assistant Secretary, Political and Secret Deptt., India Office, dated 24th May 1877, No. 568, F.S.U.P.,Vol. III, p. 661. In the light of these evidences, it is difficult to accept the view of Beale that Firoz Shah made his appearance in Sironj jungles in 1864. *An Oriental Biographical Dictionary,* 1996, p. 138.
3. Foreign Department, Political Consultations, no. 137 dt. 16-12-1861 Dispatch from Secy. of State, letter No. 137 dt. 16-12-1861, India Office – To H.E. the Right Hon'ble Governor General of India in Council (N.84).
4. Sen, op. cit., pp. 378-380
5. *Encyclopedia Britannica*, Vol. IV, 1966, p. 381.
   The Russian menace was of such a magnitude that in 1866 the Russians invaded the territory of Bukhara proper and crushingly defeated the *amir* 's forces and by the treaty of 1868 the *amir* of Bukhara became a vassal of Russia.
6. *Encyclopedia Britannica*, Vol. XVII, 1966, p. 683

7. Foreign Department Pol. A, Nov. 10, 1862, Letter from Tehran. addressed to Right Hon. the Earl of Elgin.
8. Foreign Department Pol. A., 22-31, June 1863, Letter from Tehran, January 9, 18C3.
9. Foreign Department, Pol. A., June 1863, no. 22/31. no. 24
10. Sen, op. cit., pp. 378-380
11. Foreign Deptt. Pol. A., 22/31, June 1863. Letter Tehran, dt. 16-2-1863.
12. Foreign Department. Pol. A, June 1863, Nos 22/31, Tehran March 25th 1863
13. Extracts from Office Notes from the Assistant Secretary, Political and Secret Deptt., India Office, dated 24th May 1877, No. 568. F.S.U.P. Vol. III, p. 661
14. Foreign Department, Political A, April 1863, no. 88-94, The statement of Sheikh Majood Lance Nayak of the 6th Regt. dt. 31-12-1862.
15. Foreign Deptt. Political A, April 1863, no. 88-94.
16. Foreign Department Pol. A, April 1863, no. 88-94, note dated 30-3-1863.
17. Foriegn Department Pol. A, March 1863 no. 232/233
18. Foreign Department Pol. A. 29-32, March 1864. Proceedings of the rebel Firoz Shah in Persia. No. 30. From RF Thompson to H.E. the Earl of Elgin and Kadina, dt. Tehran, the 29th April, 1863.
19. In the letter the date has wrongly been translated as 20th Rajab, San 1169. This must be Hijri 1279 (1863 AD).
20. Foreign Department Pol. A, 29-32, March 1864, A. Proceedings of the rebel Firoz Shah in Persia. No. 31, Translation of a letter of HE Maulana Goolam Alee. This date is erroneous.
21. Foreign Department Pol. A. March 1864 no. 29-32, Proceedings of the rebel Feroz Shah in Persia. N. 29 – From R.F. Thompson to H.E. the Earl of Elgin and Kidina, dt. Tehran, the 29th April, 1863.
22. Foreign Department Pol. A, May 1864, Nos. 136/46. No. 146. From Lt. EC Ross, Asstt. Pol. Agent Gwadur to S. Mansfield, Commissioner in Sind, dt. 12th April 1864.
23. Foreign Deptt. Pol. A, 1864, Nov, no. 39-48. No. 45. From Secy. to Govt. Punjab to the Secy, GOI, Foreign Deptt. submitting Letter from the British Moonshee at Cabul, dt. 26th Sept. 1864.
24. J.L. Lee, The 'Ancient Supremacy' Bukhara, Afghanistan and the Battle for Balkh 1731-1901, 1996, page 294, footnote 45. quoting a source of 19th June 1864.
25. Now in Uzbekistan.
26. Foreign Pol. A, 1864, Sept. 90-98. No. 96. From the Secy. to GOI, Foreign Deptt. with the Governor General, to the Secy. to Govt. of Punjab and its Dependencies-(No. 395, dt. Simla, the 19th Aug. 1864)
27. Foreign Department Pol. A, 27-29, November 1864, – From Cabul Diary – 3rd to 6th October, 1864 – last para.
28. T.W. Beale, *An Oriental Biographical Dictionary*, 1996, p. 138.
29. Now in Uzbekistan
30. Samarkand was occupied by the Russians in 1868. Wikipedia, consulted on 4-6-2010.

31. Foreign Secret Consultation, Sept. 1872, no. 45/46. Statement of Captain Grey's party, No. 4- List of Papers- No. 45. From Capt. Grey of 30th Aug. 1871, Para 38, p. 20.
32. Foreign Department Pol. A., no. 87-89, Nov. 1868. From the writer Mian Nowab Alee Khan, by the pen of Ghulam Hossain Khan, Karinga, inhabitant of Mohalla Kakra, Zila Shahjanpur, N. of letter 51.
Foreign Department Political Consultations, 87-89 November 1868, A. LN 413, dt. 13-10-1868 Letter to HH the Maharaja of Charkhari and Diwan Anna Saheb To H.H. Maharaja of Chirkhari and Deewan Anna Saheb
33. Sen, op. cit., pp. 378-380
34. *Imperial Gazetteer of India,* Vol. V. 1908, p. 39
35. Extracts from Office Notes from the Assistant Secretary, Political and Secret Deptt., India Office, dated 24th May 1877, No. 568 F.S.U.P. Vol. III, p. 662
36. Q. Ahmad, *The Wahabi Movement in India* (1966), p. 310
37. Ibid, p. 286 (letter 52, 13 Feb. 1869. Deptt. Inspect. Gen. Police to Inspector General).
38. Ibid, pp. 286 and 293.
39. Foreign Department, Pol. A, 140-47, January 1869. LN. 288 dt. 5-12-1868, Bombay Govt. to Government of India (Foreign Deptt.), enclosing No. 1391 dt. 13-11-1868, from Pol. Supdt., Frontier Upper Sind to Commissioner. Sind.
40. Foreign Department, Pol. A., 140-47, January 1869, letter no. 1506, dt. 19-12-1868 from Secretary to Government of India to Secretary to Government of Bombay.
41. Secret, December 1872, No 368. Extracts from office Notes from the Assistant Secretary, Political and Secret Department, India Office, dated 24th May 1877, No. 568, F.S.U.P., III, p. 662.
42. Foreign Department Secret Proceedings 1873, February 1873 Nos. 137/38. No. 138. Dated India Office, 8th January 1873, From- Under Secretary of State for India To- Under Secretary of State, Foreign Office.
43. Foreign Department Secret Consultation, 1874 Feb. No. 102/109. Confidential memo no. 109, dated Kashgar, 11th Dec. 1873. From Envoy to Yarkund, to the Secy to GOI, Foreign Deptt.
44. Foreign Deptt. Secret Proceedings, September 1875, Nos. 90/94. Note on certain Hindustanees residing in Constantinople. p. 93.
Also Foreign Department, Secret Proceedings., Nos. 5-10 & K.W., Sept., 1877.
45. K.M. Ashraf, Op. Cit., p. 97, fn 55.
46. Foreign Department Political Proceedings. B., January 1879, Cons. Nos. 39-42. F.S.U.P., III, pp. 670-71.
47. Foreign Department, Political Proceedings B, January 1879, Cons. Nos. 44-46.. F.S.U.P., III, p. 671.
48. Foreign Department Proceedings, Financial B, November 1881, Cons. Nos. 28-30. F.S.U.P., III, p. 671.

49. Foreign Department Proceedings, Financial B, April 1882, Cons. Nos. 32-33. F.S.U.P. Vol. III, p. 671
50. Foreign Department Proceedings, Financial B, June 1883, Cons. Nos. 122-123. F.S.U.P. Vol. III, p. 671.
51. S.N. Sen, op. cit., p. 170
52. Misra, Anand Swaroop, *Nana Saheb Peshwa*, 1961, pp. 503-505.
53. R. Mukherjee, *Awadh in Revolt 1857-58*. 2008, p. 150.
54. This version of the proclamation is in Abstract NWP. Narrative, Foreign, 1858: F.S.U.P., I, pp. 459-63.
55. Misra, Anand Swaroop, *Nana Saheb Peshwa*, 1961, p. 505.
56. Tara Chand, *History of Freedom Movement in India,* Vol. II, March 1992 reprint, p. 101.
57. Edward Thompson, *The other side of the Medal*, 1989, p. 57.
58. P.J.O. Taylor, *What really happened during the mutiny*, 1997, p. 8.
59. Wazir Khan's deposition, 3-3-59, Political Proceedings 30-12-1859, No. 311, letter no. 54, dt. 9-3-1859. For his deposition see appendix 1.
60. Sen, op. cit., p. 311
61. F.S.U.P. II, pp. 629
62. website: http/www.royalark.net/india4/delhi9.htm (website visited on 4th May 2012)

Appendix - 1
Depositions of Wazir Khan and Pir Zahoor Ali dated 3rd March 1859[1]

Depositions of Wazir Khan

Wazir Khan was formerly an Asstt. Surgeon of the Agra dispensary having been educated and received his diploma in Calcutta Medical College, early education at Delhi College, belongs to Firoz Shah party, left Oudh within about 3 months ago, and have since accompanied him, joining the Rao's force at Indurgarh.[2] The Rao Saheb and Feroz Shah, have however, left the camp at Paranja (?), previous to this starting for the British camp in hearing of the approach of another force from Augur.[3] Rao Saheb and Feroz Shah intended to march towards the N.E. considering that was the only safe way to retreat.

The question of surrender was first mooted when the rebels were in Bikaner territory, the Raja having sent one of his officers with a notification to the address of *Risaldars* and others of the Rao's force stating that a proclamation of pardon had been issued by the British Govt., and enclosing a copy. On the receipt of the same Firoz Shah and Rao Saheb appointed myself and 3 others to go to the Bikaner Officer not being changed with any guarantee for our safety we continued our fight towards the south hearing the approach of British force.

We discussed the matter of surrender again at Akola[4] in the middle of a forced march from Kankrauli[5] in Meywar to elude the pursuit of the another B.F. On that occasion it was determined to send into Neemuch to ascertain what terms would be granted and accordingly on passing the station in our flight two of our party were deputed on the mission. They fell into the hands of the police of Jeerun under the Neemuch Superintendency. The letter was written by myself answered by Capt. Dennega, Suptd. Neemuch and reached me after our crossing the Chambal.

When the Neemuch mutineers arrived at Agra, fought with the British troops. Wazir Khan was present in the city. The British troops retreated into the fort and the mutineers went over towards Muttra. He remained in the city till Sunday. He took flight to Muttra where he joined the Neemuch mutineers to Delhi.

On the reoccupation of Delhi by the BF, he left Delhi with the retreating rebels crossing the Jamuna at Mathura, they (rebels and Wazir Khan also) came to Bewar[6] where he was separated from the mutineers. He went to Farrukabad where he remained for about 2 months and met Firoz Shah who came there after his defeat at Agra in September (Sept. 1858).

3 days before retaking Farrukabad he left that place for Bareilly and Firoz Shah went away to Lucknow. Firoz Shah came to Bareilly where Wazir Khan met him again. After the battle of Bareilly, Wazir Khan left that place with Feroz Shah, went towards Bangarmhow. Feroz Shah remained there during the rains (rains of 1858) and returned back to Mohamdi since which time both are there.

Feroz Shah is a near relative of King of Delhi being either his grandson or nephew. About 2 years before the outbreak, he went on a pilgrimage to Mecca and on his return landed in Bombay when the rebellion was at its height. He was proceeding to his home at Delhi. When on reaching Dholpur enroute, and finding the road unsafe, he remained there for a few days, but on being informed by the Raja of Dholpur that his remaining there any longer might lead to his capture as being a relative of King of Delhi, he fled to Gwalior (*Morar ki Chhawni*), where the mutineers from Mhow had previously arrived. He accompanied them in their attack on Agra where by were defeated by the British troops. Firoz Shah then separated from the greater part of the Mhow–Indore mutineers and went into Mewat with about 10-12 followers and remained there for sometime. On arrival of the Jodhpur Legions in Mewat, he accompanied them to Farrukabad, remaining there for a short time with the intention of going towards Lucknow. When about to leave Farrukabad, the rebelled 41st NI prevented him from going and placed him at their head. On retaking of Farrukabad by the British Forces, Firoz Shah went to Lucknow where he remained till that place was reoccupied by the British. Leaving Lucknow, he went via Shahjehanpur to Bareilly. After a few days he left Bareilly with about 150 followers with the intention of going to Naseerabad. On evening of arriving at Moradabad enroute, a collusion with the Nawab of Rampur troops was forced upon him by their not permitting him to halt unmolested them during the night for rest as he wished. On that occasion in their narration, opening their guns on him Firoz Shah charging out the head of 150 horse captained them. 1600 guns routed the Nawab's troops. Moradabad fell into his hands. Thence he marched to Bareilly taking the captured Rampur's guns with him and remained at Bareilly till the place was retaken. On the approach of the British troops, Nana who had come to Bareilly a month before, and was Khan Bahadur Khan's guest, offered to march out and give battle to the British of Khan Bahadur would place his troops under his command. The Khan did so. Nana marched out at their head but instead of advancing to meet the British he tempered with the troops that had been enticed to him by promises of increased pay, caused him off into Oudh. The Nawab of Farrukabad and Naseerabad – Masum Alee Khan and other leaders who were at the time at Bareilly accompanied by Nana.

On reoccupation of Bareilly by the British troops; Feroz Shah, Khan Bahadur Khan, Ismail Khan and other leaders who had remained for its defense retreated to Mohamadi where was the

Maulana Ahmadoola Shah. From there Firoz Shah proceeded to Sundela, the police of which place fled on his approach. He stayed there during the rains, the whole distt. having fallen into his possession.

After the same he left Sundeela and went towards Mohamdi and had several encounters with the British troops, retreating there, arrived at Biswa Baree where another fight took place. Continuing his retreat he arrived at Mohemdabad from where he escaped the Ganges unopposed between Fatehgarh and Cawnpur with about 2,000 fighting men, 1500 were cavalry. When about to cross the Jamuna canal he came unexpectedly in contest with a British detachment. Firoz Shah was at the time siding with Wazir Khan, and about 50 *sawars* at a distance of about a mile on the flank of his main column. He thereupon rode to the main column to bring up his troops and returned with about 300 cavalry which alone he could collect at the moment. With these he determined to engage the detachment and formed his men in 3 divisions charging himself in front. Pir Zahoor Alee on the left, and the Wordy Major of the 12th Irregular cavalry Regt. on the right. He could not take the guns and retreated after a severe encounter to Tulfun – a British Officer was hurt in the fight and many rather on their side. On our side only one man by name Risaldar Niaz Mohd. Khan formerly *bafadar* on the 16th Irregular.

On reaching the Jamuna a little above the confluence of Chambal – the rear party on that occasion was surprised by a British detachment and a few cut up, proceeding south, then we were again surprised at Mrandi in the Gwalior Distt. by Napier – on that occasion Maulvi Fazal Haq and a good many men besides some being made prisoners among others Pir Zahoor Ali's brother who was riding on an elephant. We lost also 6 elephants, Wazir Khan had a narrow escape being in the same elephant with Maulvi Fazal Haq but not considering it safe I had dismounted.

From Marandi we continued our course on South to the Seronge Jungles where we met Nasar Mohd. Khan, thence west to Paron jungles passing through the Chuppra[7] Distt. and Nahargarh of Kota, at the latter place the Paron Raja Raujee met us and conducted us to his place in the heart of the jungle tract. Remaining two days at Paron we passed NW through the Kota territory getting into that of Jeypore via the Lakhera[8] pass, Indargarh[9].

Here we joined the Rao Saheb party – halting two days for his arrival, an information of his arrival communicated by Nawab Raheen Ulla Khan who had preceded the Rao. We all 3 marched together towards Jeypore diverted from that route by the advance of an British column, we went to Dausa, and were surprised the next morning by a British column. On that occasion the 12th Irregular Cavalry of Pir Zahur Ali were principally engaged both sides, lost several men, the sawars getting mixed up in the melee undistinguishable owing to the similarity of dress. A General on our side formerly a Subedar in the 9th Regt. by name Talyar Khan was badly wounded. He had fought all through the Delhi seize. He was afterwards killed in the surprise at Sikar.[10] Thereafter he proceeded from Dausa via Katpatee.

The Seekar affair might have been disastrous to our force but for the same covering parts of the 12th Irregular of Pirjee's and special for the presence of mind of a native officer of the 12th Irregular by name Amir Khan. Feigning the pressure of a considerable body under the command he gave word of command accordingly. The Officer commanding the advance party of the British halted and sent for guns. The delay administered of our people of getting off. But even in different direction, the Rao and Feroz Shah going towards Deedawana in Mewar, the covering party of 12th Irregular of Pirjee's whom I accompanied retreating to Laxmangarh[11] and Sikar we did not effect a function again for 2 or 3 days.

In the interval Tatya Tope was reported to have left the force at Deedawara, during the night with a few followers for what purpose was not given out.

From Deedwana[12] we went towards Beekaner when in that country the question of surrender was first moved and dropped as above mentioned.

On passing Haduo in Marwar the Thakur treated us ill in allowing his people for take money for individuals of the force for supplies and newer furnishing any. Further, in refusing the refund the money when applied to by the Rao to do so. For this reason the Rao ordered the place to be attacked. It was caused by storm, the Thakur with the survivors of storm driven within the keep and the village burnt.

In the Bikaner country 600 cavalry – the greater part of the 12th Irregular cavalry under J. Gurreef Khan broke off from our force. We don't know where they went.

Proceeding south through Mewar we were surprised again by another British column at a village with a tank a few miles from Bheelare.[13] It was fortunately in the evening and darkness, as we should have suffered a great loss. We escaped by dividing into several groups where all affected a junction the next day further to south.

To escape from the pursuit of the several British columns in the open country, the leaders decided to shape a course again for the strong country of C.I. To this end, we first attempted to pass the *ghats* eastward at Peepli but found it occupied by some local troops and were repulsed, we then tried another *ghat* some 6 or 7 Kos further south. It was reported to be closing, but the Rao gave the money to the villagers who brought the information to open it, which was done. It was very difficult for horses and camels about 8 miles ascent, branches of trees and straw which had been cleared away were found strewn at the intervals up the ascent.

On ascending to the plan of Meywar we marched straight to Kakrauli but gathering from a party of regular cavalry we surprised them that a British force was in the vicinity. We continued our fight after but 6 hours rest through we had come that day 18 Kos. It was after 30 miles further continuous flight to Akola that the question of surrender was again discussed, matters were henceforth to issue by learning that fresh British force (Bg. Sommerset) was in rapid pursuit of us and deputation was accordingly sent to Neemuch to sue for terms, the result of which has been above detailed.

Besides TT who reported to have gone at Deedwana and 600 cavalry in the Bikaner territory, Yusuf Khan, a General of the Rao Saheb left also in the Bikaner country with 50 men. Some *sawars* of the 5th Irregular detached themselves at Kankrauli. Abdul Sattar Khan of Jaora left the force between Sadree and Mandsore in the recent flight from Bg. Sommerset brought to retreat into the Banswara jungle saying as he left. Since you are going to surrender I will go and surrender through Myanna Nawab at Jaora – 14 or 15 men accompanied him. Chhota Tantiya (nephew of Tatya Tope) and Ghashani Lal Puree and lastly Pir Zahoor Alee with 300 men who have surrendered. Besides the above of note and good many have broken off signally or in small groups either beaten by the fatigue or hoping to find an asylum with friends en route.

At the time of discussion for surrender both the times, Wazir Khan was to the closest intimacy with the leaders and indeed was the medium of informing them of all concerning ourselves which appeared from time to time in English papers that found their way into our camp, the most reliable information we received of the movement of the several British columns in the field against us was from the papers and also regarding that of such of our leaders as got separated from us or were in rebellion in distant parts, thus we never enabled to effect a junction with the Rao and TT on leaving Oudh.

At first none of the leaders disposed to surrender as they were not aware of the safety of their lives, but in some of the English papers falling into my hands and on reading about the amnesty I opened the subject for surrender to Firoz Shah the only leader who know would take my advice. He willingly understood the proposal and discussed the matter with the Rao Saheb, when it was agreed that a copy of the amnesty should be procured and its contents well understood. We had no opportunity of getting one, however till we arrived in the Bikaner territory the question of surrender them mooted, was broken up as has been above related.

On the last occasion at Akola, Firoz Shah after getting all his officers to agree to the proposal of surrender sent Wazir Khan with the Darpan Gaure and Imam Alee, to speak to the Rao Saheb on the subject, the Rao after listening with earnest attention said that he could not be the first to open negotiations in the matter on account of his relations and head of his House, the Nana Rao not having made any offer of submission, but if we thought fit to open the correspondence he would have no objection to go as we did, if the terms granted were favourable, since he would then have alternative but to join us in submission. It was then agreed by all the Sardars to depute some persons with letters touching the question of surrender to the nearest station. On passing Neemuch then in our flights from the column closely pursuing us from Kankrauli, we deputed two of our party – viz. Surmat Khan and Abdul Raheem Khan to the station to seek for terms pursing our course, meanwhile across the Chambal, we had all determined to await the answer of our letters at Rooneeja[14], while en route thither, and before we crossed the Chambal the answers from Neemuch signed by Capt. Dennye reached us but did not convey the guarantee required by the leaders so we pursued the course as above related. Here Feroz Shah and Rao Saheb went off from Raoraja on learning of the approach of a column which might have cut off their retreat. I believe if they had received the guarantee of life conveyed in Gen. Michel's notification they would have come in. For the Shahzada Feroz Shah at last I an speak with confidence. He wept when he parted from me, and wished he could accompany me (Wazir Khan) with safety.

Firoz Shah's age is about 22. He is of a good disposition, he has always borne the character of Talib-ul-ilm, or a seeker of knowledge, has learnt Arabic and other general languages. He has invariably opposed to plundering during our recent wonderings, and has on several occasions severely punished his followers for committing excess.

The question of surrender by Tatya Tope was never mooted out up to the time that he was with the camp, but I should think he would never think of it unless his life was granted. Tatya Tope has much influence on Rao Saheb. He, it was who brought in the

Gwalior contingent mutineers to join the Nana Rao, up to which the Nana invested him with supreme command over that Division of force, not withstanding this Tatya Tope does not assume any degree of independence relatively to Rao Saheb but differ to his superior rank.

The Rao presented Nazar to Feroz Shah on the two forces uniting and presented all his *Sirdars* in farm who also presented Nazar. The Shahzada however, desired all of them on that occasion to retain entire central of their respective bodies of troops and never interfered with them.

I think all or most of the Mohamdans of the force besides his immediate followers which may amount now that Pirjee has come in to about 300. Some of the Hindoos leading men would also follow him if surrendering. Gauri Shanker, the Principal Military Officer of the Rao was particularly anxious to forward on the recent negotiations.

The treasure with the Rao Saheb is believed to be contained in gunny bags that are carried on 7 or 8 camels each rider by use of the Rao's own trustworthy followers (Marathas). They are escorted always by a body of 20 or 30 chosen vilayatees. However, besides the treasure supposed to be in 3 bags, the Rao carries a bag, of course white cloth constantly on his own horse and is never detached from his ride for a moment, and no one is allowed to touch it on the ground that it contained the Rao's food. It may be so from the tenacious anxiety however, with what this bag is shifted about with him in every change of place, convergence or position, it is possible it may contain jewels of value. This is the general supposition in the camp.

Rao has 5 or 6 horses to ride on, and changes them day about but his favourable and best is a dark gray Arab. At rest time, the Rao changes his dress generally adopting that of the country in which he may be moving and that of an ordinary description.

Rao's time of march changes frequently. No one but his immediate followers know where he may be riding. He is always on horse back.

The camp usually pay for the supplies wherever they are given willingly, but if it is sure to be plundered unless strong enough to resist attack. Again when villages are found deserted supplies are necessarily taken, and not paid for. This was most frequently the case within the Jodhpur territory.

Village area started from the *Ghat* was in Marwar at a distance of 7 has journey from the post of *Ghat*, it was about 9 Kos from Palee. The Rao gives Rs.500. We started from the village at 3 in the morning and reached the foot of the *Ghat* at 10 a.m. and do not get our half bathing place at the top till 6 in the evening.

The people in the country no where seemed very unfriendly but that may have been because we were strong enough to resent incivility. This source of strength and security is indeed the chief hand of union in the force. It is generally believed that if they break up all will perish, one race of people only, I heard, spoken of as unfriendly and that is the Bheels of the Meywar jungle tract. Some closed the passes against us as in the case of Marwar Pass above referred to. In the Jeypore territory we came upon 3 companies of Nyjeehe (?) marching to reinforce Kot Potlee.[15] We took them prisoners, but set them free after a day's detention. In the Jodhpur country, a party of Raj *sawars* followed up to cut of strugglers but we sent a party to attack and drive them off which they did, killing a few of the Raj sawars and taking some prisoners.

The revolt of the soldiery arose without any doubt from their belief that the Govt. desired to destroy their caste through the new cartridges. The musket for which the same are adopted are commonly called and distinguishes in the rebel camp to this day as *Bedharmi Bandook*.

When Feroz Shah joined the Rao Saheb at Indurgarh the former had between 1800 or 1900 Cavalry (Govt. mutineers) chiefly Irregulars and some 3 or 4 hundred of undisciplined horsemen.

The Rao had between 4 or 5 thousand chiefly Govt. mutineers of which there might be about 5 or 6 hundred infantry, between 2 or 3 hundred mutineers cavalry and the rest undisciplined horse. A good many of his men had been disposed in the jungles after their defeat at Burade (Bg. Sommerset) and have been separated from the main body ever since. On the occasion of his presenting the Nazar to the Shahzada, on presenting his officers of his force who also offered Nazar introduced them as belonging severally to his 3 divisions under the names of Bengal Haltha, the Maratha Hattha, the third .... At that time then the united rebel force must have been amounted to between 6 or 7,000 fighting men.

The 12th Irregular cavalry entirely was with Feroz Shah and the 5th Irregular entirely with the Rao, the rest were composed of soldiers single or as parties up to the strength of a troop from all the different regiments. These formed themselves into regiments of *Risaldar* under self elected commanders.

Orders were daily issued under the name of Rao. That for the march was ordinarily well observed at starting and indeed maintained throughout when in the proximity of a B.F. or in approaching towns where opposition was expected. Fitters were the column struggled along the road.

Bala Rao is the younger brother of Nana. He has been an active leader in the rebellion. He was commanding the mutineers at Cawanpore when the Gwalior contingent mutineers arrived, and was present in the attack on Cawnpore – garrison on that occasion.

Deposition of Pir Zahoor Ali

Exracts from Translation of the Deposition of Pir Zuhoor Ali (Pir Zahur Ali) late of the 14th Bengal Irregular Cavalry taken on the 4th March 1859.[16]

. . . A portion of the Infantry and Cavalry with 2 guns went towards Malagurh which they reached in 3 marches. On hearing that the British troops had arrived at Golowlee[17] we got ready and went there with two guns. n the evening on arrival at Golowlee and encamping, a short was suddenly fired on our Camp by the British upon which we all got under arms and opened our guns. After 5 or 6 rounds the British force retreated and we remained in our position the whole night. Marching the following morning we arrived at (a) village name unknown. Here the Nawab of Malagurh ordered us to destroy those *zemindars* who would not pay money. The cannonading lasted till late in the evening but not being able to effect a breach in the wall we returned back to Malagurh. On hearing that the British troops had arrived at Bolundshuhur the Nawab of Malagurh marched with his troops and we followed him the same evening; at 9 P.M. our force reached Bolundshuhur and advancing further from the city we threw up a breastwork and stood to our arms the whole night. The following morning our videttes informed us that the British had come. They opened fire on us, we returned it. The fight lasted for 3 hours. Cavalry from both sides then charged on each other and fought hand to hand and we took flight leaving one of our guns the carriage of which was broken and carrying away the rest of them.

Encounter at Kasganj

A portion of our force reached Malagurh and the rest scattered and got separated as well as the Nawab. Marching (p. 123) from Malagurh and descending the Unoopsuhur (Anupshahr) Ghat we reached Bareilly taking some reinforcement from that place with the intention of going back to Malagurh; and crossing the Ganges we me and fought with the British at Kasgunge (Kasganj). The latter retreated to a place 4 *koss* off and we remained at Kasgunge for 18 days. On hearing that the British were coming on with more troops we advanced o meet them with 3 guns and an action took place. We were defeated and fled leaving 3 guns in the field. We arrived at Kangeerree[18] where we were joined by some force of the Nawab of Faurruckabad. We remained with them for a day. The next day a British force reached that place and another fight took place on which occasion we were again defeated and fled leaving 18 guns in the field. Some went to Lucknow some to Bareilly and the rest in different directions. . . .[19]

Encounter near Etawa on the Yamuna Canal

. . . Joining Firoz Shah and the 12th Irregular Cavalry, at Mahmoodabad, we turned toward this side (south). When crossing the Ganges we met with some British Cavalry one of whom was killed and the rest retreated. On reaching the Jumna Canal we were engaged with the British force which was there with Mr Hume the Collector of Etawah on which occasion Lietenant Cuyle and some sowars were killed and Mr. Hume with the Infantry and guns retreated into a *Ghurrie* (*Garhi*). We continued our march and arrived at Joffaon.[20] Crossing the Jumna we halted on the other bank. The following morning we were surprised there by a British force. Retreating and crossing the Chumbul we passed between Jhansee and Dutteea (Datia) and went towards the Bujrungurh Jungles. At Narode[21] *en route* we met with a British force where we lost some elephants and other property. It was at this place we missed Moulvie Fuzzul Haq; whether he was taken prisoner or killed is not known. While marching we plundered some stores of the British en route. The following day when encamped in the dense jungle we were surprised by British troops where we lost 3 elephants and other property. Proceeding on westward we crossed the Chumbul and reached Indurgurh. Here we expected Rao Sahib and halted two days for him when he joined us. We then marched all together towards Jeypore at Daussa. When about to march in the morning we were surprised by a British force; retreating we arrived at Seekree and were surprised there again. We then took our course towards Beekaneer in which territory we received a *Hookumnama* from the Rajah to the effect that an amnesty was granted and notifications had been issued by the British Govt. on the subject. On receiving this paper all the leaders agreed among themselves and deputed Mohamed Vuzeer Khan, Surmust Khan, Gowree Sunker and Deisai Gungadhur Puth[22] to Beekaneer with letter from Rao Sahib and Feroze Shah, but the *ressaldar* of Beekaneer somehow or other sent the deputation back.

We then took our course towards the south. Two days after, the 12th Irregular Cavalry got separated from us and returned and we continued our march. Arriving at a village we were again surprised by the British troops. From thence we went to Peepleea *Ghata* but the Bheels there would not allow us to pass. Turning to another *Ghata* or 7 *koss* (from) Peepleea which was closed and known to us we opened it and got through with great difficulty one by one. From thence we passed Kunkrolwee and Akola and halted two *koss* from the latter place. Here we discussed the question of surrender and deputed two *Vakeels* to Neemuch. On passing near that station in our flight reaching Roaneeja we received a notification from Captain Showers but hearing that a British force was advancing from the Augur direction, though Rao Sahib and Ferozeshah went away, myself and followers remained back to await the arrival of he *Vakeels*. On their return with a guarantee of safe conduct from General Michel we left for the British camp at Boorha and surrendered ourselves there.[23]

Reference :

1. Foreign Department, Political Proceedings, 30-12-1859, No. 311, letter no. 54, dt. 9-3-1859.
2. *Seventy kilometers north-west of Kota, Rajasthan.*
3. This is Agar, 65 kilometers north-east of Ujjain, M.P.
4. Forth five kilometers south-west of Chhittorgarh and twenty kilometers east of Mawali, Rajasthan.
5. Sixty kilometers north of Udaipur, Rajasthan.
6. Thirty kilometers south-west of Farrukhabad, UP.
7. Chuppra may be Shivpuri, which was then called Seepri.
8. Lakheri is 10 kilometers south of Indergarh in Rajasthan.
9. Indargarh is seventy kilometers north-east of Kota, Rajasthan.
10. One hundred fifty kilometer north-west of Jaipur, Rajasthan.
11. Twenty kilometers north-west of Sikar, Rajasthan.
12. One hundred fifty kilometers north-west of Jaipur.
13. May be Bhilwara, Rajasthan.
14. Sixty kilometers east of Mandsaur, M.P.
15. Hundred kilometers north of Jaipur.
16. F. S. U. P., Vol. V, pp. 122-124.
17. Appears spelt for Gulaothi
18. Appears spelt for Gangaji.
19. The account given here deals with the battle at Musabagh, Lucknow, under the leadership of Ahmad Ullah Shah, the encountr at Bari—13 kos from Lucknow and revolutionaries' march to Muhamdi and Shahjahanpur, encountr

with British forces at Shahjahanpur and fight of the revolutionaries from that place.

20. May be Jalaun
21. Appears misspelt for Nagode.
22. Appears to have been misspelt for 'Punth' (Panth).
23. Foreign Department, Political Proceedings, 30th Dec. 1859, Part II, No. 313, pp. 4 to 6.

Appendix - 2

Depositions of Tantia Tope

at Camp Mushairi, 10th April 1859, in presence of Major Meade, Commanding Field Force.[1]

My name is Tantia topi; my father's name is Pandurang inhabitant of Jola *Pargana* Patoda *Zilla* Myeir.[2] I am a resident of Bithur. I am about forty-five years of age, in the service of Nana Sahib, in the grade of companion or *aide-de-camp*.

In the month of May, 1857, the Collector of Cawnpore sent a note to the Nana Sahib at Bithur, asking him to forward his wife and children to England. The Nana consented to do so, and four days later the Collector wrote to him to bring his troops in from Bithur. I went with the Nana and about one hundred sepoys and three hundred matchlockmen and two guns to the Collector's house at Cawnpore. The Collector was then in the entrenchment and not in his house. He sent us word to remain, and we stopped for the night at his house. The collector came in the morning and told the Nana to occupy his own house which was in Cawnpore. We remained there four days, and the gentleman said it was fortunate we had come to his aid, as the sepoys were disobedient and that he would apply to the General on our behalf. The General wrote to Agra, whence word came that arrangements would be made for the pay of our men. Two days afterwards the three regiments of Infantry and the 2nd Light Cavalry surrounded us and imprisoned the Nana and myself in the Treasury, and plundered the Magazine and Treasury of everything they contained, leaving nothing in either. The sepoys made over two lakhs and eleven thousand rupees to the Nana, keeping their own sentries over it. The Nana was also under charge of these sentries and the sepoys who were with us joined the rebels. After this the whole army marched from that place, and the rebels took the Nana Sahib and myself and all our attendants with them, and said, "Come to Delhi". Having gone six miles from Cawnpore, the Nana Sahib said that as the day was far spent, it was better to halt and march next day, they agreed and halted. In the morning the whole army told the Nana to go with them towards Delhi. He refused, and they then said "Come with us to Cawnpore, and fight there". The Nana objected to this, but they would not listen to him, and so, taking him as a prisoner, they marched towards Cawnpore, and began to fight there. The fighting continued for twenty-four days, and on the twenty-fourth day the General raised the flag of peace, and the fighting ceased. The Nana got a female who had been captured before, to write a note to General Wheeler, that the sepoys would not obey his orders, and that if he wished he would get boats and convey him and those with him in the entrenchment as far as Allahabad. An answer came from the General that he approved of this arrangement, and the same evening the General sent the Nana something over one lakh of rupees, and authorised him to keep the amount. The following day I went and got ready forty boats, and having caused all the gentlemen, ladies, and children to get into the boats, I started them off to Allahabad. In the meantime the whole army, Artillery included, having got ready, arrived at the river Ganges. The sepoys jumped into the water and commenced a massacre of all the men, women, and children, and set the boats on fire. They destroyed thirt-nine boats. One, however, escaped as far as Kala Kankar, but was there caught and brought back to Cawnpore, and all on board of it destroyed. Four days after this the Nana said he was going to Bithur to keep the anniversary of his mother's death; the sepoys allowed him to go, some of them accompanying him. Having kept the anniversary, they brought him back to Cawnpore, and took for their pay and money they had first made over to the Nana's charge, and made arrangements to fight against Hasan Fatehpur, where they heard some Europeans had arrived from Allahabad, and they told the Nana to accompany them. The Nana refused. The Nana and I remained at Cawnpore, and sent Jawala Persad, the Nana's Agent with them to Fatehpur. Being defeated there, they retreated to Cawnpore and the European force pressed them the whole way to Cawnpore, when there was a battle for about two hours, and the rebel army was again defeated, and ran away from Cawnpore. Under these circumstances the Nana and I fled to Bithur, arriving there at midnight, and the rebel army followed us. Next morning the Nana, taking some money with him, sent to Fatehpur. The rebel army followed and looted the place. The Nana, Bala Sahib, Rao Sahib and I, with all our wives, crossed the Ganges in boats, and arrived at Fatehpur in the Lucknow territory and put up with Choudhri Bhopal Singh. Some days passed, when the 42nd Native Infantry arrived at Sheorajpur, and wrote to the Nana to send three some one to take them to him.

I went and told them that the Nana had sent for them. In the meantime the English army had arrived, and the 42nd went to Bithur and fought there. I accompanied them, and having been defeated we fled, crossed the Ganges, and came to the Nana. Some days later I received orders from the Nana to go to Gwalior, and bring back to fight the English such of the Contingent as were at Morar. I went to Morar, and brought back the Contingent to Kalpi. The Nana had sent his brother, the Bala Sahib, to Kalpi, and according to his order I went with the army to fight against Cawnpore, leaving a small force and Magazine at Kalpi. At Cawnpore there was a battle which lasted eleven days, when the rebel army was defeated, and we all ran away. Next day we fought at Sheorajpur, and, having been defeated, we ran away, taking fifteen guns with us. I and the Bala Sahib and the Rao Sahib, who had been sent by the Nana to Cawnpore crossed the Ganges at Nana Mau-Ki-Ghat. We remained at Khera for the night. I got orders from the Rao Sahib to go and take charge of the small force and Magazine left at Kalpi, in obedience to which I went there. After my arrival at Kalpi I received orders from the Nana to go and attack Charkhari, and that the Rao Sahib would be sent after me. I accordingly went to Charkhari with 900 sepoys, 200 Cavalry, and 4 guns, and fighting began. Four days afterwards the Rao Sahib came to Kalpi. I fought at Charkhari for eleven days, and took it. I took 24 guns and three lakhs of rupees from the Raja. the Rajas of Banpur and Shahgarh and Divan Deshpat and Daulat Singh, the Kuchwaya Kharwala, and a great gathering of people joined me there at this time. I received a note from the Rani of Jhansi to the effect that she was waging war with the Europeans, and begging me to come to her aid. I reported this to the Rao Sahib at Kalpi. The Rao came to Jaipur and gave me permission to go to the assistance of the Rani. Accordingly I went to Jhansi and halted at Barwa Sagar. There Raja Man Singh came and joined me. The next day about a mile from Jhansi our army had a fight with the English army. At this time we had 22,000 men and 28 guns. In this battle we were defeated. Part of the rebel army with 4 or 5 guns fled to Kalpi, and I went to the same place by way of Bahder and Kunch, with 200 sepoys. The Rani arrived at Kalpi the same evening as myself, and begged the Rao Sahib to give her an army that she might go and fight. The following morning the Rao Sahib ordered a parade of all the troops, and told me to accompany the Rani to battle. Accordingly I accompanied her with an army, and there was a battle at Kunch which lasted until (sic, till) noon. We were again defeated, and I fled to Chirki, which is about four miles from Jalaun, where my people were. The Rao had a battle afterwards at Kalpi, and was defeated and he and his whole army arrived at Gopalpur; we all marched thence towards Gwalior. We had one day's fight with Maharaja Sindhia and defeated him. Three days afterwards all Sindhia's army joined the Rao Sahib, and having procured from the Gwalior Treasury through Amar Chand Batia, the Treasurer, sufficient funds, pay was distributed to the army. Ram Rao Govind was also with us. Some days after the English army arrived at Gwalior from Kalpi, and a force also came from Sirpur. (Sipri or

Sheopur). Fighting again took placed and continued for four or five days, during which the Rani of Jhansi was killed. Ram Rao Govind had her corpse burnt and we were all defeated and fled, taking 25 guns with us. We reached Jaora-Alipur, and remained there during the night. Next morning we were attacked, and fought for an hour and half. We fired five shots, the English army fired four shots , and we then ran off, leaving all our guns. We crossed the Chambal and reached Tonk. The Nawab of Tonk fought with us, and we took four guns from him. With these guns we proceeded to Bhilwara by way of Madhopur and Indargarh. We were there attacked by the English force, and I fled during the night, accompanied by my army and guns. At that time I had 8,000 or 9,000 men and 4 guns. We halted a night at Kotra, four miles from Nathdwara. Next morning we marched towards Patan, and, after proceeding about a mile, the English army arrived. We left our guns and fled, reaching Patan as fugitives. The Nawab of Banda, who had come with us from Kalpi, and the Nawab of Kumona, who had joined us at Indurkhi, were both with us. On our arrival at Patan we conquered the Raja, got possession of his guns and magazines, and surrounded the palace. Next day I told the Raja to give me some money to pay the expenses of my army. He said he could give me only five lakhs of rupees. I returned and told the Rao Sahib this. Next day the Rao Sahib sent for the Raja and demanded 25 lakhs. The Raja declared that he could not give more than five lakhs; but after some discussion it was settled that he should pay fifteen. The Raja said he would go to his place and send this sum. He went accordingly, and sent two and quarter lakhs in cash, and promised that the rest should follow. By next day he had paid up five lakhs.

Emam Ali, Woordie Major (Wardi Major), 5th irregular Cavalry, ill-treated the Raja, who fled during the night. We remained there five days, and issued three months' pay to our troops at the monthly rate of thirty five rupees to each sowar and twelve rupees to each foot-soldier. We then marched for Sironj, taking eighteen guns with us. On reaching Rajgarh the English army came up and attacked us. We left our guns and fled, reaching Sironj by way of Nija Kila. We halted at Sironj ght days, and proceeded thence to Isagarh. On arrival we demanded supplies, but the people would not give them. We, therefore, attacked and plundered the place. We halted the following day, and the Rao Sahib told me to go to Chanderi while he went found by Talbahat. I accordingly went to Chanderi and the Rao Sahib to Lalitpur. On reaching Chanderi, four shots were first fired on us from the fort, which we attacked and fought with Sindhia's Agent. After three days we marched from Chanderi towards Mangraoli, taking eleven guns, seven of which we got from Isagarh and four from Sironj. On our march to Mangraoli we met the English army. Shots were fired for a short time, when we left all our guns and fled.

I reached Jakhlaun, and next day went to Sultanpur, where the Rao Sahib also arrived. After three days the English force arrived, and the Rao Sahib took his army to Jakhlaun, and some firing took place there. I was not present in this fight. The Rao Sahib returned to Lalitpur, and the following day proceeded to Kajuria and halted there. Next day the English army came up just as we were going to march, and an action began which lasted an hour and a half. We then left all our guns and fled, and reached Talbahat. We halted there, and the following day went to Jakhlaun, and then to Etawah (Itawa), 12 miles distant, where we stopped. We there heard that the English army was coming to surround us, and marched at night. The English force came up in the morning, and our army became separated. I accompanied the Rao Sahib, and we proceeded *via* Rajgath, and crossed the Narbada and got to Khargon Bustee *via* Kundula. The troops who were with us burned the Government *Thana* (station) and Bungalow at Kandula. The Rao Sahib forbade their doing so, but they would not obey him. This was about four months ago. At Khargon Bustee there were some of Holkar's troops one hundred and forty troopers, a Company of Infantry, and two guns. These we forced to join us and took with us the following day when we marched towards Gujrat, crossing the high road where the telegraph wire ran. The sepoys broke the wire and plundered seven Hackeries (carts) which were on the road proceeding with Government property towards Gwalior, and seized the *Chaprasis* and *Chaukidars* who were with the Hackeries, and took them with them. Some of the *Chaukidars* were hanged by them. We there left the high road and proceeded westward. Next day we were surprised by the English force, and leaving our two guns we fled and reached the Narbada. An officer with a hundred men was on the opposite bank. Our force began to cross and the officer and troopers ran off. We plundered the village of Chilka, and marched thence at midnight. After proceeding 34 miles we halted at Rajpur. Next day we took 3,900 rupees and three horses from the Raja of that place, and went on to Chota Udepur. The following day the English force surprised us, some them were killed and some of ours. From Chota udepur we went to Deogarh Bari, and our army became separated. There was jungle at that place, and I halted there two days. Our troops having been assembled again, we went to Banswara. There our men plundered sixteen or seventeen camel loads of cloth belonging to a merchant. We went thence to Salombar, and I caled on Kaisar Singh, Agent to the Udeipur Raja, to furnish us with supplies. He sent us some and we started the following day with the intention of going to Udepur. However, on the way we received news of the English force, and retraced our steps to Bhilwara. We remained there two days and then proceeded to Partabgarh were we fought for two hours with a body of English troops from Neemuch. About 8 o'clock in the evening we ran off, and halted six miles east of Mandisore. We then went by three stages to Zirapur. An English force surprised us there, and we were again surprised by another force at Chapra Baraud. We fled thence to Nahargarh, at which place nine shots were fired at us from guns. We moved out of range, and halted for the night, and the Rao Sahib sent Risaldar Nanu Khan to call Raja Man Singh. The Raja came and accompanied us to a place about two miles from Paron, where we halted. We remained there two days and on the third went on to a place about 8 miles beyond Kilwari. Raja Man Singh accompanied us as far as a river which we crossed on the way, and then left us. We made two stages thence to Indargarh, where Firoz Shah met us with the Bodyguard and 12th Irrregulars. Next day we made two stages to Dausa. The English force surprised us there; some men on both sides were killed, and flying thence towards Marwar we reached a village about sixty miles from Marwar, whose name I forget. At 4 o'clock that night we were surprised by the English force, and the 12th Irregular Cavalry separated from the Rao Sahib's army. Next day Thakur Narayan Singh, Ajit Singh, uncle of Raja Man Singh and thakur Ganga Singh joined us. They were coming in this direction. I had been quarrelling with the Rao Sahib all the way from Deogarh Bari, and told him I could flee no longer, and that I should leave him on the first opportunity. The opportunity occurred here, and I left him and accompanied the above-named parties in this direction. When I left the Rao Sahib he had about six thousand men with him. I was accompanied by three men, two to cook my food and one groom, three horses and a pony. The two Pandits were Ram Rao and Narayan. Gobind left me and ran off after coming two stages. We reached the Paron jungle, and met Raja Man Singh. Ajit Singh took leave of Raja Man Singh and sent home. Narayan Singh and I remained with Raja Man Singh. The Raja said, "Why did you leave your force? You have not acted rightly in so doing". I replied that I was tired of running away, and would remain with him whether I had gone right or wrong. I heard after this that the Rao Sahib's army had gone to Patan and thence towards Sironj. I told Raja Man Singh I would send a man to obtain news of them, and he approved of my doing so. I sent accordingly, and got information that the Rao Sahib was not there, but Emam Ali, Woordie Major, Feroz Shah, and Adil Muhammad, Nawab of Ambapani, were there with eight or nine thousand men. Emam Ali, Woordie Major of the 5th Irregular Cavalry wrote to me to come and join them. I had lost my master's (the nana's) seal, and had another made up at Paron.

When I heard as above from the Woordie-Major, I sent a man to Raja Man Singh, who was at Mahudia in Major Meade's Camp, to inform him that I had received a not of this purport, and to ask him if I should go or remain. Raja Man Singh had consulted me before giving himself up to Major Meade, and had left one of his men with me, saying "Stop wherever this man takes you". Raja Man Singh replied to my message that he would come in three days to see me and we should then decide what to do.

He came accordingly on the night of the third day, and spoke a great deal to me, and told me that he had met Major Meade and that his disposition was good. When I asked him what he advised—whether I should go or remain—he said he would reply in the morning. I then went to sleep, and during the night some of the sepoys of the Government came and seized me and took me to Major Mead's Camp.

(*Signed by Tantia Topi*)

Question—By Major Meade:- Have you made this statement of your own free will and without compulsion? and has any promise been made or hope held out to you to induce you to make it?

Answer—I have of my own free will caused this statement to be written, and no one has forced me, or held out hope or promise of any sort to induce me to do so.

Signed by Tantia Topi, Agent of Nana Sahib, and two witnesses.

The above deposition or statement was made by the prisoner Tantia Topi in my presence on the 10th of April, 1859, at Camp Mushairi, of his own voluntary act and without compulsion of any sort, or promise made or hope held out to him as inducement to make it.

(Sd). R.J. Meade, Major,
Commanding Field Force

Reference :

1. *Military Department Proceedings- No. 5 of 1859. Consultation 2nd Sept. No. 144. National Archives, New Delhi. FSUP, Vol. III, pp 582-590.*
2. It may have been spelt for *Maihar*.

Appendix - 3

Pandurang Rao's (Rao Saheb) deposition

in the Court of the Magistrate, Kanpur, Dated July 4, 1862[1]

My father's name is Sada Sewak, Deccani Brahan by caste. My age is 35 years. My profession is Riyasat (Ruling class) and my residence is Bithoor.

Question : You have been charged with the crime of being a leader of the rebels of 1857 and for having fought against the government as the leader of the rebel troops. What have you to say to this?

Answer : I was neither a rebel nor a leader of the rebels and never fought against the Government. The real state of affairs is this:- During the Mutiny of 1857, I was working at Bithoor. Nana left me at Bithoor with the instructions, "If a critical moment overtakes, you will shift away with ladies and children to any place you choose, at the time I send a message to you". My name, at first, was Sita Ram but Baji Rao adopted me as his son and changed my name as Pandurang Rao. The servants and other people called me 'Rao Saheb'. When he adopted me, I received at first no allowance but I was being brought up like real sons. At Baji Rao's death Nana became the head of the family and he treated me as before. He let my boarding and lodging arrangements remain as before, but allowed Rs. 200/- p.m. extra for my monthly expenses.

Still he granted me no allowance (salary). During the Mutiny, I continued to receive these Rs. 200/- p.m. When Nana Rao and Bala Rao had fled from Kanpur to Bithoor, Bala Rao had a bullet wound. Nana, accompanied by all the ladies and myself, went to Patkapur and there we crossed the river by small boats. We stayed on the other side of the river in a court-yard built by the Nana. The next day, Jess Singh and Bhopal Singh heard about us and reached there, took us to Fatehpur Chaurasi and kept us in Bhopal Singh's house. Some days after, elephants and vehicles were sent by the Begam from Lucknow, and they took all of us there. (Then the deponent amended his statement and said that): Nana sent only the ladies to Lucknow and Tatya Tope, Nana, Bala Rao and myself remained at Fatehpur Chaurasi. After this Bala Rao went to Delhi, Nana to Lucknow and Tatya to Morar. But I stayed at Fatehpur Chaurasi. Then Bala Rao fled from Delhi and reached Fatehpur and *nana also sent the ladies back from Lucknow to Fatehpur. Nana stayed at Lucknow and afterwards himself came back to Fatehpur after some days.* Tatya Tope brought the army frfom Morar and came upon Kalpi. Bala Rao left Fatehpur and reached Tatya Tope at Kalpi.

Sheorajpur and Bilhore are in the Dewar territory. At the same time Jwala Prasad, the *Karinda* of Nana Saheb came to realise the dues. He made his entrenchments somewhere in the *Ilaqa* of Sheorajpur or Bilhore. When Tatya Tope and Bala Rao crossed at Kalpi and came chose to Akbarpur, they called Jwala Prasad to themselves and Nana sent me for realisation of dues to Sheorajpur and Bilhore, in *Pargana* Dewar. He also sent (a) Company of troops (Johnstone's) with me for my protection.

Question : If you were appointed to realise dues from Parganas Sheorajpur and Bilhore, Dewar, why were these men posted for your protection?

Answer : Nana feared that I, the deponent, might slip away to some place in *Rajwarah* and therefore he posted the Company of troops.

Question : Were these men under you or not?

Answer : They were under me but they did not leave me nd did not go to distant places even if I ordered. I was close to Garhi which is near Sheorajpur, when at dawn I received a *Parwanah* of call from Bala Rao. I left the place and saw Bala Rao the same evening at bridge on the Bhawanti. Then I remained with him till he fled from Kanpur. Both of us crossed the Ganges at Birwa *Ghat*. The same day Bala Rao joined Nana, and I stayed at Naubat Ganj and Jwala Prasad and Tantya Tope were with me. Tatya Tope crossed on this side and went to Kalpi and Jwala Prasad took me to Nana at Aura Maoo.

Question : Jwala Prasad was simply a sowar or horseman in the army who used to move about among the clerks of the Thana and Hahsildari. How was it that he got the honour of bringing a person like to you to Nana?

Answer : In the days of my grand-father, Jwala Prasad was simply a soldier drawing Rs. 6/-. Nana made Jwala Prasad a *Risaldar* after Peshwa's death. During the rebellion Tatya Tope and Bala Rao were masters of the entire army and so was Jwala Prasad. His influence was over-weaning and even if I had objected, nobody was prepared to pay and heed. Jwala Prasad and myself came to Nana at Aura Maoo. The same day Bala Rao, after the finalization of all things accompanied the ladies from Aura Maoo to *Mauza* Birwa thora. He took all the property with himself. Nana took me to Bhagwat Nagar with the intention of going to Kalpi. There we stayed in the country-side bordering the Ganges with the intention of crossing the river. During this period Nana received a letter from Tatya Tope asking him (Nana) to reach at once, and another from the ladies complaining that they had been put to much trouble by Bala Rao. Nana instantly sent Gauri Shankar, a high Military Officer, who had taken flight from Delhi, with 400 Horsemen and Foot-soldiers with me to Tatya Tope.

Question : Why did Nana send you to Tatya Tope?

Answer : I do not know. He simply ordered me to report myself to Tatya Tope at Kalpi. I reached Kalpi and stayed there for about 3 months.

Question : What announcement was made at Kalpi when you reached there?

Answer : When I reached Kalpi nothing about my arrival was announced.

Question : Was a mendicant hanged at Kalpi?

Answer : I do not know.

Question : What was the strength of the army when you reached Kalpi and what strength was retained there for 3 months?

Answer : There was a large army of about 2,000 or 3,000 but I do not know the exact strength.

Question : To which Paltan did this belong?

Answer : It belonged to *Paltan* Morar and *Paltan* Gayatri and to one more Paltan the name of which is not known to me. When Nawab Banda fled and stayed at Kalpi, he had one *Risala* and two or three hundred *Tilangas.*

Question : Was someone, suspected of spying, killed at Kalpi?

Answer : At Kalpi all those, who were killed, were put to death at the hands of one Chatta Singh, an officer of Morar army, and by the order of Tatya Tope. When the fighting at Jhansi took place, Tatya Tope went there to help the Rani. He went via Charkhari while I stayed at Kalpi. *Tatya tope was defeated by the English army at Jhansi and there from came back to Kalpi.* The mother of the Nawab of Banda wrote a letter inviting me to Banda. With Tatya Tope's permission I left for Banda and had gone a *kos* from Kalpi when I met Nawab Banda and his mother who, I learnt, had fled from Banda.

Question : You have just said that you were entrusted with no duties at Kalpi. Why did the mother of the Nawab of Banda call you in case you held no office?

Answer : Nawab Banda was my kinsman and his mother for many years had cherished the desire of meeting all the members of my family; because I was near at Kalpi, she called me. Then the Nawab of Banda stayed at this place for 3 or 4 days and, after this, sent all the members of his family to Kalpi. I stayed there with the Nawab and after eight days I reached Kalpi with the Nawab. After this Tatya tope marched again and faced the English army. He was defeated at Koonch and came flying to us. Seven or eight days after the English army came to Kalpi, and from there Tatya Tope, Nawab of Banda and myself went to Gwalior side and stayed 3 *kos* on this side of Gwalior. He encamped at a distance of 3 *kos* on this side of Gwalior. The same day a Deccani person was sent by the Raja of Gwalior to Tatya Tope with the message that he would arrange supplied for him but that he should not come to Gwalior. The next morning, the Raja's army reached this place and fought Tatya Tope's troops. A large part of his army fled but the Nawab's *risala* attacked the Raja's army on the flank and put it to flight. *The whole soldiery of the Raja joined Tatya Tope*. The Raja of Gwalior fled form Gwalior to Agra. Tatya Tope, Rani Jhansi, Nawab Banda and myself now entered Gwalior. After a fort-night, the English army attacked Gwalior from two sides. The Rani was killed with the sword a day before our flight and Tatya Tope, Nawab Banda and myself accompanied by some army fled and halted at a place 13 or 14 *kos* from Gwalior. Two or three days after the English army together with some of the Raja's troops got to this place as well. We fought and again fled to a place 10 miles off. All our field-pieces were captured by the English. Then we reached the territory of Jeypur through the forest, then went to Bondi and after this reached Rampur in the Holkar territory. Then we went to Jala Patan. Then Mussulmans of Patan, may be *Wilayatis* (foreigners) or of any descent, came to us 10 *kos* from Patan and took us together with our army to Patan. The Raja of Patan did not give us supplies. We fought him and his army came over to our side. Tatya Tope made the Raja captive and brought him to me. Then he suggested to me, "I shall use harsh words and you should use gentle language to the Raja so that he may yield money". The Raja promised to give a few *lacs* and Tatya Tope sent him home under the escort of the army. In two or three days the Raja first gave us some money but then he fled away by winning over the people of the army. His family still remained there. His *Karindas* arranged with the money-lenders and supplied us the money. Now we marched out of Patan accompanied by horses, elephants and baggage. Then two battles, one at Bilwara (Bhilwara) and another at Kotwara were fought against the English by Tatya Tope. I do not remember if these two battles were fought before the fight at Patan or after it. From Patan we came to Rajgarh and thence to Biawara (or Bilwara). On the way there was a battle with the English army and they captured all the field-pieces Tatya Tope had. Thence we fled to Sironj where we stayed for eight days and then went to Isagarh. Tatya Tope fought the army of the Raja of Gwalior at this place. His army broke open the door of the boundary wall of the town, made entry in and plundered. The next day Tatya Tope left Isagarh and marched out to Chanderi where he fought the army of the Raja of Gwalior. He ordered me to go to Bundelkhand with the ladies and to stay there. We reached Lalitpur from Saugor and a battle took place at Khajauri. Tatya Tope fled with his army once again, Nawab Banda, Tatya Tope and myself again came to the side of Sironj and 10 *kos* away from Sironj there was another battle. Tatya Tope and myself again took to flight. Nawab Banda, Tatya Tope and myself then crossed the Nerbadda and reached Fatehpur. Then we reached the bridge of the Pali river through the forest. *Now the Nawab of Banda wanted to present himself before the English, but the officers of the army intervened. Then he deserted us and presented himself before the English.* Now Tatya Tope and myself came from Khargon to Indore. There 200 horsemen came over to Tatya Tope's side and while yet on the way, we fought the English army. The next day, we crossed the Nerbadda and marched towards Baroda. Tatya Tope fled from this place to Banswara and plundered some chattels there. Then another engagement with the English army took place at Partabgarh and Tatya Tope fled. Fourth day, after, there was again a battle against the English army and Tatya Tope fled. Four or five days after we crossed the Chanbel (Chambal), and reached near a fort in the Jeypur territory. *Now we met Firoz Shah and Tatya Tope, Firoz Shah and myself came to Jeypur territory where we again faced the English army.* Then we came flying to Dhousa. There was again a battle with the English. One night Tatya Tope left us, un-informed, with half of the army and since then we have not met. *I said to Firoz Shah that we might present ourselves before the English if he so wished*; and he consented. Then we both came towards Sironj. Firoz Shah said that he had sent his *Vakil* for establishing good relations with the English. Then I sent my servant Mohd. Ishaq as a Vakil to the General at Sironj, with a verbal request of presenting myself. The General sent a *Parwanah* to me asking me to go to him and that would not be detrimental to me. Several times I made up my mind to do so but the people of my army did not let me do it. The *Parwanah* is no more with me; it has been lost. The people of the army did not allow me to draft the reply in (the) manner I wished, rather they sent one against my intentions. The next day Mohd. Ishaq who was sent to deliver the reply came back and told me that my request was not conceded to by the *Sarkar* and that the General had ordered that I should present (before him) within a period of 10 hours. But the people of the army did not allow me to present myself there. The next half of he army left me but about 200 or 300 men were still present. Next day I took 10 or 12 of my chief men with me and left the army. After this, they also dropped on the way and only three persons remained (with me) namely Umrao Mussulman, Ganesh Brahman and Pokar Ahir, my presonal servant. I wandered about, disguised as a mendicant, in the territories of Gwalior and Tonk. Then in that jungle, Umrao Mussulman and a few days after Ganesh Brahman also left me. Umrao Mussulman brought my wife and her old mother to me in the jungle. Now, considering my stay in the forest improper, I came to Pushkar near Ajmer. After this we reached Thaneshwar *via* Ajmer, Jaipur and Delhi. I had adopted the name of Lachhman Das Pandit. For 15 days we stayed at Thaneshwar then we went to Jwalaji, from there to Kangra, and then to Pur Mandal, Soodh and Mahadeo in the Jammu territory and then to Tirkata. I had a mind to go to Kashmir and therefore went to Chandenee. I sent the old lady along with a man to Kashmir and I with my pregnant wife still remained at Chandenee in the Jammu territory. Madho Rao Brahman accompanied me from Pushkar but he fell ill at Pur Mandal. I came from Chandenee to Pur Mandal to take him. Then I and Madho Rao reached Jammu to buy a buffalo. Thence we reached Sialkot, bought a buffalo and returned to Chandenee. The new temple is one and half kos from Chandenee where I used to go for worship frequently. Here Bhim Rao who was with Tatya Tope met me in the guise of a mendicant. He recoginsed me although I did not. When I came out of the temple and was going to ride my horse, he accosted me thus, "I am your old slave who had tasted your salt. Now I have come to you after much wandering about". He stayed with me for one and half months at Chandenee and then said, "I am a rebel, but a rebellion has subsided, rebels are no more being brought to account. I shall, therefore, now go to my home." Two or two and a half months after this Bhim Rao came with the Deputy Commissioner of Sialkot and took me captive.

Question: You have mentioned about the General's Parwana. Clearly say what were your terms and what terms were offered by the Government?

Answer : He had said that my life would be spared and I would not be fettered and thus my honour would be safeguarded.

Question : Did he not write, in which chases?

Answer : No.

Question : What were your terms?

Answer : The first condition was that the property of my followers including my own should not be forfeited and that somewhere between Benares and Hardwar I should get an open place on the bank of Ganges for my residence. Other things I do not remember. Although, I do not fully recollect other details, still I think the *Parwana* said that in case I did not present myself I would be considered guilty. This frightened me and so I did not surrender.

Question : Did you ever go to Hyderabad Deccan?

Answer : Never.

Question : A certain person in Hyderabad wanted to create trouble in the army in order to put it to flight. Do you know who he was?

Answer : I do not know who he was.

Question : Is the deposition, just read out to you, and made by you before the Deputy Commissioner of Sialkot, correct?

Answer : Yes, it is so. I gave this deposition.

Question : You said you had no power, but you also said that you kept the (English) gentleman and his wife in your protection. If you had no power over the army, how did you take them from the army?

Answer : I did not take them by force but entreated Abha Dhanuk Dhari to hand them over to me.

Question : You have got it written in your deposition, acknowledged by you just now, that the spy, Bhim Rao was taken captive at your suggestion. If you had no authority how was Bhim Rao imprisoned?

Answer : I had no authority, but everyone agrees to a good thing said by a person of note. I had said a right thing independently and so Bhimrao was taken captive.

Question : Do you have a witness for anything?

Answer : None.

Question : Your deposition has been read before you word by word and you have acknowledged it. Now, what answer do you have for being a rebel leader.

Answer : I am neither a rebel nor a rebel leader.

Question : If you were not a leader how did you recruit the army?

Answer : I did not recruit any army.

Question : If you were not a rebel why did you accompany the army for an attack on Kanpur and fought (sic) the English?

Answer : Just as Bala Rao had kept me at Fatehpur Chaurasi so Nana Rao also kept me with himself. I had no power independently.

Question : If you were not a rebel leader, why was an announcement made in your name at Kalpi?

Answer : All announcements used to be made by Nana's name. Bala Rao was not at Kalpi and I was alone. Tatya tope was there with me. The announcement was not made in my name. Tatya Tope was the commander of the army, stationed both outside and inside the fort. I was staying in the open outside the fort. I know nothing about the mendicant's being hanged nor do I know who did it and when. I also do not know about the fine imposed on the people at Kalpi.

Question : If you were not a rebel why were you there with Firoz Shah?

Answer : When Tatya Tope left me I thought it was in my power to join the English but I had no friend or acquaintance to introduce me. If I along would join I would be killed. Therefore, first I sent my *Vakil*, Mohd. Ishaq to the General. I could not present myself before the English because I was in Tatya Tope's captivity.

Question : Once you alone took an army to Jalaun and then once to Lalitpur and fought the English. Why did you do so if you were not a rebel and only a captive in Tatya Tope's hands?

Answer : I did not fight in Jalaun nor (*sic*, or) in Lalitpur.

Question : You have said above in your deposition that the Nawab of Banda segregated himself and joined the English. Could you not act the same way, if you were not a rebel?

Answer : I could not avail of an opportunity; the Nawab of Banda had a large number of females with him and on this pretext he stayed behind and thus availed of an opportunity to join the English. I was all alone and could fine no pretext.

Question : Who has a better opportunity of segregating himself, one who has females with him or one who is all alone like you?

Answer : The Nawab of Banda had reason for staying behind while I had none. The army had already marched forward and the Nawab being left behind, he went over to the English.

Question : You have said above in your deposition that Tatya Tope brought the Raja of Pain (sic. 'patan') captive before you and asked you, in order to squeeze money from him, to use gentle words for him and himself to address him in harsh tone. This shows that Tatya Tope and yourself were one in all matters and you and Tatya Tope exacted fine from the Raja.

Answer : I did not take any fine from the Raja, only Tatya tope did so. I had to do what Tatya Tope asked me to do. It was Tatya tope who asked me to do this, and not I who had asked Tatya Tope.

Question : The Commissioner of Jhansi has stated in the Narrative of Events of that district that in October 58 (1858), 1,000 men came down upon the Jhansi territory, under Rao Saheb, plundered some villages, killed a large number of those who had been in the service of the English, amputated and cut

off the noses of many and deformed them and then crossed the Bindha (or Bindua) river at Sirsa Ghat.

Answer : I had seen a bungalow on fire at a distance of about 10 *kos* from Jhansi. It was government bungalow but I do not know what it was built for. The people of the army had set fire to it. I do not know what else they had done. The Nawab of Banda and myself were there with the army but Tatya Tope was not there although other officers of the army were there.

Question : Who was the chief of the army that accompanied you?

Answer : Gauri Shankar and Imam Ali were the officers of the army. I had not (*sic*, no) authority and simply accompanied the army whenever it moved.

Question : (Deputy Saheb)- If you were not rebel why did you cross the river Bindua, go to Lalitpur with the army and join Tatya Tope who had brought an army from the side of the South- Deccan, and then stayed together at Lalitpur?

Answer : As I was under the authority of Tatya Tope and of the army, I had to go wherever the army went.

Question : From the Commissioner's deposition it is learnt that you fought a battle with General Mitchel at Sidhwaya where you were defeated and from where you went to Bhopal via Saugor (Sagar). What have you to say about this?

Answer : The army was staying at a place between Saugor and Sironj. The news of the coming of the English troops from the Saugor side was received in the night and therefore our army marched out at midnight. Half of the army had proceeded on, and the remaining half was still left. This faced the English troops with the result that it took to flight. I was with the first half which had already left and this also took to flight.

Question : From the depositions of the witnesses, attested to-day in your presence, it has been learnt that you were an

accomplice of the rebels and of their leaders and it was known to all the people of Jhansi and Lalitpur (where this army marched and where this gentleman was the Commissioner) that you were the chief of the army. Why was Tatya Tope or Nana Rao not known as the leaders of this army?

Answer : Bala Rao and Tatya Tope were the masters of the army and not I. As there are many of my kinsmen in the Deccan side, this may be a reason why I became known as a leader.

Question : Bhim Rao, the man who got you captured, also says you were a leader?

Answer : He tells a lie; I can't say why.

Question : Do you have any witnesses in support of this?

Answer : There were many in the army. But now I have none.

Signatures (illegible in Hindi)

Signatures (illegible in English)

Reference :

1. "Trial Proceedings in the Case *Govt. vs. Rao Saheb*". Kanpur Collectorate Mutiny Records. F.S.U.P., Vol. III, pp. 683-694.

Appendix - 4
A Poem about Shahzada Firozshah by an unknown poet.[1]

।।श्रीरामजी।।

।।कवित लीख्ते : समत ऊगनीसै साल चावदै के हाल
कछु रूप गयो षायाल रोज मैली हुई बादे की :
हुवै लाचार साउकार सब पुकार करैं
दीये डडै लाख जब तलप चुकी प्यादे की
लुटी बीलोद जीरन कनगेटी हैटी भई
खेट की सुनत है जब नीमच कै ईरादे की
रईत लुटै है राज बनीया पीटै है
जब हुंडीया पाते हैं फ्रोज सेख साहेजजादै की।।
कवत मैटकैल फीरीया फकीर खुब गये जान
कर गयो हेवानी सर सुप्रत मुसलानी के
बदल्या ओीमान बईमान सब ईसान भै
कीनी है कीसान मतै लगै सब ईरानी कै
कर हीला गला पुकारै दाम मीला कु
कलबला मचौगे प्यासै मरै अन पानी के
आगी मै जरेंगे एक रसे सै खीचीगे
हर गज बचीगै नाय तुरक तुरकानी के।।
करकै हीलागुला पुकारै दाम मोला कु
सेलाकर लोलाकर नीसान चाले गोर कै
छरै भुवारै भर मारै अगरैजन नै

कटत मुकरानी इरानी उड उड कै
कता सै सपता सीर ऊडत है बीलायतन कै
सर सै मीटैगे गोरखाड मै कुटेगे
जुमी मृगसर मै कटैगै दाम तुरक मन्दसोर कै।।
डाल तै पेट मै तेल छोरीयो के बैल जसै
आय गयै फैल भाज मुरग नीचान कौ
जाली बेग मोलीबेग पोलीस बबाद बैग
खोदै घर बदुक जसे फीरै बैल घानी कै
छोड़ दीनी हय कय कछु ऊन मानत नाय
सची 2 कैसे बयान रंग पलीटै साल रानी कै।।
नमो अेक रदन गज गवरी नंद काटो सबेज दुख दंद फन्द
सोवत सेंदुर अंग मुगती माल भोल पै चंद राजत बीसाला
समत उगणीसै सतरे के साल सब सुनौ सैठ सठी के हाल

Translation of the poem

Shri Ramji. Incidence of samvat one thousand fourteen hundrec (1857 AD) led me to write something about it. When the money-lenders were beaten, they became weak and they moaned. When they gave one and half *lac* rupees then the salary could be paid to the infantry. The troops tortured Billod and Jeeran. Now it is heard that the Shahzada is planning to attack Neemuch. The public is plundered in this state. Traders are beaten for obtaining the *hundies* of the Sheikh Shahzada. Now every body has known this fraud mendicant Emperor. Taking everything from the public this muslim has been behaving like a demon. All the rebels have forgotten their duties. They have started plundering on the name of the security of the public. This has also changed the behaviour of the public. Even the farmers are following this Persian. They invade taking the name of the Maula. But they would die in Karbala without food and water. They will burn in fire and will be pulled by rope and these Turks would not, in any case, will be saved from death.

Taking the name of Maula these rebels indulge in roits and fire on the British. Makrani, Durrani joyfully wave victorious flags.

Fighting after taking their pay, these Wilayties can be seen fighting in Mandsaur. Their heads will be severed and will burst after falling in a ditch. In the *Mrigshira Nakshatra* the value of the Turks will be reduced.

Raping the girls, their leaders Jali beg, Mori beg, Sakhawat beg keeping the gun on their shoulders wander in the streets of the town like bullucks of oil pressers. They have no shame and they don't pay heed to any one. The truth is that the things have changed after the reign of the Empress.

O one toothed, elephant headed, son of Gauri, chrimson faced, adorned with garlands, doning moon on the forehead, kindly get us rid of our pains and plight. Listen to the merchants on *Samvat* nineteen hundred seventeen (1860 AD).

Reference :

1. Photocopy of this long poem was kindly provided to me by Shri K.C. Pandey of Shri Dashpur Prachya shodh Sansthan, Mandsaur MP, who, according to him, obtained it from the collection of Shri Narendra Sipani, Agriculture Researcher and owner of Sipani Farm House, Mandsaur MP in 2008. Shri Pandey was nice enough to transcribe and translate the entire poem for me. It was also published in his article '*Pashchimi Malwa ke pratham Swantantrata sangram par san 1860 mein likhi kavita*' in "*1857 ka Mahasamar* (*Dewas Jile Ka Yogdan*)", 2007, edited by Dr. Alpana Dubhashe, pp. 96-98

Glossary

Ahalkar	An official
Bandobust	Arrangement
Baori	Step-well
Basta	Bundle
Bazar	Market
Bhowree	Hindu Marriage
Bildar	labourer
Biswa	A measure of land
Chanwar	Fly-whisk
Chakledari	Fief holder
Kutchery	Court
Dak	Post
Dargah	Muslim Shrine
Diwan	Prime Minister
Duffadar	An official
Elakadar	Holder of a territory
Faqir	Muslim mendicant
Firangee	The British
Firman	Letter/Order/Notification
Ghaut	The place from where the river is crossed/mountain pass
Haj	Pilgrimage
Harkara	Messenger
Havaldar	An army official
Hundi	Pay order
Jamadar	An army official

Jowarry	Millet
Kamavizdar	Revenue Collector
Kamdar	Manager
Keyfeeat	Description
Koss or Coss	e.g. 2 miles i.e. about 3 kms.
Kothree	Store-keeper
Kotwal	In charge of the Police Station
Kutchery	Court
Lac	One hundred thousand
Lashkar	Army
Maafee	Free holding
Marg	Road
Masnad	Throne
Maund	Unit of weight of 40 seers or about 80 lbs.
Morchal	fly-whisk
Muhzar	Proclamation
Muharram	A Muslim festival
Muharrir	Writer
Muhzur	Diclaration
Munshi	Writer
Murshid	Preceptor
Musafirkhana	Traveler's lodge
Naib Suba	Deputy Governor
Nazar/Nazrana	Gifts
Nikah	Muslim Marriage
Nishanbardar	Carrier of royal flag
Nullah	Stream
Pagri	head gear
Panchsadee	Five hundred
Parwana	Letter
Peshkar	Reader
Punj Hazari	Mansabdar of Five thousand
Risaldar	Cavalry officer

Sahukars	Money lenders
Salam	Salutation
Sanad	Grant
Sirdar	Chief or Noble
Sarishtedar	An official
Sawar	Horseman
Sebandies	A class of warriors
Shara	Shariyat
Shastra	Treatise
Shush Hazari	Mansabdar of six thousand
Sipahsalar	Commander
Suba	Province
Tahsildar	Officer in charge of Tahsil, an administrative sub division of a district
Talib-i-ilm	Seeker of knowledge
Taluqa	Fief
Taluqadar	Fief holder
Thana	Police post
Tulwars	Swords
Urgee	Application
Vakeel	Representative
Vilayatees	Foreign mercenaries
Zamindar	land holder

Bibliography

Primary Sources

Unpublished records: National Archives of India, New Delhi

Foreign Department, Secret Consultations
Foreign Department, Political Consultations
Foreign Department, Political Proceedings
Foreign Department, Secret Proceedings
Military Department, Proceedings

Unpublished records: Shri Natnagar Shodh Sansthan, Sitamau Distt. Mandsaur M.P.

Basta bundle no 115 of Keshav Abhilekhagar

Printed Primary Sources

Ansari, I.H. and Qureshi, H.A.*1857: Urdu sources* (Tr.) 2008

Ball, Charles; *History of the Indian Mutiny,* London, Vol. I and II

Forbes-Mitchel, William : *Reminiscences of the great Mutiny,* reprint 1989.

Forrest, George W. (ed): *The Indian Mutiny 1857-58, Selections from the letters, Dispatches and other State Papers preserved in the Military Department of the Government of India, 1857-58*, Vol IV, Calcutta 1912, reprint Delhi, 2003.

Forrest, George W. : *A History of the Indian Mutiny, Vol. III, Edingerg and London, 1904-1912.*

Godse, Vishnubhatt : *Ankhon Dekha Gadar* (Hindi), 2000

Hansard : *Parliamentary debates: third Series*. Vol. CXLVII of 1857, CXLVIII of 1857, CXLIX of 1858, CLII of 1859, CLIII of 1859

Hasan, Moinuddin : *Ghadar 1857*, 1999 (Hindi Tr.)

Karim Ali, Munshi : *Tarikh-i-Malwa* (Urdu) 1874. (In the Library of Shri Natnagar Shodh Sansthan, Sitamau)

Kavanagh, T.H. : *How I won Victoria Cross*, 1860

Luard, Major C.E.: *Contemporary Newspaper Accounts of the Events during Pamphlets the Mutiny in Central India 1857-59*

Lunia, B.N. (ed.) : *Freedom Movement in Madhya Bharat,* 1956

Marx and Engles : *The First Indian War of Independence 1857-59,* Fourth reprint, 1975

Mushirul Hasan (ed.) : *Mutiny Memoirs Being Personal Reminiscences of the Great Se[oy Revolt of 1857. Colonel A.R.D. Mackenzie, C.B. Honorary A.D.D. to the Viceroy*

Mutiny in India : Further papers relative to the mutinies in the East of 1857-58, and the restoration of authority, 2 vols., Calcutta, 1801.

Mutiny in India : Narrative of Events regarding the Mutiny in India Indies, 1857.

Parliamentary Papers : 1857 Vols. XXXIX, XXX; 1857-58 Vol. XLII, XLIII, XLIV; 1859 Vol. XVIII, XXIII, XXV, XXXVIII; 1860 Vol. L; 1863 Vol. XL.

Press List of Mutiny Papers, Calcutta, 1921.

Punjab Government Records 1911, Vol. I and VIII

Purwar : H.M. and Singh D.K. (ed): *Kuchh Telegram, Dastavez: Janpad Jalaun,* 2007.

Raghubirsinh (ed.) : *Malwa ke Mahan Vidrohkaleen abhilekh (Hindi), 1986*

Revolt in Central India : 1857-59, complied in the Intelligence Branch, Division of the Chief of the Staff, Army Head Quarters India, Shimla, 1908

Rizvi, S.A.A. and Bhargava, M.I. : *The Freedom Struggle in Uttar Pradesh*- The Source Material. 6 Volumes 1957-61 particularly, Vol. II, III and V.

Sayyid Ahmed Khan : *Rissalah Asbab-i-Baghawat-i-Hind.* 1858. English Translation by Graham and Colvin. Beneras, 1873.

Selections from the records of the Government of the Punjab and its dependencies New Series Vol. 7

Showers, C.L. : *A Missing Chapter of the Indian Mutiny*, 1888 *The Calcutta Gazette* 1857-59.

The Mutinies in the East Indies, Parts I, III and IV

The Trial of Bahadur Shah II 1858 (1870)

Secondary Sources

Ahmad, Q. ; *The Wahabi Movement in India, 1966.*

Atkinson, G.F. : *The Campaign in India, 1857-58*. 1859

Beale, Thomas William : *'An Oriental Biographical Dictionary*, new edition revised and enlarged by H.G. Keene, India Reprint, 1996

Choudhuri, S.B. : *Civil Rebellion in the Indian Mutinees 1857-59,* 1957

——— *English Historical Writings on the Indian Mutiny, 1857-1859,* 1979.

—— *Theories of the Indian Mutiny 1857-59,* 1965

—— *Civil Disturbances during British Rule in India,* 1955.

Depalpuri, Qazi Abul Quddus Faruqi, *Baghawat-i-Malwa* (Urdu) (Printed in the Press of Darul Uloom, Merrut) Copy with Mohammad Idris Khan, Mandigate, Mandsaur, M.P.)

Duberly, Mrs. H.F. : *Campaiging Experiences in Rajpootana and Central India, during the suppression of the Mutiny, 1857-58.* 1859

Durand, H.M. : *The Life of Sir Henry Marion Durand*, 1883

Edwards, W. : *Facts and Reflections connected with Indian Rebellion,* 1859

Fisher, F.H. : *Azamgarh Gazetteer*, 1883

Fisher, H.M. : *Azamgarh Gazetteer*, 1883

Ganguli, Anil Baran : *Guerilla Fighter of The First Freedom Movement*, 1980

Guha, R. : *Subaltern Studies I: Writings on South Asian History and Society,* 1982.

Gupta, Bhagwandas : *Jhansi Rajya Ka Itihas aur Sanskriti (1731-1857),* 2008

Gupta, Rajnikant : *Military traits of Tatya Tope*, 1987

Hardikar, Shrinivas Balaji : *Nana Saheb Peshwa* (Hindi), 1969

——— *Tatya Tope* (Hindi)

Hasan, Mahdi : *Bahadur Shah II,* 1958

Hobsbawm, E.J. : *Primitive Rebels,* 1959

Homes, T.R. : *History of the Indian Mutiny,* 1904

Innes, McLeod : *The Sepoy Revolt*, 1879

Jahidi, Ashfaq Ahmad : *Tarikh-i-Jaora* (Urdu), 1947 (Copy in the library of Shri Natnagar Shodh Sansthan, Sitamau, M.P.)

Joshi, P.C. : *Rebellion 1857: A Symposium*, 1957

Kaye, J.W. : *History of the Sepoy War in India 1857-58, 3 Vols.* 1880

Kaye, Sir John William : *A History of the Sepoy war in India, Vol. I. 19th ed.* 1880, *Vols II and III 4th ed.*, 1878.

Kaye and Malleson : *History of lthe Indian Mutiny-* in 6 Volumes, 1897.

Keene, H.G. : *Fifty Seven,* 1883

Lee, J.L., : *The 'Ancient Supremacy' Bukhara, Afghanistan and the Battle for Balkh 1731-1901*, 1996

Lowe, Thomas : *Central India During the Rebellion of 1857-58.*, 1860.

Majumdar, R.C. : *The Sepoy Mutiny and the Revolt of 1857, Second edition, 1963*

Majumdar, R.C. : *History of the Freedom Movement in India* Vol. I. 1971

Malleson, G.B. : *History of the Indian Mutiny 3 vols. Vols. I and II, 2nd edition, 1878; Vol. III,* 1880

——— *The Indian Mutiny of 1857*, 1906

——— *The Revolt in Central India*, 1908

Mehta, Ashok : *1857, The Great Rebellion*

Metcalf, T.R. : *The aftermath of Revolt : India 1857-1870,* 1964

——— *Land, Landlords and the British Raj: Northern India in the Nineteenth Century,* 1979.

Mishra, A.S. : *Nana Saheb Peshwa*, 1961

Mooswi, Shirin (ed) : *The Facets of the Great Revolt*, 2008

Mukherjee, Rudrankshu : *Awadh in revolt 1857-58*, 2008

Nayar, Pramod K. : *The Great Uprising,* 2007

Paget, Leopold Mrs. : *Camp and Cantonment: A Journal of Life in India in 1857-1859,* 1865

Parasnis, D.B. : *Jhansi ki rani Laxmibai, (Hindi) samvat 1997*

Russell, William Howard: : *My Diary in India in the Year 1858-59*, 1860

Sahiwala, Arjunsingh *: Jeevan Charit, Reprint Samvat 1967 (1910 AD) Parts 1-3* (In the library of Pratap Shodh Sansthan, Udaipur)

Savarkar, V.D. : *The Indian war of Independence 1857,* 1947

Sen, S.N. : *Eighteen Fifty Seven*, 1958

Sengupta, K.K. : *Recent Writings on the Revolt of 1857: A Survey,* 1975.

Shadwell, L. : *The Life of Colin Campbell, Lord Clyde, 2 Vols.,* 1881.

Shrivastava, K.L. : *The Revolt of 1857 in Central India-Malwa.*1966

Sinha, Shyam Narayan : *The Revolt of 1857 in Bundelkhand*, 1982

Stokes, E. : *The Peasant and the Raj: Studies in Agrarian Soceity and Peasant Rebellion in Colonial India,* 1978.

Tapti Roy : *The Politics of a Popular Uprising: Bundelkhand in 1857*, 1994

Tarachand: *History of the Freedom Movement in India* Vol. II

Taylor, P.J.O.: *What really happened during the Mutiny.* 1997.

Thomas Louis : *Central India during the Rebellion of 1857-58*

Thompson, E. : *The Making of the Indian Princes, London,* 1943

—— *The Other Side of the Medal,* London, 1930.

Thornton, T.H. : *General Sir Richard Meade & the feudatory states of Central and South India,* 1898.

Thorpe, Ralphe H. : *Bengal Past and Present*, July-Dec. 1969, part II, no. 166.

Tope, Parag : *Tatya Tope's operation Red Lotus*, 2010

Wilson, H.H. : *A Glossary of Judicial and Revenue Terms of British India,* 1875

Gazetteers, Newspapers and Magazines

Asiatic Journals
Calcutta Review
Friend of India
Journal of Indian History
Royal Asiatic Society of India , Bombay Branch
The Nineteenth Century and After
Encyclopedia Britannica
Imperial Gazetteer of India
Madhya Pradesh District Gazetteers
Uttar Pradesh District Gazetteers
Rajasthan District Gazetteers
Survey of India Maps

Index

Illustrations

1. Ahmadulla Shah of Faizabad

2. Begum Hazrat Mahal

3. Jhansi Rani

4. Khan Bahadur Khan of Bareilly

5. Lord Clyde

6. Nawab Tafajjul Hussain Khan of Farrukhabad

7. Mandsaur Fort

8. Residency, Lucknow

9. Sir Hugh Rose

10. Tukoji Rao Holkar II